D0460485

PRAISE FOR *WORRY-FREE MONEY*

"It's so nice to see a personal finance book from
an author who has spent a lot of time on the front lines
of financial planning. **Shannon Lee Simmons offers pragmatic
solutions, or, more accurately, 'fresh ways to think'
while dealing with one's money.** Well done!"

—DAVID CHILTON, author of *The Wealthy Barber*

"Shannon Lee Simmons is amazing. She truly cares about
helping Canadians worry less and build more confidence in their
money. This book has a **simple, straightforward message
about building a strong financial foundation**, with help for
every generation at every life stage. Deal with your FOMO,
Unhappy Spending and F*ck-It Moments. Seriously."

—KERRY K. TAYLOR, personal finance expert
and creator of Squawkfox.com

"Shannon Lee Simmons really gets the deeper reason
why we worry about money. This **charming, fast-moving
and laugh-out-loud** guide is for anyone ready to
take charge of their finances!"

—KELLEY KEEHN, award-winning author
and personal finance educator

"If you're ready to **end the financial drama and feel
good about your money**, you need this book. Immediately.
You cannot afford to miss this one!"

—SANDRA HANNA, CEO, Smart Cookies

WORRY-FREE MONEY

WORRY-FREE MONEY

The Guilt-Free Approach to Managing Your Money and Your Life

SHANNON LEE SIMMONS

Collins

Worry-Free Money
Copyright © 2017 by Shannon Lee Simmons.
All rights reserved.

Published by Collins, an imprint of HarperCollins Publishers Ltd

First edition

No part of this book may be used or reproduced in any manner whatsoever
without the prior written permission of the publisher, except in the case
of brief quotations embodied in reviews.

HarperCollins books may be purchased for educational, business,
or sales promotional use through our Special Markets Department.

HarperCollins Publishers Ltd
2 Bloor Street East, 20th Floor
Toronto, Ontario, Canada
M4W 1A8

www.harpercollins.ca

Library and Archives Canada Cataloguing in Publication
information is available upon request.

ISBN 978-1-44345-445-2

Printed and bound in the United States of America
LSC/C 9 8 7 6

For Mom,
because this book would not have been possible
without your endless support, love and motivation.

Contents

Everyone Is Worried about Money

How do you feel about your money situation? I'm not asking for the answer you give your friends, family or colleagues, but for the truth. At three a.m., when you wake up and can't sleep, how do you feel about your finances?

"There's always something and we can't seem to move ahead."

—couple; household income: $80,000

"I feel like I'm spinning my wheels. I'm sick of being broke."

—single; personal income: $45,000

"We have good incomes and we don't live extravagantly, but I feel like we are always strapped. I feel broke."

—couple; household income: $110,000

"How are other people doing it? Why am I falling so far behind?"

—single; personal income: $60,000

I run a financial planning firm and I hear the above statements every day when I meet with clients. Over the past 10 years I've had thousands of conversations as I sat down with everyday people to talk about their money. And we get it all out on the table—every financial secret, embarrassment, fear, win and loss. The process can be cathartic, enlightening and truly amazing.

I get to cut right to the chase with people. "Hi, nice to meet you. How much down payment did you put on your house? How much money do you make? What are your hopes, dreams and fears? Do you lease or own your car?" (I'm lots of fun at parties.)

People don't lie or sugar-coat their finances when they talk to me. I get to peek behind the curtain into their financial lives and realities. Like a financial confession booth, I am privy to the true financial story, not simply what's posted on social media or spoken in person at dinner parties—"Yeah, things are great" or "We spent more than we wanted but it was worth it." They trust me with the real deal, the nitty-gritty numerical details, and it's not a responsibility I take lightly. I love that I'm able to create a space where it feels safe to disclose things like these:

"I feel like I can't win."

—client in his mid-30s

"I feel like we did everything that we were supposed to, and yet here we are."

—couple in their mid-40s

"I don't think we have enough to stop working."

—soon-to-be-retired couple who remortgaged their mortgage-free house to help their children pay off massive student loans

---

Sound familiar? When you allow yourself to be honest, the words you might find yourself using to describe your finances include *frustrated, exhausted, scared, resentful* and *guilty*. All these are just other words for *feeling broke*. Feeling broke means you're worried about money. You're convinced there just isn't enough. You believe that if you just had a bit more money, surely you'd be less stressed, more fun, healthier, a better partner, a better parent. Happier. Successful. Less anxious. Safe. Maybe you could slow down, safe in the knowledge that you have the things you need. And maybe you could breathe. If you just had more money.

A decade ago, my clients didn't feel as squeezed, hopeless and frustrated with their financial lives as they do now. The drastic increase in the use of the word *broke* caught my attention a few years ago. People in urban centres, the suburbs, the country; single, married, with or without kids—it didn't matter. Client after client was saying to me, "I feel broke." They all had this feeling of financial frustration and unease.

The interesting thing is that, on paper, these people are not actually, numerically "broke." But *being* broke and *feeling* broke are two different things.

Let me be clear. In this book—and most of the time in my office—I'm not talking about the finances of individuals and families who don't have enough to pay for basic necessities like food, shelter and health care. That situation, while still hopeful, requires a different set of financial solutions, financial planning and support that we won't dive into here. In this book I'm talking about the financially frustrated middle class, those who earn a living wage right up to the downright privileged, but who all feel like they cannot get ahead. They feel stuck and they worry—a lot—about their financial future.

So what's actually happening when you're feeling broke? The real problem is that you don't truly know if you are on track or not. Are you going to be okay financially? Or are you actually falling behind?

It feels like there's no real way of knowing. Just because you have some credit card debt doesn't mean that you're never going to be able to retire. And just because you have savings doesn't mean you're financially okay either. When you don't know if you're on track, you never know what you can afford.

If you don't know what you can and cannot actually afford, every purchase feels terrifying. Was the $40 takeout a bad financial decision that you should beat yourself up for, or was it okay? Will an extra $100 in rent really push out your dreams of home ownership for years, or will it make no difference at all? How guilty and afraid should you actually be when you spend money? This constant sense of vague guilt makes it feel as if there's no plan and no strategy to your finances.

And it doesn't stop with spending. That guilt spills over into your savings—or lack thereof—too. I'm sure you know the benefits of saving and I'm sure you're already worried about saving enough. How can you not be when low wages, rising home prices and the creeping fear that robots could take over your job dominate the modern economic reality and populate every news cycle? It starts to feel as if every single dollar you earn should be stored away, protected and saved for a rainy day—hell, a rainy decade. But life costs money and you have to spend money at some point. It's a trap. You worry if you spend and you worry if you don't. As a result, you find yourself worried about money, and often.

In the past when things felt financially scary, you may have turned to hardcore budgeting to gain control of your finances, but this type of budgeting simply does not work. It's not the answer. Budgeting makes you feel truly broke, which leads to overspending, under-saving and general anxiety about the future.

Being both a certified financial planner and a certified life coach, I often make the joke that in my financial planning practice I use my life-coaching skills 80 percent of the time and that the rest is just an Excel spreadsheet. But there is truth to this. I listen. I hear you and people like you, and I've seen the mounting guilt, anxiety and frustration when it comes to money. I know what's making you worry and I know how to help, so you can stop budgeting and start living life without financial worry.

It's about changing your financial perspective and learning to say no. And it came to me years ago after I got into a massive fight with my then-future husband in an IKEA store.

An IKEA Fight

It was a Saturday afternoon. I was staring intensely at a Billy bookcase as if it were a piece of art that I needed to appreciate, terrified that an IKEA sales associate would ask me ever so cheerfully if I required assistance. If that happened I'd have to speak, and if I had to speak, I'd cry. A public IKEA cry. Ugh! The worst. Thankfully it was busy and the sales associates were swamped as they helped other people: people buying new kitchens, planning for babies, sprucing up bedrooms.

Only 30 minutes earlier Matt and I had been laughing in the car as the radio blared a Kim Mitchell song. We were driving to IKEA because we needed a new couch. Simple enough, right? But that couch took on a life of its own.

Our current couch was a 25-year-old hand-me-down. It was starter furniture. The statement piece of a couple who had moved in together right after postsecondary and gratefully accepted whatever they could scrounge from friends and family. In our small apartment it fit right in with our camp chairs, a folding picnic table and a mattress lying on the floor as our bed. Back in those early days I'd stumble home from my Bay Street job every night and we'd cook up a stir-fry or meatballs, and then we'd curl up on that couch to watch *Planet Earth* DVDs (we didn't have cable, and streaming wasn't a thing back then). We'd laugh and talk about our day, completely happy with our big dreams and our cast-off furniture.

Three years later we had paid off our student debt. We moved to a flat with wood floors and bought a bed frame (a big day for us). Then I quit my high-rollin' Bay Street job to start my own company. This, I can assure you, had not been part of the plan.

By that Saturday at IKEA, I had been running my business for just over two years. I was doing okay, keeping my head slightly above water, but had nowhere near the income or financial security I'd had with my Bay Street job. I worried nearly constantly that I had thrown us off course financially with my decision to quit.

I worried that we were falling behind. Moments when we had to say no to social events or purchases were like a punch to my gut. A brutal reminder that the reason we couldn't afford to spend money was because I had quit my job. I felt inadequate and utterly insecure. And, to drive home that overwhelming sense of inadequacy, I was inundated daily by social media posts from peers who had stayed the course at their professional jobs. They all appeared to be managing just fine. I would wake up at three a.m. in a panic and scroll through photos of vacations, weddings, home renovations and fabulous designer couches—$2,500 couches. The kind I could have afforded if I hadn't quit my job.

In the morning I would tell myself to stop being ridiculous. Everything was fine. Yes, things were taking longer than expected with the business, but we were debt-free. Things weren't so bad. We were planning a wedding and we could afford a new couch. Just not a $2,500 designer couch—and therein lay the problem. Despite our lack of debt and my gradually growing business, deep inside I feared that we were not only falling behind but might never truly recover. And it was all my fault.

That was why I was about to cry in the IKEA store. The lump in my throat had nothing to do with furniture and everything to do with money fear, guilt and the pressure to keep up.

You should know that our home was and still is wall-to-wall IKEA furniture. I love that place. But in that moment I didn't want one of their couches. I wanted a couch from a designer store. A gorgeous $2,500 grey couch with an ottoman. I had been Internet-stalking it for months.

When Matt and I went to look at it, he said, "Um, this couch is $2,500, Shan."

And I replied, "That's because it's high quality and has a 10-year warranty."

He looked skeptical. "It's an investment," I insisted. "If you amortize the price over 10 years, it's only $250 a year, right?" (Wrong. I hadn't added in tax or delivery. That couch was actually going to cost about $3,000.) "Wouldn't you pay $250 a year for a beautiful couch?" I continued.

"I don't know," he said. "We should check out some other stores to compare. We haven't even gone to IKEA yet."

I did not want to go to IKEA. I knew that we would find a lovely, reasonably priced couch and my dream of owning the expensive grey designer couch would be destroyed. But he insisted. So off we went. Compromise.

Upon arrival, we headed straight to the couch department, where I saw in the IKEA distance just what I had feared: a lovely grey couch very similar to the $2,500 ($3,000) designer couch. My heart sank. I tried to rush past it and distract my husband by making some silly joke about nothing.

"Oh, hey!" he said. "Look at this one!" Crap. He'd spotted it.

"What about it?" I asked.

"It looks exactly like the one from the other store." He picked up the price tag. "Sweet! It's $600! So much more affordable." He looked at me expectantly, like he wanted to fist-bump or something. I was not interested in fist-bumping.

I protested. "This is the same couch that—" I listed three friends who owned this exact couch. (That was true.)

"So?"

"So we can't have the same couch as everyone else." (That was my insecurity talking.)

He looked at me curiously, as though he didn't quite recognize me. "We're talking about a difference of $1,900. I don't think we should spend that much more on a couch when this one is almost exactly the same. We can't afford it." (That was a punch to the gut.)

This was where Logical Shannon exited the scene completely. My face burned hot. "Of course we can afford it," I insisted. "I make money, you know. Our couch is disgusting; it's falling apart. It embarrasses me when people come over." I remember it clearly—I was seething. People were staring at us.

"Sure, but why can't we just get the more affordable couch?" he asked. "I don't get it. You're acting so strange right now."

"Because we aren't broke," I growled. (There's that word.) "You need to grow up!"

That was when I turned and headed straight for the bookcases, fighting back tears, leaving him with his mind whirling, insulted, humiliated and confused. It was terrible. I cringe just thinking about it.

Before you judge me as the most snobbish, out-of-touch woman on earth, let me admit that in that moment I had lost all perspective. I wasn't myself. I was being ruled by an overwhelming sense of money fear and inadequacy. And, as I was coming to realize while I stared at the display books on the shelf, when we feel inadequate, we make bad financial decisions.

As my blood pressure came down, I started to realize that this was a familiar feeling. Having couch envy was like being 12 years old again. When I hit Grade 7, I began to understand the difference between those who had money and those who didn't have as much.

"Look," one of my friends said, pointing to a group of really cool girls at school. "They all have Tommy Hilfiger jeans. Those cost like a hundred bucks. Their parents must be loaded." Since most people in my public school were not "loaded," rich parents held big currency in the popularity department.

It was funny. I hadn't noticed the brand of jeans the other girls wore until it was pointed out to me. To my surprise, my friend was right. This was some sort of secret expensive-jeans club. I begged my parents for a pair. They said no a million times until finally, for my birthday, I got a pair. It was such a big deal.

I wore the jeans to school and the leader of the secret expensive-jeans club said "Nice jeans" to me. I beamed.

I realized in the IKEA store that the grey designer couch was simply my grown-up version of Tommy Hilfiger jeans. I wanted the couch to help me feel that I could keep up, to fit in with those who seemed more successful than me. Maybe I could point it out when one of my ex-colleagues came over and hope it would prove that starting my own business had been okay, that I hadn't made a huge mistake by leaving Bay Street, putting us financially behind forever. All of a sudden, in the midst of the Billy bookcases, I could see that this overwhelming pressure to keep up was making me feel inadequate and broke. It made me want to overspend on the designer couch to prove my financial worth, even though I knew we shouldn't.

I literally shook my head. *Wait, what? That's ridiculous.* Enter: Perspective.

This realization gave me a moment to pause and ask myself: Could we actually not afford the designer couch? While buying the couch wouldn't make or break our retirement, that didn't mean we could *really* afford it. As I continued to "examine" the bookcase, I did some quick calculations in my head. In order to pay for it without credit, we would have to eat into our wedding fund or our emergency fund by $3,000. I was not willing to do either. The wedding was coming up soon, and as a self-employed person, I knew the importance of an emergency account.

The other option was to pull out the credit card and swipe. But I also knew that we couldn't realistically reduce our spending money by more than $300 a month without increasing the likelihood that we would go into even more debt. That meant that it would take us approximately 10 months to pay down the couch. I didn't want that either.

Because of my job, I knew that overspending like that would simply leave me feeling more anxious about money and guilty every time I sat on the fancy couch. It would be a physical reminder that I had overspent and made a foolish financial decision. We could not afford it. Buying the designer couch meant short-term happiness in the moment in exchange for longer-term pain. Not worth it.

So I said no. I took a breath, apologized for my epic meltdown and said, "Let's do the IKEA couch."

All these years later, I'm curled up on that IKEA couch as I write this. While it might not be the ergonomically friendly way to sit with a laptop, I'm comfortable and I like this couch. I don't resent it now and I didn't resent it then either. I didn't ruminate about how I couldn't get what I'd wanted, and I made a point of no longer looking at designer couches online. In short, I appreciated what I could have and I didn't feel like I was settling, and that was key.

Buying the more affordable but still lovely IKEA couch meant that we were living within our means. For us the IKEA couch was the compromise between financial responsibility and happiness. We still got a great couch and I didn't create more guilt and money anxiety by overspending. That's why it felt good.

So why am I telling you such an embarrassing story right off the bat? Because that IKEA fight shifted the way I gave financial advice for years to come. I believe it's the main reason why my business, the New School of Finance, has a waiting list. It was the birthplace of Worry-Free Money—the idea that it is possible to live within your means without hating your life, and that all you need is a little self-knowledge.

The couch fight showed me the importance of understanding the underlying reasons for wanting to overspend. Once I understood why I felt compelled to overspend, it was much easier to find perspective and say no. I wasn't really upset about the couch. I just wanted to overspend on the expensive one to prove to myself that

I wasn't a financial failure. My own financial sh*t was making me feel broke and afraid.

Saying no to overspending allowed me to continue living within my means and to appreciate what I did have, instead of comparing what I *didn't* have to what others *did*. Powerful stuff. That experience laid the groundwork for how I give my clients advice and financial solutions to this day.

•

Imagine living a life that makes you feel happy while still being financially responsible. Imagine feeling hopeful about your financial future. Imagine feeling that you have control over your finances once and for all. It is possible. It's Worry-Free Money.

This book explores the reasons why you feel broke and want to overspend, while also showing you how to stop budgeting and start living without fearing for your financial future. In the coming chapters you'll discover how to—

- Understand the underlying reasons for why you want to overspend.
- Understand what you truly can and cannot afford, without budgeting.
- Spend money on things that make you happy.
- Say no to overspending (and yes to saving).
- Stop comparing yourself to others.

Mastering all five will give you control over your finances, enjoyment of your life and hope again for the future. That's Worry-Free Money.

•

A few housekeeping items before you deep-dive into the awesome financial world of Worry-Free Money.

Since I'm a certified financial planner, I use many client stories in this book, which means you'll be getting a glimpse into the private financial lives of everyday people. It's important for you to know that every story in the book is told with the express permission of the client who inspired it and that all the names have been changed.

My company, the New School of Finance, works with clients from all walks of life who are diverse in age, location, privilege, sexual orientation and cultural background. The financial stories in this book reflect that diversity. From those who are struggling to make ends meet to others who are big, big earners, *everyone* is worried about money.

Last, there is a super-helpful Resource Library at the back of the book to help you create your own financial plan as you read. Bust out your calculators, people. It's time for Worry-Free Money.

My mission is to offer you the kind of empathy, support and realistic financial strategies you need in order to survive modern life, to move you from simply understanding financial concepts to implementing positive changes in your life without resentment. By the end of this book, you'll be living within your means without hating your life, and truly believing that everything's going to be okay. I promise.

NOTE: No savings accounts were harmed during the making of this book.

Part One

Stop Feeling Broke

Living a life of financial frustration leads to bad financial outcomes. I've seen it again and again. Money fear, scarcity mindset, worry, feeling broke—whatever you want to call it. If you constantly feel as if you can't live the life you want to live without sacrificing your long-term financial security, you'll be financially frustrated. And eventually you'll give up on trying to be financially responsible because . . . what's the point?

"When our debt hit $5,000 on the line of credit, I felt something let go. It was like, fine, what's another $400?"

It's hard to stay motivated about your financial plans when you feel broke. That's the real trouble. Eventually you develop a tolerance to feeling bad about your finances. It doesn't mean you like it; it just means that you're resigned to the fact that you have given up or are giving up more often. It's the reason why you abandon financial plans, stop checking credit card statements and constantly dip into savings accounts, all the while hoping every time it rains that the basement won't flood. In some ways it's just easier. And sometimes it leads to actually being broke.

When you constantly feel as if you can't afford the life you want or thought you would be able to live, there can be a subtle but destructive shift in your approach to spending. Instead of stressing the details, you shrug and think, *Why bother? Spend now and worry about it later.* Before you know it you've overspent and under-saved and your financial goals keep getting pushed farther and farther out to make room for your short-term needs.

The good news is that once you understand why you keep falling off the financially awesome wagon and recognize the reasons why you want to overspend, you won't be tempted to shrug off financially responsible decisions. You'll give up less often, or maybe not at all. You'll be motivated and confident about the future. And when you start putting some rainy-day money aside, you'll understand that it isn't "doing nothing." It's letting you sleep at night.

This is how you usher in a new era of money happiness, of Worry-Free Money. An era that will last because you won't want to give up before you even begin.

CHAPTER 1

Feeling Broke
Leads to Being Broke

Modern life sets up a horrific financial trap, blending an overwhelming pressure for you to overspend with a crippling fear for the future when you do. In other words, you feel afraid when you spend money and guilty when you don't. Now throw in a bunch of daily headlines—"Debt Is Bad"; "Housing Prices Rise Again"; "Not Enough for Retirement"— and you've got a frustrating cycle of guilt and fear. You feel broke all the time. It's no wonder you're worried about money.

But if you're like most people, your financial worry and financial decisions don't always align. Like the mom in tears who feels so strapped because she has once again dipped into her emergency savings, this time to drop $300 on her niece's wedding gift. "We should be able to give Nessa a gift for her wedding, no?" Or the professional who doesn't have enough money for next month's rent but still lays down a credit card for new work clothes. Both of these people are worried about their finances, yet they overspend, and their spending decisions make them feel out of control with their finances and frustrated.

Imagine this: You are terrified of having mice in your house but you still leave crumbs all over the floor. Then you're up half the night, worried that you're hearing mice, because you know the crumbs are on the floor. You know you should have cleaned up the crumbs so you could sleep soundly, but you didn't. Your actions directly created more anxiety. It's the same with your finances.

If you find yourself in a cycle of worrying about money but still overspending or under-saving, it's not because you are bad with money or lacking in willpower. There's something else at play here, something bigger than grit or financial literacy. I believe that we, as a collective whole, are slowly giving up on our finances—day by day, swipe by swipe, crumb by crumb. And every one of those crumbs is a F*ck-It Moment.

The F*ck-It Moment

The F*ck-It Moment is when you feel as if there's no point in trying to be financially responsible and you end up overspending, even though you're worried about your financial future.

Like when you're working hard and following the rules but feel that you will never be able to afford the life you want. *I can never actually afford a vacation, but I need one. F*ck it, life is too short.* Swipe!

Or when you're in the middle of a home reno and you reach the point where all you can think is "in for a penny, in for a pound." *We've already spent $10,000. What's another $1,000? F*ck it.* Swipe!

*Sure, I know that cooking what's in the fridge versus ordering pizza is the better financial decision. But I'm tired and I had a terrible day. F*ck it. I'll worry about it later.* Swipe!

Typically, when you think of people who overspend, images of a mall-obsessed ditz binge-spending on expensive purses and fancy cocktails comes to mind. "But that's not me," you may say. "I don't live extravagantly."

That's probably true, but from a financial perspective, over-spending doesn't mean extravagance. It simply means you're not saving enough overall. Maybe you don't have debt, maybe you're already saving, but that doesn't mean you're not overspending or worried about money. In order to survive financially and sleep at night, you need to ensure that you are saving enough to reach your financial goals, such as paying down debt (if you have it), preparing for emergencies (because you will have them), saving for big lifestyle goals (a house, school, a new business) and securing retirement. That's a tall order. It doesn't matter if you forgo fancy cocktails and expensive taxi rides. If you're not covering your financial butt, you're overspending. And F*ck-It Moments are a big part of the problem.

The solution is to stop spending and start saving. Easy-peasy, right? Wrong. If it were that easy to stop spending and save money, everyone would be doing it and no one would ever worry about money again. But that's not realistic. Life is messy and expensive and never follows the rules.

Real life forces you to make hundreds of small financial decisions every day. Renew the gym membership? Join co-workers for a drink or say no again? How much to give at the bar mitzvah? Now add in groceries, kids' activities, birthday parties, weddings, grooming, the new screen door, even pants, and it's easy to see how messy, overspending F*ck-It Moments happen.

Understand that I'm not talking only about the big expenses where you wind up house-poor, car-poor or baby-poor. Overspending can certainly happen there, but it also happens one small transaction at a time. Day by day, swipe by swipe, none of which is large enough to set off alarm bells like the shopping addict who buys $3,000 shoes online at one in the morning. Therein lies the problem. These small financial decisions add up over time. You probably can't point to one specific transaction in your bank account and say, "Yes, that's the moment where I screwed myself out of financial security forever."

You often don't notice your F*ck-It Moments until it's too late and you're already frustrated, worried . . . broke.

Like my client Leanne, an entrepreneur who runs a successful retail clothing store. The store pulls in about $200,000 a year in revenue. Sounds awesome, right? But after she pays her rent, her staff, her suppliers and her marketing costs, Leanne makes $40,000 a year. She busts her butt every day, often working evenings and weekends, putting in roughly 55 hours a week. That means about $14 an hour, which is less than what she pays her staff. The amount of effort, brain space and exhaustion that her job demands, combined with the responsibility of making the rent and paying bills, doesn't always seem worth it to her. She could work for another retailer and make more money with much less stress. She's tired and burnt-out.

Leanne arrived at my office for our first meeting carrying a shopping bag. She had just dropped $150 on a blazer. Granted, this $150 purchase was unlikely to rob her of her retirement, but it was an impulse buy after a very long day at work. A perfect example of over-spending and under-saving, but at the time she was too tired to care.

"Retail therapy," she said with a shrug. "Pun intended." Then she looked down at the bag. "I dunno why I bought it. I just work so frigging hard and I love this blazer. I was just like, *Whatever, I deserve this*. It's only $150. It's not like I bought a million-dollar house." She was angry—I could tell by her body language. Not at me, but at the situation.

When we work hard, we want to be rewarded. Buying things and experiences that fill us up emotionally are ways of celebrating our achievements, enjoying the fruits of our labour. Money is the reason why we work.

"I should be able to afford a damn blazer without feeling crappy about it," Leanne said. "But I already know I'm going to beat myself up for this later." Her eyes filled with tears. "It's just so annoying, you know? I work so hard. How is it possible that spending $150 is such a big deal? I'm 35 years old and I feel broke because I bought a new jacket. Pathetic."

I get it. Modern life is a grind. Being in constant demand from work through phones, email and other electronic devices can leave you exhausted, physically and mentally. You work hard for your money, and having your income remain stagnant while the cost of living rises can frustrate anyone.

I'm sure you've had a F*ck-It Moment or two. We all have. You know, those times when you weren't able to say no to spending money on something you knew you really couldn't afford. You felt the pressure to spend and gave in because it just felt easier, and probably more fun, than being financially responsible. So why was that? Why did you reach a point where you felt like your financial plan wasn't worth it, where you lost the motivation to stick to the plan?

F*ck-It Moments, big or small, are caused by an overwhelming pressure to spend money. The pressure takes over and in the moment outweighs your rational, logical thought that you should say no. Leanne should have said no to the blazer (it was an overspend for sure), but in that moment she felt inadequate—financially inadequate, as if she couldn't afford the life she wanted to live. She felt broke.

The more intensely and frequently you feel the pressure to overspend, the more broke you feel, because you have to say no more and more often. Daily life begins to feel akin to being on an all-lettuce diet. Eventually you'll see a pizza and eat the whole thing because you've felt deprived for too long. It's the same with money. The more frequently you have to say no to the urge to overspend, the more likely you are to hit the F*ck-It Moment again and again, sabotaging your finances.

The bottom line is that avoiding the F*ck-It Moment is critical for your financial survival, whether it's happening in daily transactions or large, sweeping purchases. In order to reach the F*ck-It Moment less and less often, you need to figure out exactly why it is that you feel deprived all the time, so you can stop feeling broke and stay motivated.

Feeling broke is characterized by two things: the frustrating awareness that there isn't enough money for the life you want to live, and the nagging fear that you could wind up financially screwed (literally broke), regardless of how hard you work. Both of these reactions are reasonable, normal and absolutely human. That's why money, more than anything else, can make you frustrated and anxious. The very things that drive your financial decisions are at war with each other: spend money to enjoy life or save so you don't end up with nothing. Is it any wonder you feel deprived? The more you have to say no to spending, the more you feel that you can't win. Or the more you say yes to spending, the more you worry about your financial future. It's a trap.

Interestingly, the rise in our collective anxiety has given birth to more investment advice, budgeting apps, and tips and tricks than ever before, all available 24/7. Yet they are not helping to curb rising debt levels in North America or ease our worries about the future. Why? Because they don't look at the reasons behind our "bad" or "irrational" financial decisions. They don't help us understand *why* we choose to overspend or to give up.

Knowing how to find the best ETFs, brokerage accounts and insurance packages is useless if you don't have enough money left at the end of the month to put into investment accounts or towards those premiums. Information about those resources is worthless until you can get control over your finances in a sustainable way, forever.

A healthy dose of worry is important for your financial future, helping to ensure that there is indeed enough money. Without a bit of worry, you may end up overspending, constantly living from F*ck-It Moment to F*ck-It Moment because you have an unrealistic sense that the universe will ultimately provide. But there is a happy medium. No one wants to end up as the grasshopper who sang all summer while the ant worked hard. But if you find yourself feeling guilty for spending any money at all or are up nights worrying about financial outcomes you can't control, like rising interest rates, you have likely gone too far towards the ant—one who is constantly anxious, worried and afraid—regardless of how well you're doing financially.

Over-worrying makes every single dollar that you have to spend to live your life feel precious. It leads to resentment, frustration and even more F*ck-It Moments, because you feel afraid or guilty every time you spend money. Here's the thing: underspending is neither sustainable nor realistic. Housing, transit and a new pair of pants all cost money. After a while, living on a shoestring, constantly saying no to things you would like to have or do, can't help but make you feel deprived, frustrated and inadequate. That's why underspending can be as dangerous as overspending. Both make you feel deprived. Both make you feel broke and both lead to more frequent F*ck-It Moments.

The pressure to underspend and over-save is fairly obvious—we all want financial security in the long run. But where does the crippling pressure to overspend come from? Why do we feel deprived when we have to say no to overspending? What is driving our urge to give up and throw in the towel on being financially responsible? It's something I call the Inadequacy Influence.

The Inadequacy Influence

The Inadequacy Influence is when you feel like you can't keep up or like you're not good enough, and spending money (regardless of affordability) seems like the solution. In that moment, spending money makes you feel that you are in fact enough. Inadequacy can rear its ugly head in a lot of ways, leaving you feeling guilty and insecure. Like you're a bad friend, a bad parent, a bad spouse or bad at your work.

Lacking confidence about the way you look before a first date? Overspend on a new outfit. That's a financial decision made under the Inadequacy Influence. Feeling guilty about leaving your adult child who's just had a baby so you can go to Florida for the winter? Overspend to fly them all out for a visit. A financial decision made under the Inadequacy Influence. Feeling insecure when your friends come over about how damaged your kitchen floor looks? Overspend on some new tiles before the wedding shower you're hosting. A financial decision made under the Inadequacy Influence.

The Inadequacy Influence is often a precursor of the F*ck-It Moment. You feel as though you're not enough, so you overspend to make the problem go away, but that leads to sleepless nights and fear about the future. You feel trapped, like you can't win. Eventually you lose motivation. You give up. My client Gabrielle is a perfect example.

Gabrielle came to my office last year, upset over her decision to purchase her son a PlayStation. She knew she couldn't afford it, but

12-year-old David had been asking and asking for months. Gabrielle felt guilty that she couldn't afford to give her son something he so desperately wanted, but she stood her ground, saying no again and again because it wasn't a good financial decision. Then came that fateful day when David had friends over after school.

As the boys were trying to decide how to spend the afternoon, Gabrielle overheard them making fun of David for not having a game system, saying that his house was boring and they should go to Liam's instead. When the boys left, David was upset, but Gabrielle even more so. She felt like the world's worst mom. Her son was being left out and made fun of, not because of something he'd done but because of something *she'd* done—being unable to afford the PlayStation. The Inadequacy Influence told her she was a bad parent. To appease her crushing guilt, she did what a lot of parents do to protect their kids from hurt. She bought a PlayStation for $400.

In Gabrielle's case, the situation worsened. Because she and her partner were hosting a birthday party that same month and attending a friend's 20th anniversary celebration, that extra $400 on her credit card wouldn't be going anywhere soon. There it sat, collecting interest alongside her other purchases, month after month. A clear reminder that she had been financially irresponsible.

Naturally money worry came in the middle of the night when she couldn't sleep and had no perspective. The little voice inside her head, whispering, *There isn't enough money, and there will never be enough money, and you're so bad with money,* sounded like the voice of wisdom—one that knew her all too well—plunging her into a frustrating cycle of financial guilt and fear. She wanted to give up. What was the point in trying?

When you make financial decisions as a response to feeling inadequate, you probably overspend, and that's why it creates fear. If you could afford it, it wouldn't make you feel less than you are and it wouldn't be scary. But you can't really afford it, yet you say yes anyway. That's why you feel broke. That's why you feel as if your finances could spiral out of control at any minute, and it's what makes you worried for the financial future. The fear and the struggle are real.

Limiting the impact of the Inadequacy Influence and recognizing your own triggers will help you gain perspective and identify those F*ck-It Moments before they hit. Think about the last five purchases you've made—not groceries and gas, but things beyond the basics. What was driving each purchase? Was it need? Want? Or was there maybe something else creeping in at the edges? Looking back can help you understand what the Inadequacy Influence feels like in action. And learning to recognize that feeling helps give you control. Once you can see those moments coming, you'll be able to limit their impact, say no to overspending and avoid the fear and anxiety that comes with it.

Understanding the reasons behind the pressure to overspend and how the Inadequacy Influence can negatively impact your finances is an important first step toward Worry-Free Money. The next step is recognizing where the Inadequacy Influence comes from and how to avoid it.

CHAPTER 2

The Joneses and the Life Checklist: A Double Blow to Your Finances

One of the questions I hear most often at client meetings is "Are we/Am I on track?" What this question is really asking is "Are we where we should be financially according to our age and social group, or are we screwed?"

"Are we screwed?" is a big and scary question. Will we be able to keep the house in our old age? Will I struggle for the rest of my life? Will we ever be able to escape the hustle? Can I stop being secretly resentful of my friends' success because I'm finally getting ahead too? In other words, "Will I ever stop feeling like I can't keep up?"

The Joneses

Whether it's family and friends or what you see in advertising and the media, the group that you align yourself with or identify with become your peers. To get specific, Judith Rich Harris, author of *No Two Alike*, proposes that human beings calculate their status based on an average of the group against whom they measure themselves. These are the people you are subconsciously trying to keep up with. They are the ones whose status is most likely to make you fall victim to the Inadequacy Influence.

If you're thinking this is a bad thing, let me be clear: comparing yourself to others is not a negative or jealous act and it doesn't make you shallow. Keeping up is an innately human, completely natural way to avoid falling behind the pack. It's survival of the fittest.

Think about a toddler who wants everything that the kid beside him touches. Not because he's learned to be greedy but because his sense of self is telling him that whatever that other kid has might be better than what he already has. He's comparing himself to a peer and quite naturally wants to keep up or, better yet, get ahead. This innate instinct is why we teach children sharing and manners, and why we keep reinforcing concepts like kindness and respect.

But no matter how old, educated, sophisticated or disciplined we like to think we are, the need to compare ourselves to others never truly goes away. It's keeping up with the Joneses.

Now I know that there's a lot of judgment around the phrase "keeping up with the Joneses." Images of shallow people competing with each other to have nicer fences, cars and lawns. Of being totally consumed by how much stuff or status they have. But I'm talking about a different type of keeping up. It's not petty and it's not about an empty, consumer-driven pursuit of status simply for its own sake. It's about fitting in with your people. That's reasonable, normal, human. You probably have your own Joneses, even if you don't think you're trying to keep up with anybody.

Meet Les and Reese, clients who live in the country—self-proclaimed bumpkins and damn proud of it. Last year their household income was about $80,000. Their mortgage is manageable and they do not consider themselves extravagant spenders. Yet when they came to see me, they felt as if they weren't moving forwards with their finances.

"We don't buy fancy clothes and we don't drink expensive coffee like you city folk," Reese joked. "So why are we having such a hard time saving?"

Les and Reese were both 43 at the time, with no debt outside of their mortgage. With Reese being the sole breadwinner and having no employer pension plan for retirement, they were well aware that her income needed to cover not only their daily life expenses but also savings for their future. Knowing, however, had not translated into reality. Even with $10,000 in their savings account, they were not hitting their annual targets for retirement savings.

I suggested we start by putting that $10,000 into a retirement account, but Reese stopped me cold. "No," she said. "That's the ATV fund. We can't mess with that." As she hurried to explain why, I realized we had just run headlong into the reason why they couldn't save.

Les and Reese loved everything about their rural life—the open spaces, the fresh air, the sense of community with friends and neighbours—all of which were made richer by memberships in the local snowmobile and ATV clubs. Weekend excursions with their friends were what Les and Reese did for fun with their family. It was how they maintained their social group.

Where they lived, people couldn't care less about which restaurant you went to or what event you attended on the weekend, but they cared very much if you held up the crew because your ATV kept breaking down on the trails. After a while the invitations to join the outings would start to dwindle, until eventually you weren't invited at all. It wasn't personal. They liked you just fine, but if you couldn't join them on the trails, what was the point of an invitation?

Reese laughed when I suggested that the members of those clubs were her Joneses. "They're our friends," she said. "We're not competing with them for anything."

I explained that keeping up wasn't about competition. It was about fitting in with the people she and Les identified with, the ones they compared themselves to on a daily basis. They didn't need fancy coffees, designer clothes or bigger and better houses in order to fit in with their group. But an expensive piece of machinery was a must-have if they wanted to keep up, both literally and figuratively. No wonder they were hell-bent on sinking their savings into a depreciating asset.

Was the ATV a good financial decision? No. Was it a good social decision? Absolutely. The social expectation within their peer group was that you owned an ATV. Because Les and Reese valued their spot in the group as much as the lifestyle that came with it, their savings goal simply could not compete with the pressure to keep up. This was a financial decision made under the Inadequacy Influence, and it was directly related to the pressure to overspend (which we all feel) in order to keep up with our people. So when you're thinking about your Joneses, don't just look at your lawn or your car to try to figure out how you might be being influenced. Think about how you need to participate to feel like you're part of your community, whatever that community might look like.

The Life Checklist

Everyone has their own version of what it means to be on track, but it's always based on the same things: who you are, who you compare yourself to, and the expectations or social norms of the people you love and care about it. Together they add up to something I call the Life Checklist.

The Life Checklist is different for everyone. It's a collection of achievements or lifestyle expectations that define what success is for you. Maybe it's a house and a car. Or a horse and a truck. Or eating organic food. Whatever it may be, your list started taking shape a long time ago, back when you were young and absorbing everything around you. As you grew, that list morphed and changed, based on the social norms and expectations of your upbringing and the peers you came to identify with.

Like it or not, that list acts a benchmark for your finances and how good (or bad) you feel about what you've accomplished. It's how you know whether you're keeping up with or falling behind your pack, your people. Saying no to spending money on something that will uphold your Life Checklist means that you feel like you're depriving yourself, your family or someone you love of something necessary. It's hard, and maintaining your Life Checklist is typically why overspending happens. You simply don't say no.

Like my clients Mona and Brandon. Five years ago they were expecting their first child and felt as if they were "late" buying a home when they compared themselves to their peers. They were renting affordably, had relatively good cash flow on a monthly basis and about $25,000 of savings. As an added bonus, they were debt-free.

They had just received a very generous $50,000 gift from Mona's parents. It was unexpected and everyone was excited, assuming that they could now buy a house close to family and friends in the city they loved. While Brandon and Mona both have healthy incomes of $50,000 and $60,000 respectively, when we crunched the numbers, a mortgage of $400,000 was the most they could afford without being unrealistic about how they spent money. That meant finding a house for around $450,000 ($50,000 + $400,000). They left my office excited about the plan.

Three years later they were back. They had indeed purchased a house and their kid was adorable, but they were swimming in debt. They had been rolling their monthly credit card debts into an ever-increasing line of credit. It was a secret and heavy burden. Their incomes were healthy but they were barely getting by, living from paycheque to paycheque. They were stressed.

"My parents didn't raise me to be financially irresponsible," Mona said. "I feel like I've squandered their gift." Her shame was palpable.

"What happened?" I asked, passing her a tissue. (I keep them on hand in the office at all times. Tissues and whisky . . . just kidding.)

"I got tired of feeling like we didn't have our sh*t together," she said.

Once they had started their home search, the Inadequacy Influence reared its ugly head and the pressure to overspend was intense. After searching and searching for a home within the $450,000 price range I had given them, they ended up saying "F*ck it" and paid $650,000—$200,000 over what we had agreed was financially responsible.

They had considered whether they should rent for a little longer, but "comments like 'You're throwing your money away renting' and 'Prices are only going up' got to me," Mona confessed.

Mona had grown up in a middle-class suburb of Toronto. Her formative years were privileged. Most of her friends had managed to buy homes in their late 20s and early 30s. When she hung out with her people, they were talking about real estate prices, home reno horror stories or daycare costs. Without a house of her own, Mona felt excluded from these conversations, like she wasn't keeping up.

"We'd come home from a dinner party and feel pretty low because our friends were talking about plumbing issues, and I was tired of making the joke that I just call my landlord. It started to become really evident that we didn't make as much money as our friends." Mona was failing to keep up with her Life Checklist, putting her directly under the Inadequacy Influence. She felt that if she and Brandon only had more money, they could have bought a house long ago and none of this would have been an issue.

"Everyone assumed that because we're both employed and over 30 we should be able to afford a house," she said. "I felt like that too! I mean, how crazy is it that we couldn't get something we wanted with a $50,000 down payment? That's a lot of money! It doesn't make sense. Five years ago we would have been laughing."

To be clear, no one in their social group was saying those things to be a jerk. In fact, most thought they were being helpful. But one by one, those comments only served to validate the sinking feeling that they were falling behind.

"And then my best friend called," Mona said. "She told me the house down the street was up for sale. 'Come be our neighbour! Our kids will go to the same school!' she said, and that was the turning point."

"It was a steal for the neighbourhood," Brandon assured me, but even with the $50,000 down payment, they still started off with a $600,000 mortgage, which made them house-poor.

Even if they had wanted to rent a while longer or to consider moving farther out to keep their mortgage within their means at $400,000, it was impossible to escape the pressure from friends and family. Plus, who was kidding whom? They wanted to be near their friends and family, and neither was willing to commute two hours each way to work every day. And Mona had long dreamed of owning a three-bedroom home that they could grow into. The pressure to overspend was also coming from herself—one giant inadequacy-fuelled pressure cooker.

They bought a house they could not afford to shut everyone up, including their own nagging feelings of inadequacy. It worked for a while, but the fact that they were totally financially stretched caught up with them. When it no longer worked, they kept pretending they were fine, to friends, family and Facebook followers. Only they knew the financial truth . . . and now me. They loved their house, but at what cost?

After explaining what the Life Checklist was, I asked Mona to describe what hers looked like, with emphasis on those lifestyle expectations that made her feel as though she "had her sh*t together." After a few moments of thought, she started to write.

Mona's Life Checklist

1. Goals I am proud of having achieved in my life:

✔	Have a career that I enjoy
✔	Be free of student debt
✔	Annual travel with Brandon
✔	Have a beautiful wedding, shower and bachelorette party
✔	Buy a home near family (i.e., without a two-hour commute)
✔	Have children

2. Lifestyle expectations I want to meet:

	Continue to take family vacations
	Try to eat good-quality/organic food where possible
	Pay for kids to go to school and for their first down payment
	Retire happily and rich at 60 or 65 (60 would be better)

Here's the thing: each of the items on Mona's Life Checklist came with a price tag. Life costs money.

"Okay, this all makes sense," I said.

"What does?" Mona asked.

"The weight of your Life Checklist is the reason you're in over your head right now. Everything on this list has equal importance. They all seem to be things you feel you need to achieve in order to be successful. The fact that you hadn't bought a house yet and your friends had was bound to make you feel inadequate. It's no wonder you stretched the budget. You see, when your parents gave you that $50,000 gift, it validated your Life Checklist and your expectation that you needed to own a home in order to be successful. The gift was meant to help you and Brandon buy a home, not to pay down student debt or travel or pay rent."

"Actually, we wouldn't have received the gift unless we used it for a down payment. I guess I never thought about it adding to the pressure."

"Exactly. There was so much pressure, internally and externally, when it came to buying a home."

While well-intentioned, the gift of a down payment only brought Mona's Life Checklist into sharper focus. She was already feeling that she and Brandon had fallen behind their friends. If she couldn't buy a home then, she would miss checking an important box on her Life Checklist. It was a box that made her feel very financially inadequate—broke, even though they absolutely weren't.

At the end of the day, that's how your Life Checklist works. It's ruthless and it doesn't lie. Tick those boxes or people will know that you don't make or have enough money. It feels as though it doesn't matter that you earn enough to pay your bills, have a life that makes you happy and even save some money. You obviously don't earn enough to do all the things your peers seemingly can. And if you can't do *all* the things, then you feel inadequate, as if you are falling behind. Otherwise you'd put your talented kid in hockey, get the nice baby stroller, go on a trip, own a home where you actually want to live.

That is what's hard about your Life Checklist. When you can't afford to do or achieve the things you always thought you would, it can make you feel like a financial failure, even when you're not. Did Brandon and Mona need a $700,000 house? Of course not. They could have happily rented. Did they need a house where they didn't have to commute to work? No, but they wanted it. Living within a short commute from work and family was a huge box on their Life Checklist, making their *wants* feel like *needs*.

Everything on your Life Checklist can feel like a need rather than a want. When you fall behind or fail to reach the benchmarks, your sense of inadequacy is real, and most times you throw money at it to make it go away. It's the root cause of the Inadequacy Influence.

Identifying Your Triggers

In order to break free from the Inadequacy Influence, you need to be able to spot the areas in your life where you are most likely to wind up feeling as though you can't keep up. These areas of your life are triggers, things that make you vulnerable to the Inadequacy Influence and to overspending. If you know your triggers in advance, you can see them coming. You can anticipate the pressure to overspend and shift your perspective so you don't end up feeling deprived, and you will therefore reach the F*ck-It Moment less often.

Imagine that you were terrified of public speaking. If a friend at a wedding unexpectedly puts you on the spot to make a speech, you probably react in a way that isn't ideal. Maybe you stammer and freeze. Maybe you hide in the coatroom. Or maybe you're so angry at your friend that you hold a grudge for a while. The point is, you didn't see it coming and that's why your reaction is so strong. You didn't have time to brace yourself. If, however, your friend asks you months before the wedding to make a toast, you'll probably fare just fine. You practice because you know it is coming and you're prepared for the sweaty hands and racing heart. It doesn't catch you off guard when the emcee announces your name, and therefore you have control of your emotions and your reactions.

This is how identifying your inadequacy triggers can help you avoid feeling broke. If you are able to identify areas in your life where you are prone to falling victim to the Inadequacy Influence, you can predict them, brace yourself and get perspective. Take my client Nate, for example. When he first came to see me, he was 29, financially frustrated and complaining about his job.

"I wish I could just win the lottery, quit my job and travel."

"Do you hate your job?" I asked.

"No, my job is fine. It's just that, I don't know, it's so limiting."

Nate worked a nine-to-five desk job with a very secure pension plan and wonderful benefits. He earned $50,000 a year. Since he was unionized, he was on a pay grid. All this was good—great, in fact—but he was constantly frustrated with his financial lot.

"My friends work in jobs they really love. Jobs that pay more, that allow them to travel and take time off work. I feel like I'm stuck. Super-secure golden handcuffs."

Nate had bought a condo he could afford and had been dutifully paying down the mortgage. He had achieved some amazing things already and yet he wasn't satisfied.

"What would a higher-paying job allow you to achieve that you can't right now?" I asked.

"I'd buy a nicer car, that's for sure." He laughed. "And travel more."

"Is your car falling apart?" I asked.

"No, but my friends are in sales, finance or tech. They make more money than I do, for sure, and as we get older, the gap is becoming much more noticeable. Ugh, I hate admitting this, but they all have sweet cars and I can't help but feel like the odd man out. I love cars. I'd like to have a nice one before I have kids one day and only drive a minivan. I mean, I've got the line of credit. Can't I just buy a new car and pay it off over time?"

Nate's Life Checklist

1. Goals I am proud of having achieved in my life:

✔	Have a job with a great pension
✔	Own property

2. Lifestyle expectations I want to meet:

	Drive a nice car
	Have a job I actually like
	Run a marathon
	Go to Burning Man
	Play in a band
	Move to a home in the suburbs (with three bedrooms)
	Travel six months of the year
	Get married
	Have kids
	Save enough to retire at 65

After looking at his finances, I knew that Nate couldn't realistic-ally afford the car he wanted. Not if he hoped to achieve some of the other financial goals he had mentioned. He was clearly a financially responsible guy, yet here he was debating spending tens of thou-sands of dollars on a car. Nate was falling victim to the Inadequacy Influence and was *this* close to a F*ck-It Moment.

While he didn't realize it, having a nice car was a huge box on Nate's Life Checklist. His peers had managed to check that box, leaving him feeling that he'd fallen behind, and he was now ready to throw money at the frustration. I wondered what other lifestyle expectations were waiting to trip him up, so I asked him to figure out his Life Checklist.

"Do any of these items surprise you?" I asked.

"No, but I guess I never really thought about my life as being a series of goals and lifestyle expectations. It's kinda cool . . . Kinda freaky."

"What's freaky about it?" I asked.

"Well, there's like two different sides of me reflected here. The part that wants the house in the suburbs and the family, and the other part that wants to be more carefree and travel for six months a year." (He's a Gemini. So, you know, it made sense.)

"I see that too," I said. "So, let's dig in. I want you to circle the goals or expectations that you assumed you would have achieved by now. Then put a note beside the ones you're worried aren't financially realistic."

He groaned and I laughed (not maniacally or anything). "Yes, I know. It's a bit of a buzz-kill."

He went through the list and circled the following as things he felt he should have achieved by now and added his notes on why they felt out of reach:

- Have a job I actually like (not sure I can give up the pension)
- Drive a nice car (not unless I borrow a ton of money)
- Travel six months of the year (I'd have to quit my job and the pension)

"Interesting," I said.

"What?" he asked.

"The very things you were complaining about—the car and the travel—are the things that you are most insecure about. You feel like you should have achieved them by now, which means that some part of you feels like you've maybe done something wrong or made bad choices."

"So?"

"So you've just identified the financial areas of your life that are most likely to make you feel inadequate, which makes you feel broke and frustrated. But here's the reality: you're not really willing to give up your secure job. Just as you're not willing to give up on a house in the suburbs or starting a family or going to Burning Man or playing in a band. You don't feel stress around them because, in your mind, those things are definitely going to happen. The other goals, such as extended travel, a fun job and a fancy car, are things you'd like to achieve but cannot afford. That's why they make you feel broke—because they are out of reach unless you compromise on what's really important to you. Travelling for six months a year and having a nice car are things you feel that you *should* be able to afford. But you can't, so they're a constant reminder that you don't make enough money to do all the things you want to do.

"When you compare yourself to your friends who have beautiful cars or travel every winter, you feel low, like somehow you've made bad choices with your life and career. But you didn't make bad choices, Nate. Just different ones. Ones that allow you to achieve some of your Life Checklist, but not all of it. That's powerful information."

"What's powerful about it?" he asked.

"Knowing ahead of time what things will trigger your feelings of inadequacy is empowering. Whenever you encounter people—not just your friends—who travel, drive a fancy car or talk about how much they love their neat, interesting job, you're likely to feel a pang of insecurity and frustration with your own finances, because those people are managing to do the very things that you can't afford. Cars, travel and job love are your current financial sore spots, areas that could potentially push you to overspend in an attempt to keep up. These are your triggers."

Nate looked at me for a moment. "Hmm, that's so true. I don't feel crappy when someone gets married or buys a house. But travel photos get me every time. They make me want to quit my job or spend way too much money on a last-minute flight somewhere."

"Exactly. Now you can anticipate those crappy feelings, and the pressure to overspend that comes with them. You can actively work to not let it bother you and to appreciate everything on your Life Checklist that you've already achieved or will achieve, instead of focusing on the few things that you have not or cannot."

Nate left the meeting happy, knowing that next time one of his friends was off to Thailand or got a bonus or a new sports car, he could be happy for him instead of resentful.

Sure, those things he cannot afford would still be on his Life Checklist, but they weren't realistic right then, given all the other things he wanted to achieve. That didn't mean he was broke; he'd just made different choices. And he'd still get to go to Burning Man, so that was a win.

Take a minute and think about what this means for you. Ask yourself: What are my lifestyle expectations? How do I measure my financial success relative to my peers? Who are my Joneses?

There are bound to be some Life Checklist goals that you have already accomplished and some that you fantasize about achieving, even if they aren't realistic in terms of what you can actually afford. Those things might include travel, becoming debt-free this year, renting a bigger apartment without roommates, starting a business, putting your kids in Montessori school, buying or renovating a home, rock climbing, a year in Provence—the possibilities are endless. Chances are your people—your Joneses—will have many of the same boxes on their own lists. When you see them ticking off the boxes faster than you are, beware of falling victim to the Inadequacy Influence. You may feel anxious, frustrated and ready to throw money at them, simply to prove that you can have all those things too. When you feel that happening, focus instead on what you have already achieved on your list and what's truly important going forward. And know that you haven't failed at life. You've just made different choices.

What Is Your Current Life Checklist?

Part 1: Your Life Checklist
1. Goals I am proud of having achieved

Write down a list of goals or lifestyle expectations that you have already met and are proud of. These can be simple things like "I love being a part-time musician" or "I love growing my own vegetables" or "I love being fit." They can also include values that are important to you. Things like "I like knowing I'm a good friend," or "I like the fact that I rescue cats." The list will definitely include massive achievements such as "moved across the globe to go to veterinary school in Australia" or "bought a home."

The list should reflect both things you've achieved and those you want to maintain. For example, a lifestyle expectation of being a part-time musician is not something you can achieve once and then cross off your list, like getting your master's degree. It's ongoing.

2. Lifestyle expectations I want to meet

Write a list of lifestyle expectations or goals you would like to achieve or wish you could achieve. The items you've listed in these two sections are a snapshot of your current Life Checklist.

Part 2: Where Do You Feel the Sting of Inadequacy?

Circle the expectations in the second list above that you think are not financially viable. This is important, because you're identifying expectations that you have (or others may have for you) that are not realistic given your financial reality. These are the areas where you are most vulnerable; unless you overspend to tick that box, your people—your Joneses—will know that you can't keep up. And you'll be admitting to yourself that you can't afford to live the life you want to live.

The point of this exercise is to recognize your lifestyle expectations, where you've achieved them and where you may feel that you are falling behind. This way you can identify not only the things you have achieved but, more importantly, the nonnegotiable goals, the ones that are truly important to you. Once you know what those are, you'll also recognize the expectations that may not be financially realistic—the boxes that can sabotage your happiness and your finances.

Putting down your Life Checklist on paper allows you to see the things that matter most to you, pointing out the areas where you're most vulnerable to the pressures of your Life Checklist and therefore the Inadequacy Influence. Once you know where your potential pitfalls lie, you can sidestep those feelings of inadequacy and resist the need to overspend in order to tick the boxes on your Life Checklist faster—or at all.

CHAPTER 3

Social Media:
Your Life Checklist on Steroids

Your Life Checklist on its own is not a problem. Having goals keeps you motivated and excited about what's coming next. The problems start when your Life Checklist pushes you to make financial decisions that are detrimental to your financial health in an attempt to keep up with unrealistic expectations. Make no mistake, modern life has messed with our lifestyle expectations big time by ratcheting up the cost of daily life and making us feel financially inadequate most of the time. I blame a lot of this on social media.

Social media take the concept of keeping up with the Joneses and put it on steroids. It's just about the worst thing to happen to our bank accounts since overdraft protection. From where I sit, it has slowly but surely made daily life more and more expensive over time, and I don't think it's simply an adjustment for inflation.

A study by the Columbia Business School found that people with high social media usage have higher credit card debt than people who use social media less often. In addition, the study also found that social media use reduces self-control, which I know directly relates to your ability to stick to a budget.

The hold that social media have on us is powerful and dangerous because it fans the flames of the Inadequacy Influence. Through our many social media feeds, we're all painfully aware of how many other people—our people—are succeeding at their Life Checklist and how we may be falling behind or missing out.

Scroll through your social media feeds. Bet you'll see tons of noteworthy and awesome things that your friends and peers are up to. Carefully curated photos of fabulous dinners, exciting family outings, nice cars and happy babies, or maybe a selfie taken while cooking an outrageously delicious and beautifully presented meal. But those pictures tell only a fraction of the story. Behind every great photo is a bill. And rare is the person who will publicly admit that they're carrying a balance on their credit card because they just bought a computer they couldn't afford.

Social media are like one giant lifestyle advertisement in which your friends are the models. House porn, food porn, trip porn, gadget porn . . . as you scroll through, it's hard not to compare your own life and your own financial situation to that of your friends.

FOMO (fear of missing out) is perfectly natural and boringly human. For example, if there's a social outing that you want to attend with family or friends, you will likely go even if you can't afford it, in order to avoid feeling left out. This is FOMO, and our budgets are most affected when it comes to—

- parties
- family gatherings
- anything related to weddings (bachelorettes, showers, the wedding itself)
- dinner out with friends
- trips
- buying houses/condos/property
- starting a family
- retiring early

Much of this is social spending with your people. Your people are hanging out together and having a good time, and you don't want to miss out on the fun or be seen as not caring enough.

Thanks to social media, you are now much more aware of missing out. Staying in while your pals are out apple-picking or at a play or at a stag-and-doe feels so much worse when you're watching Netflix at home in your sweatpants while eating Cheerios out of the box.

It's one thing to say "Nope, I'm staying in, wearing sweats and not answering my phone" because you *want* to. It's a whole other thing to stay in when you really want to go somewhere but can't afford it. That's the real FOMO, the financially caused FOMO. That's what makes it hard to say no to spending and makes you feel broke.

Most people aren't posting photos to purposefully make other people feel inadequate or to show off. But unconsciously that's exactly what we are all doing. When we share something on social media, it's usually noteworthy or pretty or fun. It heightens the awesomeness and lifestyle expectations of daily life. And with those, the cost.

A good example of how social media can raise your daily cost of living is something I call the "I see, therefore I want" effect. A great example of this is seen in my client Cheri. Over a few years of scrolling through her social media feeds, she noticed that charcuterie boards were popping up more and more when her people were hosting an evening. Seems mundane, no? Like, who cares if her people put out some meat and cheese when they host a party? But these beautiful boards seemed to have become a new hosting standard among the people she followed.

Five years ago she hadn't felt the need to buy anything other than chips and dip for a girls' night. And her girlfriends probably didn't care, but now, thanks to her social media feed, Cheri did.

She wanted to show them that they were important to her and that she was a good host. These days when her girlfriends are coming over, she picks up some nice meat, cheese and pickles without a second thought. She doesn't resent doing it; it actually makes her really happy. But it is a new expectation she has set for herself, an expectation created entirely by social media, and now it costs her $40 when she hosts, versus the usual $15 she spent three years ago.

Trust me, no one was posting photos with charcuterie in the background to make her feel inadequate or raise the financial stakes in her life, but that doesn't mean it didn't have exactly that effect. Perhaps charcuterie boards aren't your thing, but maybe constantly seeing people's beautiful latte photos makes your daily cup of joe seem lame. Or maybe the photos of new parents with the latest and greatest baby strollers make your hand-me-down stroller seem inadequate. And doesn't your discount gym membership seem a little unexciting when you see all your people hitting up neat fitness and wellness classes on the weekend? This is how social media sneak in and up the financial costs of your daily life. If you followed only one person, you would probably see something that gave you a pang of jealousy or ratcheted up the financial cost of life only once in a while. But because most people follow a lot more than that, odds are that a simple scroll through your feeds will show you countless photos of people doing noteworthy, awesome things in beautiful places that cost money. It's inescapable and it's dangerous, especially when it comes to your Life Checklist.

If you're single and looking for love, photos of engagements and weddings can exacerbate your fear of never finding "the one," making you feel as if you're falling behind. If you want to buy a home but know you can't afford it, photos of first-time homebuyers your age will make you feel more than inadequate. Social media prey on your weaknesses—your Life Checklist triggers—and heighten your sense of inadequacy. Social media make you much more aware than ever before of how the people you compare yourself to are living.

A Family Vacation Hijacked by Social Media

In a recent financial planning meeting I met with Bailey and her partner, Kim. It wasn't our first meeting, but despite the plan that we had created for them, Kim and Bailey had spent way beyond their means for a family vacation. A month later, faced with the looming credit card bill, they were anxious and feeling guilty about it. Between mortgage payments, car payments, afterschool daycare programs and grocery bills, there wasn't a lot of wiggle room to pay down the new credit card bill. It was going to take them six months at least, and during that time they'd have to put off their planned savings for their emergency fund.

The last time Kim and Bailey sat down with me, they had planned to save $1,000 for a family camping vacation. Somehow they ended up spending $4,500 at a resort instead, and the additional $3,500 all went on their credit card.

Bailey, Kim and their son, Will, loved camping, and they had all been perfectly happy with the trip they were planning. I asked them how they had ended up at a resort, shelling out tons of money for boat rentals, stand-up paddleboards and dining out. They looked at each other and Bailey finally said, "We saw all these photos of our friends and their families on these amazing family vacations. Disneyland, cottages, even Mexico! I didn't realize how exciting other people's family vacations were until we were scrolling through my news feed, and I felt like, *Jeez, we are bad parents*."

And there it was—*we didn't know, but now we do, and we're not good enough*—all thanks to social media. I knew that Will was happy, well-fed, loved and healthy. All the signs of good parenting were present, and yet they had felt tremendous guilt about their lack of an annual family blowout, as if they were depriving their child of a basic necessity.

Fifteen years ago, if Kim and Bailey had wanted to see photos of their friends' amazing vacation, they would have had to physically go to their homes and demand a three-hour slide show complete with shots of hotels, water slides and fabulous meals. And 15 years ago it would have been a one-time slide show. They would have had no access to those photos once the evening was over (unless they asked for copies, which would have been creepy).

But fast-forward those 15 years and Bailey now follows 328 people on social media. She figures that about 50 percent are parents in a similar socioeconomic bracket. These are her people, her Joneses, the ones against whom she measures her Life Checklist status. A quick scroll through her news feed while brushing her teeth in the morning lets her see March Break vacation photos for 20-plus families. The Turners are skiing, the Singhs are in Cuba, and—oh, look!—the Yees are riding horses.

Bailey didn't have to go to someone's house to see those photos; she didn't even have to ask to see them. They were just there, in her face. Making her painfully aware of how unexciting her own family vacation plans felt. And all before her morning coffee.

Post by post, social media were stoking the fire under Bailey's fear that she wasn't good enough, that her financial inadequacy was depriving Will of the kind of experiences his peers were enjoying. Which paved the way for that trip to a resort becoming a need rather than a want.

That's how social media change our perceptions, making daily life more expensive. Simple things like having a few friends over becomes a $40 evening instead of a $15 one. And a Life Checklist goal of travel with the family ends up costing $4,500 instead of $1,000. It took Bailey and Kim eight months to recover from that unexpected credit card debt. For others, the financial impact of the social media parade can last much longer.

Social Media Detox = Financial Lifesaver

Meet Lulu, another client who suffered from overspending heightened by the pressure of social media. When she came to see me, Lulu had $7,000 in credit card debt, all of which had accumulated in the past year. Month by month, swipe by swipe, F*ck-It Moment after F*ck-It Moment, the balance continued to climb.

Lulu admitted that she liked online shopping and subscribed to email bulletins from all her favourite stores. Her credit card info is saved on most of their sites to make purchasing easy. A little too easy. "It's never anything huge," she said. "Just little things here and there."

Her last purchase was a rug for her apartment. "It's hard to resist when I see all these beautiful products from my favourite stores on my friends' social media feeds. Somehow it makes me feel like I'm failing at life. Or maybe we all just have debt? I don't know."

I asked her when she does most of her online shopping. "I'm a sucker for a sale," she said.

After a little more digging, I knew a major source of her financial woes was social media. "I think social media are affecting your finances in a bad way," I told her. "I'd like you to try a social media detox and see if that helps break the cycle of overspending."

She stared at me a moment and finally said, "What do I have to do exactly?"

I explained the rules:

- Two weeks *fully* off social media. No cheating.
- Unsubscribing from all her favourite retailers that currently sent notifications to her inbox.
- Deleting her credit card information from all apps and online stores.

"The goal," I told her, "is to see if the urge to spend goes down over the next two weeks. And if you do have an urge to spend, hopefully you'll have made the process more difficult."

She was definitely skeptical and not looking forward to it, but she agreed to give the detox a try.

After two weeks, we had a meeting to check in. Here's what she reported: "Being totally off social media for two weeks was painful at first. I was so angry at you for the first four days, and I cheated a few times. But I finally realized I was actually addicted to it, around the same time that I realized I didn't feel as down about my circumstances anymore. That was really interesting.

"And then I almost bought a new bathing suit online, but since my credit card info wasn't in the store's checkout data, I didn't end up purchasing it. My wallet was in another room and I was sitting in front of the laptop and TV, being like, *Oh great, now I have to get up from my cozy spot and get my credit card.* I realized I didn't want to be bothered, which is so lazy!" She laughed. "I took that as a sign that I didn't really want the bathing suit, you know? So I shut the site and decided that if I still wanted it the next day, I'd buy it then. But I didn't."

"Did you notice that your urges to buy decreased?" I asked.

"Not while I was on the detox, but once I logged back on I immediately noticed that I had urges. I was back on Temptation Island with all these beautiful products constantly in front of me."

"Can you be more specific?" I asked.

"Well, I follow two lifestyle bloggers and now I'm so much more aware of how they impact me. I've also noticed that a few of my friends are actually triggers that make me feel like crap. Maybe I'm a bit jealous? Not in a 'mean girls,' catty kind of way. It's just that they have really nice lives and I guess I compare myself to them a lot. I never thought about that before the detox. But they are my friends, so what can I do about it? I'm not going to unfollow them."

Totally fair. The people we compare ourselves to the most, our Joneses, are often our closest friends, relatives and peers. Since staying off social media forever is not an option for most of us, we have to learn to use it responsibly.

So what can you do to avoid falling prey to social media spending pressure? A different kind of checklist can help:

- Unsubscribe from the email newsletters of your favourite stores. Ignorance is bliss when it comes to sales.
- Unfollow any lifestyle brands or retailers that trigger you to overspend.

- Unfollow people (except your friends, obviously) who trigger your sense of inadequacy, such as people from high school whose unbelievable success makes you feel like crap.
- Don't use social media until you've been awake for an hour and have had some caffeine or whatever you use to wake yourself up.
- Shut off all social media one hour before going to bed.
- Use a timer. If you're about to deep-dive into social media, that's okay! Set the timer for 15 minutes. That way you'll be aware of how much time you're spending mindlessly scrolling.

Lulu and I added a financial plan to the social media detox to keep her from slipping back into overspending habits. I met with her six months later to follow up.

"I've been killing it," she said.

I leaned forward. "Tell me everything."

"I followed all your rules, and I can honestly say that I have fewer urges to spend and I feel better about my financial life. Actually, though, I think my awareness of special sales was a huge issue. Like you said, I'm blissfully ignorant now and I don't feel as sorry for myself because I can't afford the things I see on sale. And making it harder for me to buy online was key. It really alerted me to how mindlessly I was spending money before, just because it was way too easy. I deleted my automatic taxi and food delivery accounts from my phone too. That made a huge difference."

"And how's the debt repayment going?"

She beamed. "I've paid off $3,000 and haven't had a single shopping binge. I've bought stuff, for sure, but nothing that I regret or that was purchased because I was having a low moment."

"This is wonderful news!"

"I thought your whole social media detox was a bit over the top when I was here before, but honestly, being off it and being more mindful of what it's doing to me have been total game-changers. I feel that I can log in now and recognize when I'm under the Inadequacy Influence and when I'm not. I control it, not the other way around. Plus I know in advance that I need to brace myself when I'm about to look at some of my friends' profiles, because they are triggers for me."

"Amazing!" I said, and we hugged it out.

The combination of comparing herself to others on social media and the ease of online shopping had become a financial nightmare for Lulu. And no wonder! Spending money online is so streamlined it's almost effortless. *Click, click,* done. Add in free shipping and it feels like the perfect pick-me-up when you're having a weak, fearful or emotionally charged moment.

A social media detox can get you out from under the Inadequacy Influence by helping you gain perspective and recognize your spending triggers. Following that up by deleting your credit card information from your favourite online stores makes it harder to spend money, ensuring that every purchase is made mindfully. But to keep the Influence under wraps for good, you have to curb the all-too-human need to compare yourself to others—something that is easier said than done.

Social media are a fun but powerful way for us to compare ourselves to others. You need to be mindful of the ways in which the cost of your lifestyle expectations may be creeping up, as well as the effect that social media are having on your overall sense of inadequacy. The more often you have to say no to spending and the more aware you are of what other people have, the more deprived, broke and inadequate you feel, making you more likely to overspend in order to keep up. Awareness of those feelings can help you gain perspective about what your triggers are and when they're being pulled.

Taking a social media detox can help you break free from the Inadequacy Influence, but it's not forever. Lessening your social media usage and using responsibly will help, but at the core, the ultimate key to controlling the Inadequacy Influence is twofold: (1) learning how to stop comparing yourself to others in person, online, at work and in the middle of the night, and (2) appreciating what you have. Once you stop comparing and start appreciating, you'll not only feel better about yourself, you'll also find that the pressure to overspend will reduce dramatically. Without that added pressure, F*ck-It Moments will find you less and less often. You'll be able to stick to your financial plan without feeling deprived when you say no to overspending.

CHAPTER 4

Stop Comparing Yourself to Others: The Beyoncé Factor

If someone you know (or follow on social media) is nailing all the goals you have on your own Life Checklist, you're probably wondering, *How are they doing it?*

My job gives me the wonderful advantage of peeking into the private financial lives of ordinary people on a daily basis. I see the real money and what's going on behind the scenes. I know *exactly* how they're doing it—and often the reality is that what you see is far from their financial truth.

Knowing the intimate financial details of thousands of people both older and younger than me is the main reason why I don't operate under the Inadequacy Influence as often as I used to. I don't feel as broke as some of my peers because I actively try not to compare myself to them. But most people don't have the luxury of this knowledge about their peers, because we don't talk about money. All we know is what our friends and family tell us or the boxes we see them ticking off on their Life Checklists—the clothes they wear, the cars they drive, the vacations they post on social media.

Swanky Dinner Out
(photo on social media)

Photo Caption: "We fancy—fab dinner with the BFFs!"

The Pressure: "I do fun things and I have my financial sh*t together."

The Hidden Reality: "I'm living from paycheque to paycheque."

**The Home Reno
(discussion at a dinner party)**

Statement: "The new floors are in. So glad the reno is finally over!"

The Pressure: "My house is beautiful and we have our financial sh*t together."

The Hidden Reality: "We've maxed out our $150,000 home equity line of credit."

**The Fab Vacation
(photo on social media)**

Photo Caption: "Off to the beach. See ya later, snow!"

The Pressure: "I live an exciting life and I have my financial sh*t together."

The Hidden Reality: "I had no work lined up for January. This whole thing is chilling on a credit card."

That's why I started a project called "Real Selfies" a few years ago. I wanted to do something to remind people that we cannot compare our financial lives to those of friends and family. Why? Because comparison can make us feel inadequate, and you never actually know what's going on behind the scenes.

As part of the project, whenever I did something noteworthy, I'd post a photo and then I'd come clean about the bill. One of my favourites was the classic "passport at the airport" shot, a popular photo setup when someone is about to fly somewhere. Usually there's a drink and a passport plus some text about where that person is flying to. For me, the Real Selfie photo had a glass of wine and my passport with the comment "Heading out for vacay" underneath. Beside it I posted the reality: "$341 for flight to Florida. This Shiz Costs Money."

The project really resonated with people. I wasn't surprised, because every photograph highlighted the fact that we don't talk much (if at all) about how we're managing financially. The Real Selfies project reminded people that they don't know the answers to that nagging question "How are they doing it?" Maybe the folks ticking all the boxes have debt. Maybe they got help. Or maybe they just spent money on different things. Either way, the Real Selfies project allowed people to say *Maybe I'm not bad with money after all. Maybe I'm not falling behind.*

I know that a lot of people like to blame lifestyle shows, bloggers and the ever-present celebrity culture for the pressure to live "Pinterest perfect" lives that are completely unattainable and unrealistic. While I definitely believe that all these factors contribute to ratcheting up the cost of the expectations on someone's Life Checklist, here's the thing to remember: Keeping up isn't about matching the lifestyles of the rich and famous. It's not about yachting or diamonds or ponies. It's about keeping up with the people you watch daily, the people in your community, both online and in person. Remember, your Life Checklist revolves around the social norms and expectations of your peers, not celebrities.

At our last meeting my client Andrew said, "My co-worker goes on these epic trips. I mean, they must cost thousands a year. She also just bought a townhouse. I don't get it. How is she affording it? We have the same job and I think we make around the same amount a year, but I can barely save $5,000 for retirement each year. What am I doing wrong?"

I said to him, "Don't believe everything you see. No one posts a photo of their credit card bill after the vacation, just the good stuff."

He looked doubtful. "I guess so."

"You should ask her how she affords it."

"I can't do that," he insisted. "It's rude!"

"There's no way of knowing whether or not you should be comparing yourself financially to her until you know if the playing field is level."

"What do you mean?"

"If Beyoncé bought a yacht, would you feel bad about not owning one?"

He laughed. "Of course not."

"Why?"

"Because Beyoncé is a mega-millionaire. She's in an entirely different financial sphere from me."

"Exactly. You think that you and your co-worker are in the same financial sphere because you have the same job. But you don't know what she makes or whether she has debt or had family help for the townhouse. For all you know she's swimming in debt, or her rich great-uncle passed away and she inherited a million dollars. Because you don't know what her financial life looks like, she may as well be Beyoncé. Unless you're 100 percent certain that your finances are exactly the same as hers, she's not someone you should compare yourself to."

And that is the Beyoncé Factor. Beyoncé buying a yacht doesn't make Andrew feel like he's financially inadequate or falling behind with his Life Checklist, because Beyoncé isn't in his financial sphere. Until you know *without a doubt* that the people you compare yourselves to are in your financial sphere, you should simply assume that they may as well be Beyoncé and you cannot compare yourself to them. That is how you shut down the Inadequacy Influence.

Andrew did ask his co-worker how she was pulling off the trips and the townhouse. He learned that she wasn't pulling it off at all. In fact, she confessed that she had struggled a lot when she first bought the townhouse, because it was really expensive (no rich great-uncle). To make life easier she got a roommate, giving her an additional $1,000 a month. She put $600 of that towards the mortgage and the other $400 went into an extravagant trip fund.

"She told me that if she had to, she'd keep renting that room for the rest of her life, because she liked being able to treat herself to an epic trip every year."

"How do you feel, now that you know the truth?" I asked.

"Relieved. You're right, she's Beyoncé. I can't compare myself to her. I don't want a roommate, so I don't have an extra $400 a month to save for trips. Totally different financial sphere."

"Exactly."

But here's the thing: Before asking the awkward question, Andrew saw only the beautiful photos from Portugal or Iceland and heard the amazing stories at the lunch table. He assumed that he and his co-worker were in the same financial sphere, yet he couldn't afford either a townhouse or exotic travel and felt like he must be doing something wrong, as if he were somehow bad with money. Lack of knowledge made him feel financially inadequate when in reality his co-worker was a Beyoncé. The truth had set him free.

If you're comparing yourself to someone who makes you feel financially inadequate or makes you feel broke, you need to turn that feeling around. How? Just ask yourself two questions:

The Beyoncé Factor Check-In

1. Do you know the intimate, numerical financial details of this person's life and how they accomplished their goal(s)?

   No? Don't compare yourself to them. They may as well be Beyoncé.

   Yes? Go to Question 2.

2. Are you in the *exact* same financial situation as them? (Include income, debt, assets and potential gifts or inheritances.)

   Yes? Okay, compare yourself to this person. Find out what they are doing differently. Maybe they have tips that can help you move forwards.

   No? Don't compare yourself to them. Again, they may as well be Beyoncé.

   It's just that simple.

See Ya Never, Inadequacy

I wish I could promise you that, once you reduce social media usage and stop comparing yourself to others, your finances will fall magically into place. But I'm all about keeping it real. Your lifestyle expectations (and Checklist) will shift over time, as will your goals and financial constraints, which means you'll constantly need to keep the Inadequacy Influence in check.

The good news is that now you not only know how the Inadequacy Influence arises and when it might rear its very ugly head, you're also equipped with the tools to say *I'm feeling bad about my finances right now because I'm comparing myself to someone else*. If that happens, do the Beyoncé Factor Check-In and see how you feel afterward.

Recognizing your personal Inadequacy Influences—your triggers, your Joneses and the boxes on your Life Checklist that refuse to be ignored—will help you keep them in check so you can stop feeling broke and avoid those destructive F*ck-It Moments. Once you know how to stop feeling broke, you will be ushering a new era of financial happiness into your life. One that will work. One that will not fail, because you won't want to give up before it even begins.

This is how you get control of your finances and keep them on track. This is how you win.

Part Two

Stop Budgeting, Start Living and Get Control

Now that you are motivated to make changes, what changes should you make in order to get control of your finances and keep them on track?

The next steps to Worry-Free Money are the logistics. This part of the book will walk you step by step through how to get control over your cash flow, stop budgeting and start living. This is the nitty-gritty, awesome how-to part. Personal finance geeks, rejoice! It's time to bust out your calculators and/or spreadsheets, pour a drink and make your plan.

All the hard work you've done to stop feeling broke can be undone if you don't feel that you have control over your cash flow. When you don't (or feel like you don't) have control over your cash flow, you continue to feel afraid or guilty when you spend money. You worry, even though you know to stop comparing yourself and to identify your inadequacy triggers.

Feeling out of control doesn't necessarily mean that you feel like you have no clue about what's happening with your finances. It could mean that for you, but it could also mean that you feel as if nothing you do is done on purpose. You have no strategy, no real understanding of how your daily financial decisions impact your overall financial health. Well, my friend, all that is about to be answered for you.

Gaining sustainable control over your cash flow is how you stop budgeting and start living without worrying about the future.

You do this by—

- establishing how much you realistically can and cannot afford to spend;
- ensuring that your spending makes you happy; and
- learning how to say no to overspending.

Mastering all three will empower you to gain control over your finances and restore your faith in your financial future. Getting control of your finances means living within your means without hating your life. Permanently.

CHAPTER 5

Why You Need to Stop Budgeting

Other than "Are we on track?" the second most common question I'm asked is "Where does my/our money go?"

In an age of endless budgeting apps and online trackers, it feels like we should all know exactly where our money goes. Yet you probably feel as if the money comes in and then, before you can say "Let's order pizza," it's spent. *Poof.* This is the Spending Vortex, where your money seems to evaporate before your eyes. It feels like you have no control over the money flying out of your chequing account.

Here's the thing. The question "Where does my money go?" isn't about not knowing where your money actually goes. If you look at your credit card or bank statement, you can see where it went. The real question is "Where is my money *going* to go?"

Unforeseen expenses creep in, every single month. "I don't know where my money goes" really means "I never know exactly how I'm going to have to spend my money tomorrow, next week or next month."

It's the same with statements like "I want my money to work for me" or "I want to be strategic with our money." What you truly want is control over your finances. To feel like you aren't wasting money and making financial decisions without purpose. You want confidence about the way you are managing your cash.

Understanding how to successfully manage your cash flow is the single most important thing you can do to get your finances on track.

Once you have control of your cash flow, the rest of the financial pieces will fall into place. Then the Spending Vortex and the worry it causes will be things of the past.

If I gave you $100 with instructions to give me back $40 later that day or else you'd be in serious financial trouble, you'd probably happily spend the other $60 without a second thought and hand over the remaining $40 with a smile. No guilt, no stress, no uncertainty. Now imagine I give you $100 with instructions to give *some* of it back to me at a later date or else you'll be in serious financial trouble. You don't know how much money you'll have to give back or when I'm going to ask for it. All you know is that some amount of money will have to be available at a moment's notice when I come calling for it.

If this were the case, you'd probably spend much less than $60, just to be careful. Maybe I'll ask for only $20 back and you could have spent $80, but you simply won't know. The result would be apprehension every time you spent *any* of that money, because you *might* be overspending. I might come back demanding $95, making even a $10 purchase risky. Uncertainty breeds guilt, fear and constant worry. It's exhausting.

The Spending Vortex creates this worry. Because you can't predict what you might need next month, *all* spending starts to feel irresponsible. You end up feeling as guilty about a $2 daily coffee as you do about a $200 luggage set. Even though neither may affect you in the long run, you feel guilty because you just aren't sure.

This is why budgets don't work. That's right—I said it.

Budgets Are Broken

Typically when you feel that your cash flow is out of control or you aren't moving forward financially, you turn to budgeting. You've been trained to think that a budget is *the* answer to all your fiscal problems. That it is the only way to regain control over your financial future. Budgets are trumpeted as the prescription for the overspending dilemma. But guess what? Traditional budgets are making things worse.

Budgeting usually means that you track your historical spending, categorize your expenses, forecast your monthly spending, set spending targets based on that historical data and then try to live within those limits. Try, fail, repeat. Why? Because this kind of budget is totally unrealistic for modern life. Budgeting like this usually means unrealistic spending targets, like $25 a week for clothes or $10 a week for toiletries, and cutting up all your credit cards. The very idea of cutting up your credit cards and using only cash makes me roll my eyes. This isn't the nineties (sadly).

These traditional types of tracking and credit-abstinence systems are not only dated, they are built to keep money at the forefront of your brain all the time. Especially when your app (or a family member) sends you text messages letting you know that you've overspent on toiletries already and it's only the tenth of the month. These kinds of budgets have too many rules and involve far too much work. It's over-budgeting, which is not only a waste of time but can actually be detrimental to your financial well-being. Budgets like this lead to F*ck-It Moments.

No matter how often you pore over your credit card or bank statements, no matter how committed you are to your financial goals, you can't know exactly where your money will be spent next month. Unless, of course, you can see into the future, in which case you probably have a winning lottery ticket and this book is now irrelevant because you can afford your dream life (woot!). But for us non–lottery winners, you can only guess where you will be spending money tomorrow, next week, next month, next year. That's why you are doomed to fail with typical budgets that force you to categorize, forecast spending and then reconcile your spending based on historical data.

Because you can't see into the future, frustration and failure are inevitable. Amounts set aside for specific expenses can suddenly come up short, so you end up "borrowing" from other categories. *I overspent on Misc. Shopping this month so I will have to borrow from Entertainment*. Juggling back and forth month after month leaves you thinking about money all the time, living in constant scarcity mode. It's a horrible game that negatively affects both your sense of self-worth and your ability to manage money.

This kind of budgeting may work for some, and that's great. But most people I meet will inevitably throw in the towel, F*ck-It, stop tracking altogether and end up feeling like financial failures. As though they're to blame when things don't go according to plan. When you fail at budgeting, you feel insecure about your finances, which validates a fear that you are "bad with money"—something that is both terrifying and shaming and not true at all.

If budgeting isn't working for you, it's not you. It's the budget. One of my clients, Jordan, came to me with exactly this kind of problem. While she could afford her life (translation: pay her bills and live) without going into debt, she wanted to start saving money. So far she hadn't been able to do it, even though she had started hardcore budgeting months ago.

Turned out that she had spent an entire Friday night setting up an epic spreadsheet. She looked at past spending and forecasted what she anticipated the next year had in store for her. Then, each month, she reconciled her forecasted budget with what really happened.

"I never managed to meet the targets. Not once," she told me. "Plus the time it took to fill in the spreadsheet was ridiculous. I'd forget for a couple of weeks and it would take hours to catch up. Eventually I was just like, *Nope, this isn't for me.*"

Tired of the time and effort her spreadsheet method took, she tried an app. Technology to the rescue! Another Friday night spent setting it up and entering all her numbers. ("Thank god for Netflix.") That weekend she had her family over and blew through her grocery budget for the week in one fell swoop. Sure enough, she got a sudden notification from her app: *Bzzz. You've overspent on groceries.* A literal reminder to herself that there was not enough money. An instant slap on the wrist to make her feel guilty for spending money on her family.

A week later she wanted to buy a dress for work. It cost $80. She hadn't bought any clothes for months and her job required a "professional appearance." But the dress was "over" her $50 per month clothing budget, so another notification came through: *Bzzz. You've overspent on clothing.* Instantly she thought to herself: *I don't make enough money.*

After reviewing her budget, I lovingly joked that there had been some small wins. On a month-by-month basis, she hadn't overspent on gifts or holidays. "Yeah, because it's March." She laughed. "Weddings and holidays are still months away, and then there goes my budget. I will be literally broke all summer."

She was so irritated by the amount of work the budgeting required and the overall feeling of failure every time those notifications came in that she dismantled the app altogether and threw in the towel on budgeting—and, by extension, saving. "It got to the point where every time I spent money I felt like crap, because I was always doing something wrong but couldn't fix it. My life doesn't work the same way each week, so it's almost impossible to know in advance how much I'll need for shopping or groceries this month versus next."

That kind of tracking didn't work for Jordan and it doesn't work for most people. In addition, this kind of budget can lead to all-out warfare for couples. It's too much work and far too restrictive for real life, because our lives aren't predictable. Things change month to month, day by day. You don't have a crystal ball. With one paycheque you may need to buy a lot of cheese. With another, a DustBuster and no cheese. Life is random.

I asked her, "So this budget sucks. Why does that make you upset?"

"I don't know. I just feel like I'm blowing through my money and not moving forward." There it was—that out-of-control feeling. The one thing that really mattered. You use budgets as a way to gain control of your finances. When you can't stick to them, you feel as if your finances are out of control, which is frustrating and frightening.

The true solution to managing your cash flow is to let go of the idea that you are in control of your daily spending. You're not. Say it with me now: *I'm not in control of my daily spending.* You need to accept the fact that your spending money must be fluid, flexible and able to respond to the ever-changing demands of daily life.

Obviously you shouldn't be spending *all* your money, but you're definitely allowed to spend *some*. We aren't on this earth merely to pay our phone bills.

I don't care how you spend your money each month (and no one should). It's your money, after all. The only thing I care about is that you're spending money that you can afford to spend.

If you could find a way to feel like you're in control of your cash flow while also saving money *without a budget*, you'd never have to put yourself through that agony again. It is possible. You just need to figure out how much money you can spend without sacrificing your financial security. That's the answer. Once you know this, you'll never have to budget again and you won't worry about money. What a magnificent concept!

CHAPTER 6

The Hard Limit:
How to Stop Budgeting

You don't need to care about where your spending money goes as long as the important, financially responsible work is happening in the background. Are your bills being paid? Are you saving enough to hit your financial goals? Great! Then you are living within your means and you have nothing to worry about. Spend away.

All you need is a line in the sand so you know when you can spend money and when you can't. Yes or no. Green or red. Go or stop.

That line is something I call your Hard Limit. No, not in a *Fifty Shades* kind of way. Well, maybe a little. Think of it as your new financial safe word. The Hard Limit is the line in the sand that separates the money you cannot spend from the money you can spend. The Hard Limit is the answer to the question "Can I afford this?"

What Is a Hard Limit?

Let's simplify. When it comes to money, there are only four categories to consider: Fixed Expenses, Meaningful Savings, Short-Term Savings and Spending Money. That's it. Every single dollar you earn gets slotted into one of those categories. The key is to isolate the daily Spending Money from all the other money that has a job.

Fixed Expenses is money you must pay out whether you like it or not, every single month or year. Money set aside for Fixed Expenses has the job of paying your bills and other fixed obligations, things like rent, cellphone, utility bills, etc. It's definitely not daily Spending Money.

Meaningful Savings is money set aside for increasing your net worth. Meaningful Savings has the job of improving your overall financial well-being—debt repayment, retirement savings, saving up to buy real estate. Also not your daily Spending Money.

Short-Term Savings is money set aside for spikes in your spending. Its job is to keep you out of debt when you need to spend money on Big Purchases, emergencies or travel. It's not daily Spending Money either.

Spending Money is what's left over. After you've put aside enough money each month or each payday for Fixed Expenses, Meaningful Savings and Short-Term Savings, the money left over is your daily Spending Money. It's meant to be spent and has no job except to ensure that you're fed, getting around and having fun. This money is your Hard Limit.

This is how setting up a Hard Limit works to signal what you can and cannot afford: It removes all the money that has a "job," leaving you with money that you can blow down to zero every month without feeling guilty. If you splurge on groceries you don't have to worry that the hydro bill won't get paid; the work is already being done. There's no need anymore to budget every single dollar you spend, because now you know the difference between the money you can spend on daily life and the money that you need to leave untouched. Respecting that division ensures that you are covering your financial butt.

When one of my clients says "If I know that I'm putting money into the kids' education savings, I feel less guilty splurging on the loot bags," I know what that translates into: when you know you are being financially responsible, you don't have to feel guilty about how you spend your money.

The Hard Limit is awesome. Let's figure out yours. (I'm actually stoked—nerd alert!)

How to Determine Your Hard Limit

Step 1: Calculate monthly after-tax income

First things first: you need to know what you're working with each month. It's crucial that you get this right. You don't need the gross amount of your paycheque (that's your annual salary divided by the number of paycheques). What you need to know is how much money actually drops into your bank account(s) every month—the net paycheque.

If you're an employee, this is fairly simple. Look at your bank statements to see the amount deposited into your bank account. That is your net paycheque.

If you're **paid twice a month**, you'll receive 24 paycheques a year, or two per month. Multiply your net paycheque by 2 to get the monthly amount. For example, if your net paycheque is $1,500, your monthly after-tax income is $3,000 ($1,500 × 2).

There may be some variances in your paycheques. If you max out your Canada Pension Plan (CPP) and Employment Insurance (EI) in the first part of the year, your net paycheque could increase in the latter part of the year. My advice is to use the amount from when your net pay is at its lowest. Build your Hard Limit around that. Then for those last few months of the year, you'll get "bonus money" each payday that you can use as you wish to top up Savings or top up Spending. As I mentioned above, if you've covered your financial butt with your Fixed Expenses, Meaningful Savings and Short-Term Savings, then it's okay to use this end-of-year windfall as additional Spending Money.

There may be other variances too. For example, if you are **paid biweekly**, you'll receive 26 paycheques a year. However, I suggest that you still multiply your net paycheque by 2, using 24 paycheques instead of the 26 to calculate your monthly after-tax income for planning purposes. Why? Because for 10 months of the year you will get only two paycheques per month, and you don't want to overestimate how much money you'll have to spend.

For example, my client Dan kept failing at the budgets he set up for himself because of this very problem. He had a net paycheque of $1,250 and was paid biweekly—26 paycheques a year. In order to set his budget, he multiplied 26 × $1,250 and came up with $32,500 a year as his annual after-tax income. Then he divided the $32,500 by 12 months and arrived at a monthly take-home income of $2,708. Great, right? Wrong.

Dan budgeted his life on $2,708 per month like this:

Fixed Expenses	$1,150
Meaningful Savings	$600
Short-Term Savings	$200
Spending Money	$758

But here's the thing: for 10 months of the year he gets only two paycheques a month, which is only $2,500 ($1,250 × 2) per month. As a result he was $208 short of his expected Spending Money for 10 months of the year. That's a lot! Dan ended up dipping into Short-Term Savings to cover regular life and so he constantly felt that he was bad with money. For him this became one more failed budgeting attempt—not the way you want to go. Building a budget or financial plan like this will set you up for failure, because you're planning on having more money than there actually is each month.

Yes, if you're paid biweekly you'll receive two additional paycheques annually, but I suggest putting those towards Short-Term Savings (which I deal with in Chapter 7, so hang tight). And you may be wondering what happens if your mortgage payment comes out biweekly; I deal with that in Step 2. For now, just focus on what's going into your bank account 10 months of the year. Similar issues can arise if you're paid weekly as well. See the table below for examples.

Here are four ways that you can calculate your monthly after-tax income based on how often you are paid. Assume that the net pay is $1,500 for those paid bimonthly or biweekly, $3,000 for those paid monthly and $750 for those paid weekly.

Pay Frequency	Net Pay	Cheques/ Month	Monthly After-Tax Income	Additional Cheques/Year
Bimonthly	$1,500	2	$3,000	0
Monthly	$3,000	1	$3,000	0
Biweekly	$1,500	2	$3,000	$1,500 × 2
Weekly	$750	4	$3,000	$750 × 4

If **you're self-employed** as a sole proprietor there's a bit more work involved, because you're going to have to forecast your income. Think about what you can realistically earn in the next 12 months, after you pay for business expenses and after putting aside sales tax and/or income taxes. For example, if you think your annual revenue

or sales will be $60,000 (not including sales tax) and you antici-
pate $10,000 in business expenses, you will have a taxable income
of approximately $50,000 per year ($60,000 – $10,000).

Use an online tax estimator to figure out roughly how much
federal and provincial income tax and CPP you'll need to put aside
to pay your tax bill. For example, if the calculator suggests that your
estimate of $50,000 in income will land you with an approximate
bill of $14,000 for income taxes and CPP, you're left with $36,000, or
$3,000 per month ($36,000/12). Here's how the calculations look:

Estimated revenue (excluding sales tax)	$60,000
Estimated expenses (excluding sales tax)	–$10,000
Estimated income (before income tax and CPP)	$50,000
Estimated income tax and CPP	–$14,000
Estimated annual after-tax income	$36,000
Months in the year	÷12
Monthly after-tax income	**$3,000**

Step 2: Add up Fixed Expenses

Fixed Expenses are those that you must pay every month, quarter
or year, and they tend not to fluctuate much. They are predictable,
which means you can plan to put aside enough money to cover them.
Here are some examples of predictable Fixed Expenses:

- mortgage payments or rent
- daycare
- consistent monthly pet walking or boarding fees
- condo fees
- insurance (car, home or renters')

- property tax
- consistent transit costs
- car payments
- life and living insurance
- debt or loan repayments
- utilities
- spousal or child support
- consistent gym membership fees
- subscriptions (cable, apps, print media)
- consistent monthly charitable donations
- bank fees

The key is that these are *predictable* and *guaranteed* expenses. Anything that fluctuates does not go in this category. Fixed Expenses should be approximately the same each month, regardless of what's going on in your life. This is why you may see things like a gym membership in Fixed Expenses but not things like groceries, gas, ad hoc transit or parking. Even though these are expenses you likely must pay for every month, their costs fluctuate.

When deciding which expenses are Fixed Expenses, it comes down to the nature of the expense. Predictable versus unpredictable; it has nothing to do with important versus unimportant. One month you may spend $800 on groceries, the next $1,000 because you hosted a party. There's no way of knowing exactly how much you'll spend. It's potentially the same with your transportation costs. I'm not saying that getting to work is optional; I'm saying that the cost each month may vary wildly. Perhaps sometimes you bike or walk and sometimes you drive. Sometimes the price of gas is up and sometimes down. The point is, as with groceries, you may not be able to predict your monthly transportation costs, and that's why you may not need to include them in Fixed Expenses. This doesn't mean that they are optional expenses; it simply means that they are not predictable. Fluctuating but necessary expenses like groceries, gas, toiletries and transportation are dealt with in depth in Chapter 9. For now, focus on figuring out your Fixed Expenses according to these criteria—predictable and guaranteed.

Have a look through your bank statements. Make note of which expenses are repeated, predictable and guaranteed. It's also helpful to check your credit card statements for repeated transactions, especially in an age when many services charge monthly membership or subscription fees.

It can be easy to miss some Fixed Expenses when you're eyeballing your statements, so be specific when you're adding them up. Be sure to pay attention to how often the payments come out of your account. For example, if your mortgage comes out biweekly, then there will be 26 payments a year. You need to multiply your mortgage payment by 26, then divide by 12 to get the monthly amount. Don't simply multiply your payment times 24 (i.e., twice a month for 12 months), as this won't give you enough money to cover the extra payments that come twice a year, when two months each have an extra week.

Remember to think about annual or quarterly expenses as well. For these, add up the annual cost and divide by 12. If you're worried because some of your costs, such as the hydro bill, are more in the summer than the winter, they are still considered Fixed Expenses because they are, for the most part, predictable. For bills that may fluctuate a bit based on the season, add up the entire previous year and then divide by 12 to get the average monthly amount you need to squirrel away. This way you're putting more away than necessary in some months so that you can use it in other months when you need it. You'll see that the way we handle cash flow for your Fixed Expenses will neatly leave the extra untouched.

Let's use a simple example. Imagine that these are the transactions from your bank and credit card statements:

Monthly Transactions		
Phone	$60	predictable/guaranteed
Rent	$1,130	predictable/guaranteed
Grocery store	$200	not predictable
Clothing store	$50	not predictable
Gym	$45	predictable/guaranteed
Grocery store	$15	not predictable
Car insurance	$125	predictable/guaranteed
Loan payment	$10	predictable/guaranteed
Bank fees	$5	predictable/guaranteed
Gas	$40	not predictable
Parking	$10	not predictable
Grocery store	$25	not predictable
Other Regular Transactions		
Gym membership	$22 biweekly	predictable/guaranteed
Renters' insurance	$300 yearly	predictable/guaranteed
Hydro	$600 average	predictable/guaranteed

So your monthly Fixed Expenses would be:

Rent	$1,130	
Hydro	$50	($600/12)
Renters' insurance	$25	($300/12)
Phone	$60	
Car insurance	$125	
Loan	$10	
Bank fees	$5	
Gym	$45	
Total	$1,450	

Keep in mind that the items that make up your Fixed Expenses can change over time. You could move, cancel your gym membership or reduce your bank fees. That $1,450 represents the predictable, guaranteed expenses in your life right now that you know you have to pay and aren't planning to change. That $1,450 per month is already promised to someone else. It cannot be spent on anything else but these expenses.

In my practice I have found that if your Fixed Expenses are higher than 55 percent of your after-tax income, you will likely struggle more to make ends meet. When Fixed Expenses are higher than 55 percent, most of your after-tax income is not yours anymore. When your paycheque hits your bank account, more than half is already spent, promised to someone else. In our example you can see that you would not be overextended. Your Fixed Expenses are only 48.3 percent of your after-tax income of $3,000. Yay!

If you're worried because you've just tallied up your own personal Fixed Expenses and they've come out at well over 55 percent, don't worry. We will look at this kind of situation in more depth later in Part Three. Just breathe. It's okay, trust me.

Step 3: Identify Meaningful Savings

Meaningful Savings are the savings that will move you forward financially. These are savings that will increase your net worth by reducing debts that you owe, adding to the assets you have, or accomplishing a larger financial goal like paying for your child's education. Examples include—

- paying down debt (of any kind) above the minimum payment
- saving for retirement
- saving for a down payment
- paying down your mortgage
- saving for your child's education fund

This is money being put aside to make you financially secure— your nest egg. When you know that you've got savings dedicated to improving your financial situation now or in the future, you don't have to worry anymore, because you know that you're covered. *Ahh,* a sigh of relief.

I usually see people budgeting by assessing how much they spend each month on bills and discretionary purchases and then saving what's left over. But often what's left over is not enough. It's important to set your financial savings goals *first*, letting the goals drive the amount that you're aiming to save, rather than your bills and spending.

When setting Meaningful Savings goals, ask yourself:

- What am I saving for?
- How much money do I need to save in order to accomplish this goal?
- How many months will it take to achieve it?

Debt Repayment

If you want to put money towards debt—credit cards, lines of credit or your mortgage—start by figuring out how much you owe and how quickly you want to pay it off. Once you've set those, it's best to use a debt-repayment calculator like the one described in the Resource Library (page 303) to calculate how much you need to put away each month. This calculator will help you understand the role that interest pays in your debt-repayment plan. Simply dividing the amount of debt you have by the number of months won't work.

It's a two-step process. If you have a $6,500 student loan charging 5.2 percent annually with a $65 minimum payment and you want to pay it off over 5 years (60 months), you input that information into the Debt-Repayment Calculator, which will tell you that $123.26 (let's call it $125) needs to go towards your loan each month. To figure out how much to put into your Meaningful Savings, first subtract the monthly minimum payment of $65, since that's a Fixed Expense (Right? You remembered to include it there?) and not Meaningful Savings. In this example, the $125 total loan payment needed, minus the $65 minimum payment, comes to $60 extra. So the Meaningful Savings you'd put towards your student loan debt would be $60 per month. Repeat this for any and all debts that you are looking to pay down.

Major Financial Accomplishments

If you are saving for a major goal like a down payment, home renovation or your kids' education, after you've established the amount you will need, your next step is to figure out your time horizon—how quickly you want to achieve that goal.

For Meaningful Savings goals that have a short time horizon (up to three years), set your savings target by simply dividing the amount you want to save by the number of months to your time horizon. For example, if you want to save $21,600 towards a down payment over the next three years (36 months), you'll need to save $600 per month ($21,600/36).

Even though you'll be setting this money aside in a savings account, I would assume a zero rate of return for Meaningful Savings goals that have such a short time horizon. Why? Money that is needed within the next three years should not be invested in the market. Investment returns vary—your savings might go up but they might also go down, and you don't have time to leave them in the market long enough to even out. The money you are saving for these goals should be in a safe, liquid savings account. Sure, it may earn some compound interest, but that interest is likely to be nominal, so you don't need to bother including it in your calculations.

If, however, the time horizon for your goal is longer than three years, it may make sense to include interest or investment returns in your calculations. Since the money will be invested for a longer time, you can take on a bit more risk and therefore more potential reward. For example, if you wanted to save $34,000 towards your child's education over the next 15 years (180 months), it's likely that you would choose to invest your money. Invested money will hopefully give you an average rate of a return over the long run, which means that you can save less each month but still reach your goal.

For example, without investment returns, in order to reach $34,000 in 15 years you'd need to save $188.88 per month ($34,000/180 months). But if you added in a 4.2 percent net rate of return on your investment—the amount earned on average after fees—you'd only need to save $139.41 each month! That's a big difference, and one that could make the likelihood of hitting your Meaningful Savings goal much more realistic.

So how do you calculate that on your own? There are savings calculators for exactly this purpose. Just plug in your savings goal amount, the number of years, and your estimated net rate of return (I think 4.5 percent is safe to use if you're invested in a balanced asset mix over five years), and they'll help you calculate your monthly payment. Check out the Savings Goal Calculator in the Resource Library (page 305) to see how compound interest and investment returns affect how much you'll need to save.

Retirement Savings

Goal-oriented savings like paying down debt or saving for a major accomplishment can seem easy enough to estimate, since you know how much you want to save. But a lot of people freeze when it comes to the retirement question, because they aren't sure how much they should be saving for the long run.

A tried-and-true rule-of-thumb is to ensure that you saved at least 10 percent of your gross income for retirement. Your gross income is your annual salary before deductions; it's not your take-home pay. For our simplified example, let's say that you are 35 years old and earn $50,000 per year (gross income). If you wanted to save 10 percent per year, you'd need to save $5,000 each year, which is approximately $416 per month ($5,000/12 months). As your income rose over time with inflation, so would the dollar amount you put in, so if you got a raise to $55,000, you would increase your savings amount to $5,500. Assuming a 5 percent rate of return on $5,500 per year that will increase with inflation at a rate of 2 percent per year, your savings could build to approximately $483,286 in 30 years (use the Long-Term Savings Calculator for detailed calculations; see page 306).

While I believe the 10 percent rule is still a good check-in, it really depends on your age and situation. If you're between 25 and 35 years old and are starting your retirement savings, putting away 10 percent of your gross income could be a good jumping-off point. For someone older who is just getting started, though, that may not be enough.

Unfortunately I can't tell you an exact amount you'll need for retirement. I know that may sound like a bit of a cop-out, but everyone's situation is different. How much you need to save for retirement depends on so many variables. Things like your lifestyle expectations, government pensions, life expectancy, whether you own your home, and potential inheritances all affect that amount. You may need to save way more than 10 to 20 percent of your gross income, or perhaps a lot less. For instance, if you've just inherited $600,000, then perhaps

Rules-of-Thumb for Minimum Retirement Savings	
Age at Which You Are Starting to Save	Recommended Amount
25–35	10–15% of gross income
36–45	15–20% of gross income
46+	20% or more of gross income

you don't need to tuck away 20 percent for retirement in each of the next 20 years. Maybe sticking with 10 percent will get you where you need to be. Or, if you want to retire early or travel a lot in retirement, 10 percent at any point in your life may simply not be enough.

Maybe you're thinking, *This is impossible. Between the mortgage, bills, car payments and groceries, there's no way I could put aside 20 percent.* Welcome to real life. As I said above, these are only guidelines, rules-of-thumb. Don't give up or feel frustrated if they don't feel doable right now in your life. There are other measures down the road that you may be able to take (we will tackle those in Part Three). For now, focus on the ideal solution.

When in doubt, the answer to how much you should save for retirement is simple—as much as you can, even if it falls short of these guidelines. Something is always better than nothing, and a little bit goes a long way.

Step 4: Work out Short-Term Savings

Short-Term Savings are perhaps my favourite type of savings. Having a Short-Term Savings account is the best (and only) way to stay out of debt permanently and truly take control of your cash flow. I have seen it so many times: clients who have solid Short-Term Savings consistently stick to their financial plan, and they worry way less about money than those without Short-Term Savings. I want that for you too.

The money saved to Short-Term Savings is the money that you put aside today in order to pay for things that will spike your spending down the road. This money isn't actual savings; it is glorified Spending Money. Yes, you're "saving" money, but it's earmarked for something that won't increase your net worth. It's not going towards debt, a down payment or retirement. Instead, you're preparing yourself for spikes in spending—the good ones, the bad ones and the ugly ones.

Spikes in your spending aren't a budgeting problem until they are. Ever felt like you're on track with your finances, doing okay with your "budget," and then *boom*, a huge expense comes out of nowhere and totally throws you off course? Budgeting fail. Maybe the brakes need repairs, a destination wedding invite comes in the mail, summer camp fees are due. It can feel like it never ends.

Over the years I've found that these types of spikes in spending are the number one reason why people go off track and feel out of control when it comes to their money. So let's kick that stress out of your life for good.

Calculating Your Short-Term Savings

There are two types of Short-Term Savings: savings for predictable spikes in spending and emergency savings. Predictable spikes in spending include things like—

- vacations
- kids' camps
- large purchases (furniture, a new deck, a boat, ATVs, unicorns)
- holiday spending
- wedding season

Emergency savings cover things like—

- home repair and maintenance
- health costs
- car repair and maintenance
- job loss

In order to figure out how much you need or want to put towards your Short-Term Savings, you have to identify the predictable spikes in spending and separate them from the emergency savings. Predictable spikes in spending are relatively easy to forecast. You know they are happening because you're planning for them or you've RSVP'd an invitation. You are able to set limits based on what you want to spend and what you think is reasonable.

For these types of spikes, set the amount that you will need to accomplish the goal and then divide it by the length of time you want to accomplish it in. For example, if you want to spend $2,400 on vacations every year, you'll need to save $200 per month ($2,400/12 months). If you want to spend $540 on a new mattress in nine months, you'll have to put aside $60 a month ($540/9). If you know that every May brings Mother's Day, four family birthdays and your wedding anniversary, which usually cost you $360 over two weekends, put aside $30 a month ($360/12 months).

For our example, let's say that you are most worried about the holidays, since the money you spend during December usually ends up chilling on your credit card for all of January and most of February. In the past few years you've spent an average of $600 during the holidays. Imagine how great it would be if you had $600 sitting in a savings account at the start of the holiday season. You could spend money guilt-free! In order to do this, you'd need to put aside $50 per month ($600/12 months) for a year in advance. If you didn't think of this until June and had only six months, you'd need to put aside $100 per month ($600/6 months).

The other type of Short-Term Savings is not as predictable or easy to plan for. Your emergency savings account is the key to Worry-Free Money and peaceful nights. You'll know that you will have enough money available for emergencies without going into debt.

When planning your emergency account, you may need to take four things into consideration, if they apply to you: home repairs, car repairs, health care and job loss. Your **home repairs** account, if you own your home, does not include renos, furniture or decor. I'm talking termites, leaks, mould and other nasty surprises. If you have a car, your **car repairs** account is for the repair and maintenance you have to put into your car to keep it on the road. **Health care** means thinking about how a medical emergency could impact you financially, including treatments not covered by provincial or private insurance plans. This doesn't mean a massage at the spa that you want to treat yourself to (that would be Spending Money). I'm talking about health-care *emergencies*. Last, **job loss**. You should aim to have at least three months' worth of living expenses saved, or five if you're self-employed or in an industry where finding a position is difficult if you're laid off. Your emergency account will likely be big, and it should be. When it comes to car repairs, home repairs and health care, you may have to continually replenish your emergency account if you used the money.

The only way to set a savings target for an emergency account is to work out an average based on your spending history. For car-repair, health-care and home-repair emergencies, the amount you had to spend over the past two or three years can be a good indicator of what's to come. For example, if you spent about $12,000 over the past three years on home repair and maintenance, $4,000 a year ($12,000/3 years) is a good estimate for annual home-repair emergencies. Some years you may spend only $2,000, and others $5,000.

As for job loss, you need to first figure out how much you need per month to pay for your Fixed Expenses, then add up the amount of money you need for basic life: groceries, necessary transportation and limited spending money. Basically, how much would you need to keep your head above water if you lost your job or had no work? Multiply by three to five months, and that is what you need to set aside as your minimum.

In our example, your monthly Fixed Expenses are $1,450. Let's say that you need $800 for basic life ($400 for basic groceries, $50 for minimum gas and $350 for realistic daily spending). If you lost your job, you would need a minimum of $2,250 ($1,450 + $800) each month for at least three months, which is $6,750 ($2,250 × 3).

Keep in mind that this amount could potentially be reduced by any money that you'd still be able to collect even in the event of a job loss—things like your partner's income, government pensions, spousal or child support, or Employment Insurance (if you qualify). For our example, let's assume that you qualify for $1,450 per month Employment Insurance and that you have been laid off from your job. Your emergency savings for job loss will be reduced from $6,750 to $2,400 because the $2,250 per month you need will be reduced by $1,450 in Employment Insurance, and therefore you only need to cover $800 each month. If you are planning on coverage for three months, this amounts to $2,400 ($800 × 3 months). To build up your savings towards job loss over a year and have $2,400 in your emergency account, you need to put aside $200 per month ($2,400/12 months). It's important to note that Employment Insurance can take several weeks to kick in and that not everyone qualifies. Be sure to find out!

In our example, your Short-Term Savings would be $250 per month: $50 per month for holidays and other predictable spikes and $200 per month for emergencies. Preparing a Short-Term Savings account is critical to feeling that you are in control of your finances. It's how you avoid those moments when the budget falls apart. Consciously putting aside money that is earmarked for spikes in spending and emergencies is important so that you know the difference between money you can spend today and money that you will spend later, furthering your control over your cash flow.

Step 5: Calculate your Spending Money Hard Limit

You're so close. Here's the final step. Add up your Fixed Expenses, Meaningful Savings and Short-Term Savings and deduct them from your monthly after-tax income. Everything left over is your Spending Money—your Hard Limit.

In our example, $2,116 is money you cannot spend (Fixed Expenses of $1,450 + Meaningful Savings of $416 + Short-Term Savings of $250). Therefore, $884 is money you can spend, your Spending Money. This is the only "budget" you ever need, the line in the sand between money you can spend (Spending Money) and money you cannot spend (Fixed Expenses, Meaningful Savings and Short-Term Savings).

As long as you are paying your bills and putting aside money for savings, who cares whether the rest of your money is spent on takeout or grooming or contact lens solution? Your life will change unpredictably from month to month, just like everyone else's. As long as the money you spend stays within your Hard Limit, it doesn't matter if it's budgeted, tracked or forecasted.

Your numbers will fluctuate over time to make room for new bills, additional savings goals and perhaps raises, but the concept remains the same. Every year you should check in with your Hard Limit to account for rising costs of living, raises in your pay and changes to your savings targets. Go through the process you've just finished. Check all the numbers and add in any new costs, removing any that don't belong anymore.

By spending money only within your Hard Limit, you stop the cycle of guilt and fear that keeps you worrying about money all the time. If you were worried that you're not saving enough, the fact that you've siphoned off enough money from each pay period to cover all your bills and savings, as well as money towards future spikes in spending, means you can relax, knowing everything is covered. There *is* enough! *Phew!*

Your Hard Limit is your financial "safe word." It's money you know you can safely afford to spend each pay period without fear, allowing you to live your life guilt-free because you've covered your butt financially, giving you peace of mind.

I know calculating your Hard Limit requires some work upfront, but establishing it is one of the most important things you can do for your finances. It's the very first step in getting control over your money so you can stop budgeting and start living without fear for the future. It's so worth it—I promise!

Let me show you an example of how much it helped my client Jesse. His is a relatively simple example. We will examine a more complex case in Chapter 8, but Jesse's story is a great place to start.

Meet Jesse

Jesse
Age: 30
Relationship status: single (but looking, in case you know anyone)
Kids: 0
Annual gross household income: $55,000
Assets: $3,000 in emergency account
Liabilities: $6,500 in student debt

The first time I met Jesse, he was frustrated about his finances. "I never know if I can afford something or not. I mean, I make a living and I don't have a ton of expenses, but some months I'm taking on debt and others I feel like I'm okay. It's feast or famine and I'm always second-guessing myself. Can I afford to go away with my friends on a trip or not? And sometimes I use my credit card because I'm afraid my debit card will come up 'insufficient funds.' I'm 30 years old and I feel broke. I don't want to live like this anymore."

Jesse's problems were twofold. He didn't know what he could and couldn't afford, and he felt as if his cash flow was all over the place, feast or famine. No control. No strategy. A perfect example of the Spending Vortex. In order to solve his first problem, we calculated his Hard Limit.

Step 1: Calculate monthly after-tax income

Since Jesse's paycheque amounted to $1,875 twice a month (not biweekly), he received 24 paycheques a year. His monthly after-tax income was $3,750 ($1,875 × 2).

Step 2: Add up Fixed Expenses

We went through Jesse's bank accounts and credit card statements looking for the repetitive, predictable and guaranteed Fixed Expenses each month.

Jesse paid $1,500 annually for car insurance, so we divided that amount by 12. "You'll want to put aside $125 each month so that in March you'll have $1,500 ready to go. That way it won't feel like a surprise," I told him. We added up his other Fixed Expenses:

"Okay," I said, "you have to put aside $1,650 each month or else you can't pay your bills."

"Is that bad or good?" Jesse asked.

Jesse made $3,750 after tax and had $1,650 in Fixed Expenses.

FIXED EXPENSES: Money You Cannot Spend	
Rent	$1,000
Phone	$100
Subscription	$10
Student loan minimum payment	$65
Car payment	$350
Car insurance ($1,500/year)	$125
Total	$1,650

We divided his Fixed Expenses by his after-tax income and found that 44 percent of his after-tax income was going towards Fixed Expenses each month, which is less than 55 percent, the afford-ability cut-off. "You're living within your means as far as Fixed Expenses go, so that's a win!" I told him.

Step 3: Identify Meaningful Savings

"This is the fun part," I said. "What are you saving for?"

"I'd like to pay off my student loan by the time I'm 35," he said. "And I'd like to start saving $6,000 a year for retirement."

Jesse had a $6,500 government student loan that charged 5.2 percent interest. In order to pay this off in five years, he would need to put approximately $125 per month towards his debt for the next 60 months (5 years × 12 months). Since he was already making a $65 minimum payment, an additional $60 per month was needed ($125 – $65). To calculate this, we used the Debt-Repayment Calculator in the Resource Library section (page 303).

Since Jesse earned a salary of $55,000, saving $6,000 per year towards retirement was more than the 10 percent minimum of his gross income that I would suggest. In fact it was 10.9 percent—way to go, Jesse! To hit this Meaningful Savings target, Jesse had to save $500 per month ($6,000/12 months). Therefore, Jesse's total Meaningful Savings were $560 per month: a combination of the $60 extra that he would put towards his student loan and the $500 to retirement savings.

MEANINGFUL SAVINGS: Money You Cannot Spend	
Retirement savings	$500
Extra money towards student debt	$60
Total	$560

Step 4: Work out Short-Term Savings

One of Jesse's problems was that he had feast-or-famine months when unexpected spikes in spending would happen. He had an emergency account with $3,000 in it that was earmarked for job-loss emergencies, but he didn't want to dip into that for things like holiday spending.

Jesse typically spent around $480 annually for his car repairs and he figured it would be about the same for the upcoming year. We calculated that he needed to keep saving $40 per month ($480/ 12 months) towards his emergency savings for car repair. In addition, since he anticipated spending $300 on gifts in the next 12 months, he also needed to put aside $25 per month ($300/12 months) for predictable spikes.

All in, Jesse needed to put aside $65 per month towards Short-Term Savings so he would never again be blindsided by a large purchase.

SHORT-TERM SAVINGS: Money You Cannot Spend	
Car repairs ($480/year)	$40
Gifts ($300/year)	$25
Total	$65

Step 5: Calculate the Spending Money Hard Limit

"So, Jesse, $3,750 comes into your bank account each month: $1,650 for Fixed Expenses, $560 for debt repayment and retirement savings and $65 for Short-Term Savings. That leaves you with $1,475 each month in Spending Money!"

Monthly after-tax income	$3,750
FIXED EXPENSES: Money You Cannot Spend	
Rent	$1,000
Phone	$100
Subscriptions	$10
Student loan minimum payment	$65
Car payment	$350
Car insurance	$125
Total	$1,650
MEANINGFUL SAVINGS: Money You Cannot Spend	
Retirement savings	$500
Student loan above-minimum payment	$60
Total	$560
SHORT-TERM SAVINGS: Money You Cannot Spend	
Car repairs ($480/year)	$40
Gifts ($300/year)	$25
Total	$65
SPENDING MONEY: Hard Limit	$1,475

"So out of all my money, I can really only spend $1,475 of it each month?"

"Yup," I said. "But I don't care how you spend it. Spend it on whatever you like. As long as you're fed, getting around and having fun, you'll be fine. There's no need to budget."

"Awesome! I never thought about not budgeting my spending money, but this is great. As long as I don't spend more than $1,475 each month, I'm safe to spend my money, so why bother categorizing?"

He paused, then asked me one of the best questions ever. "So when I get paid, how do I know what is Spending Money and what is not? Do I have to take out this $1,475 in cash or something?"

"Hell, no," I said. "You need a strategic banking plan."

CHAPTER 7

What Can You Actually Afford?

The wonderful thing about calculating your Hard Limit is that you now know how much Spending Money you can blow to zero each month without worrying that there isn't enough to pay your bills, hit your savings goals or prepare for spikes in spending in the future. Woo-hoo!

In theory you have answered the nagging question "What can I afford?" But you still have to go one step further in order to ensure that the plan is easy to maintain and that it's easy to figure out if you can or can't afford something in the moment when you are about to spend money.

Here's the trick: each pay period, you need to isolate your Spending Money in a separate bank account. That way you never have to worry about whether or not you're spending money earmarked for bills and savings. When all your money flows into one bank account, bill payments, savings and Spending Money blend together; there is no strategy and no obvious indicator of affordability. It perpetuates the Spending Vortex.

For example, when all your money is in one bank account and you know the mortgage payment will come out tomorrow morning, it's tempting to put most other variable expenses today (such as groceries or gas) on a credit card, just in case. But when you isolate the money you are allowed to blow to zero in a separate bank account, there is no need to worry about whether or not the mortgage will be covered or what you can afford to spend. You can see the balance as plain as day in the Spending account. This gives you a clear yes or no answer to "Can I afford this?"

Can I afford to go out for dinner tonight? Is there enough in the Spending account? Yes? Great. Can I afford to buy this coat? Is there enough in the Spending account? No? I'll wait until the next paycheque.

It's that simple.

Your Strategic Banking Plan

Here's how to set up your strategic banking plan.

Step 1: Isolate the money you *cannot* spend in your original chequing account

In order to do this, you need to have two chequing accounts. Your original chequing account is likely where your money from work is deposited every month and where your Fixed Expenses are paid from. This is where you'll keep the money you cannot spend each month to cover Fixed Expenses, Meaningful Savings and Short-Term Savings.

Rename this bank account "Bills and Savings." If you have combined finances with a partner, this could be a joint account.

In our example, your Fixed Expenses are $1,450, your Meaningful Savings $416 and your Short-Term Savings $250. The total amount of money you cannot spend each month is $2,116 ($1,450 + $416 + $250). This is the monthly amount that you need to set aside in your Bills and Savings account.

You should consider the money in the Bills and Savings account dead to you. Never touch it. None of it is Spending Money. Every dollar that stays in that account has a very specific job to do—even if it doesn't do that job for months at a time, in the case of annual Fixed Expenses.

Step 2: Isolate the money you *can* spend in a second chequing account

You'll need to open a second chequing account. As with the Bills and Savings account discussed above, if you've combined finances with a partner, this could be a second joint chequing account. Ensure that this is your *primary* chequing account. That means your debit card is affiliated with it, so when you withdraw money from an ATM or spend money at a store checkout, you are taking it from this account only. Name the account "Spending." This account is where all your Spending Money goes—all your guilt-free money in one spot. Woot!

Watch out for bank fees. Ask your financial institution if there is a way for you to have multiple bank accounts for one set fee. If not, see if you can get the overall fees reduced. Often if you've got multiple products with one financial institution, such as a mortgage, savings accounts and credit cards, they may be willing to discount your fees.

If you can't find free (or cheap) banking that will work for you, try to keep your monthly fees on this new plan below $15 to $20. It may seem counterintuitive for a financial expert to recommend multiple accounts that may cost you a bit more money each month, but the financial benefit of your strategic banking plan will outweigh the cost. Trust me. Think of it this way: Would you pay an extra $15 for an app that lets you never have to worry about affordability and money again? If the answer is yes, then the bank fees you may have to pay are likely worth it.

In our example, your monthly after-tax income is $3,000 and $2,116 of that is the amount that needs to be in your Bills and Savings account, which means $884 ($3,000 – $2,116) goes into your Spending account. This is your Spending Money, isolated in a bank account so that you know it's all money you can blow to zero!

Step 3: Figure out what to put in your bank accounts per pay period

This third step is my favourite—it's the key to really giving you control over your cash flow. You need to figure out how much money you can spend and blow to zero *for every pay period* in your Spending account. Knowing on a monthly basis just isn't good enough. A month is a long time: lots of different expenses can come at you.

On payday it can feel like you have lots of money, but then the whole next paycheque has to go to rent or mortgage or daycare and you will feel like you are broke until the next payday. By isolating your Spending Money for each pay period, you put an end to the feast-or-famine spending habits that can happen when you "budget" on a monthly basis.

Arrange to have all your income deposited into your Bills and Savings account. Then, each pay period, simply move your Spending Money from the Bills and Savings account to your Spending account. In our example, your Spending Money is $884 per month, so you divide that amount by two because you get two paycheques a month. So, with each $1,500 paycheque, you'll move $442 ($884/2) from your Bills and Savings account to your Spending account. This leaves $1,058 ($1,500 – $442) in the Bills and Savings account for that pay period to deal with the bills and savings that will be coming out of the account or to build up in there. Some people like to manually move their money each payday, while others like to automate the transfer. It's totally up to you. So here's what happens with each paycheque: $1,500 comes into Bills and Savings account, you move $442 to the Spending account, and that leaves $1,058 in Bills and Savings.

If all your bills come due at the beginning of the month, worry not. I will walk you through Jesse's strategic banking plan to show you how to deal with that, later on in this chapter.

If you're paid every other week, you get 26 paycheques a year. But as I've said before, for 10 months of the year you will only have two paycheques per month, so it's safest to plan for two paycheques per month, and then the extra two paycheques can be earmarked for Short-Term Savings as they come in. It's the same if you're paid weekly. Plan for four pay periods a month, but know that four times a year you will get five paycheques in a month. Those additional four paycheques should go to Short-Term Savings. For each weekly paycheque in our example, you'll move $221 ($884/4 weeks) to the Spending account.

If you've got additional paycheques to play with, here's how they can help with your Short-Term Savings. Figure out in advance when those additional paycheques will come during the year, and mark the days on your calendar. Go to your calendar and look up your last payday. Then count out each payday for the next 12 months. There will be two months when you have three paydays if you're paid biweekly, or four months when you have five paydays if you're paid weekly. On the days of the additional paycheques, move your usual amount of money to the Spending account, but instead of leaving the rest in your Bills and Savings account, move it to Short-Term Savings (there's more about set-ting this up in the next step).

For example, let's say that March and August have three pay-cheques. The third paycheques come in on March 30 and August 31. On those specific dates, $1,500 will go into the Bills and Savings account as usual and you will move $442 to your Spending account, also as usual. However, the $1,058 left over will go to Short-Term Savings instead of remaining in the Bills and Savings account. Why? Because you've already put $1,058 from each of the first two pay-cheques that month into Bills and Savings. Your Fixed Expenses, Meaningful Savings and Spending Money needs are already covered for the month, so the extra $1,058 from that third paycheque can go straight to Short-Term Savings. This can help to offset how much you need to put towards your Short-Term Savings each year, or you can use it for those purchases that inevitably crop up beyond typ-ical planning (Hello, best friend's bachelorette party! Hello, soccer camp!). See the section "Extra Paycheques" in the Resource Library section for more details.

Self-Employed? No Worries

If you're self-employed, it's easiest to move money on a monthly basis. It's good practice to have a totally separate bank account for your business income and expenses outside of your personal bank accounts, so there will be three accounts instead of the usual two. All the revenue you earn should go into your business bank account. Then, once a month, you will "pay" yourself a consistent after-tax income.

Think back to the example we discussed in the previous chapter. If your revenue was $60,000 a year, you ended up with $36,000 in after-tax income (after $10,000 in business expenses and estimated taxes and CPP of $14,000). That left you with a monthly after-tax income of $3,000.

Annual revenue	$60,000	
Annual expenses	– $10,000	
Annual before-tax income	$50,000	
Annual expected income tax	– $14,000	(estimated with online calculator)
Annual after-tax income	$36,000	($50,000 – $14,000 income tax and CPP)
Monthly after-tax income	**$3,000**	**($36,000/12 months)**

The $3,000 in monthly after-tax income will move as follows from your business account: $2,116 to your Bills and Savings account each month to cover your Fixed Expenses ($1,450), Meaningful Savings ($416) and Short-Term Savings ($250). You'll also move $884 each month to your Spending account. By only moving what you need for your personal bills and savings and spending, you leave enough money in your business account for your forecasted business expenses ($10,000) and your income tax and CPP ($14,000) over the year.

No More Worrying about Affordability

By isolating the amount of money you can spend to zero in your Spending account each pay period, you don't have to guess about affordability anymore. If it's the day before payday and your Spending account has only $5 in it, you needn't worry, because all of your bills and savings are taken care of. You've already done the hard work, so just eat soup or what's in the freezer that night and wait for your next instalment of Spending Money on payday.

If you like to use a credit card, go ahead. I also love earning points, but be sure to transfer the money from your Spending account to that credit card *every night* (provided that the banking fees for transactions aren't atrocious). That way the Spending account is always a true representation of the money you have available until the next paycheque. Why is this so, so important? One of the most common overspending blunders I see is using a credit card for every transaction with the intention of paying it off at the end of the month. But inevitably there isn't enough money in the Spending account to pay it down to zero, so debt starts to creep up.

You see, unlike a chequing account, your credit card typically does not have a Hard Limit that is low enough to keep your spending in realistic check. This is exactly what makes handling money so stressful. You never really know if you can afford your life or not. If you pay off the credit card as you go, you still get all the benefits of using a credit card (convenience, points, etc.) but you also have that go-to place where you can see your Spending Money going down in real time. That way you always know where you stand financially until the next pay period.

Step 4: Automate everything in the Bills and Savings account

If you want to take all the guesswork out of your finances, get automated. Yes, this is the most overused and obvious financial tip in the world, but it still holds true. Just like advice to put on your underwear first, a good tip is a good tip.

If possible, every transaction that comes out of your Bills and Savings account should be automated. It's a good idea to set the preauthorized payment dates that you have flexibility in choosing at the end of the month, so that your Bills and Savings account has time to accumulate the max amount of money.

When it comes to your Fixed Expenses, utilities may be tough to set as a preauthorized debit amount because they can fluctuate a bit. But otherwise, most of your Fixed Expenses should be so consistent that you can automate a specific amount with preauthorized debits. For utilities or other Fixed Expenses that fluctuate slightly, you'll have to pay them manually from the Bills and Savings account each month, when they are due. But since you've put enough aside to accommodate the high and low fluctuations, you will have enough in the account to pay them.

As for Meaningful Savings, the amounts that you are sending to debt, retirement savings, TFSAs or your mortgage should also be preauthorized debit transactions. It's a good idea to have your Short-Term Savings automatically transferred to a safe, liquid savings account. This is a great way to see what you can and can't afford when it comes to spikes in your spending. For example, if you've got money specifically put aside for vacations in a separate short-term saving account, you can plan what type of vacation you can afford simply by looking at the balance.

"Can we afford to go to Chicago?"

"How much money is in the vacation account?"

"$1,200."

"Yep, we can do Chicago on $1,200."

Some people really get into this and like to have a bunch of short-term savings accounts, one for each goal. As long as the banking fees aren't crazy, this can work.

My recommendation is to have two Short-Term Savings accounts: a "spikes" account and an emergency account. The first is for the predictable spikes in spending that you're saving up for, things like vacations, Big Purchases and big events coming up, then a separate account for your emergency savings. It's a personal decision. There's no right or wrong way when it comes to stashing your Short-Term Savings. All that matters is making sure the money is automatically transferred out of Bills and Savings.

No more feast-or-famine paydays. No more moving money from account to account to cover payments. No more wondering if you can or can't afford something. A system. It's simple and hella effective.

Jesse's Strategic Banking Plan

Here's how I set up Jesse's strategic banking plan. First, as a refresher, here's how Jesse's Hard Limit shook out:

Monthly after-tax income	$3,750
FIXED EXPENSES: Money You Cannot Spend	
Rent	$1,000
Phone	$100
Subscriptions	$10
Student loan minimum payment	$65
Car payment	$350
Car insurance	$125
Total	$1,650
MEANINGFUL SAVINGS: Money You Cannot Spend	
Retirement savings	$500
Student loan above-minimum payment	$60
Total	$560
SHORT-TERM SAVINGS: Money You Cannot Spend	
Car repairs ($480/year)	$40
Gifts ($300/year)	$25
Total	$65
SPENDING MONEY: Hard Limit	$1,475

Step 1: The Bills and Savings account

We know that the money Jesse cannot spend stays in the Bills and Savings account and the money he can spend goes to the Spending account.

Monthly Amounts	
After-tax income	$3,750
Bills and Savings account	$2,275
Spending account	$1,475

Jesse is paid twice a month; $1,875 drops into his chequing account on the 15th and 30th of each month. If Jesse's Bills and Savings account needs $2,275 each month to cover his Fixed Expenses, Meaningful Savings and Short-Term Savings, then we divide that amount by the number of paycheques per month (two) in order to find out how much he needs to leave from each paycheque to ensure that everything is covered. So Jesse must leave $1,137.50 ($2,275/2) in the Bills and Savings account from each paycheque in order to ensure that he has at least $2,275 to meet his Fixed Expenses, Meaningful Savings and Short-Term Savings.

	Monthly	Per Paycheque
After-tax income	$3,750	$1,875.00
Money you cannot spend (Bills and Savings)	$2,275	$1,137.50
Money you can spend (Spending Money)	$1,475	$737.50

Easy, right? Wrong.

"When are your bills due, Jesse?" I asked.

"All my bills are due at the start of the month, hence the feast and famine."

"Are there automated transactions in the Bills and Savings account that you could change the timing on?" I asked.

"I can adjust the withdrawal date for my retirement savings, the extra money to my student debt and the money going to Short-Term Savings. The other transactions have to come out on the date that is set on the bill," he said.

"Okay, so let's plan for all your savings, Meaningful and Short-Term, to come out at the end of the month," I said. "Then we will map out the cash flow in your Bills and Savings account each month to see if there's a shortfall."

If Jesse gets paid on the 30th and puts $1,137.50 into Bills and Savings, he will end up short. This is because $1,550 ($1,000 rent +

	Amount	Day of the Month
Monthly after-tax income	$3,750	
Money You Cannot Spend		
Rent	$1,000	1st
Phone	$100	20th
Subscription	$10	2nd
Student loan minimum payment	$65	4th
Car payment	$350	2nd
Car insurance	$125	5th
Retirement savings	$500	28th
Student loan above-minimum payment	$60	28th
Car repairs ($500/year)	$40	28th
Gifts/holidays ($300/year)	$25	28th
Total Money You Cannot Spend	$2,275	
Total Money You Can Spend	$1,475	

$10 subscription + $350 car payment + $65 student loan + $125 car insurance) is due before his next paycheque on the 15th. So he will be short by $412.50 ($1,137.50 – $1,550).

"So you're short by $412.50 when you kick off this new banking plan," I said.

"Yikes! Okay, how do I get around that?" he asked.

"You will need to start this new banking plan with a $412.50 buffer in the Bills and Savings account. You can use $412.50 from your $3,000 in emergency savings."

"Won't that happen every month?" he asked.

"No, it will only be a problem for the first month. Watch." I mapped out Jesse's cash flow for the whole month on the banking plan.

Bills and Savings	Transaction (Date)	Balance Remaining
Buffer deposit	$412.50	
Paycheque	$1,137.50 (30th)	$1,550
Next Month		
Rent	$1,000 (1st)	$550
Subscription	$10 (2nd)	$540
Car payment	$350 (2nd)	$190
Student loan minimum payment	$65 (4th)	$125
Car insurance	$125 (5th)	$0
Paycheque	$1,137.50 (15th)	$1,137.50
Phone	$100 (20th)	$1,037.50
Retirement savings	$500 (28th)	$537.50
Student loan above-minimum payment	$60 (28th)	$477.50
Car repairs	$40 (28th)	$437.50
Gifts/holidays	$25 (28th)	$412.50
Paycheque	$1,137.50 (30th)	$1,550

"See? At the end of the month you'll have $1,550 again that will get you through the next month, and so on and so on. It's only in the first month that this is an issue."

"Ahh," he said. "Got it."

If this is something that you're worried about too, map out every planned transaction that you have earmarked to come out of the Bills and Savings account and how often you will put in money from your paycheques. If there's a shortage, you will need to start off the plan with that amount of money in the Bills and Savings account as a buffer. If you've got Short-Term Savings or a balance in your chequing account already, then you can use that. If you don't have it saved up, see if you can change any of the dates of those transactions to come out later in the month, once you've had a chance to deposit two paycheques.

If there isn't any wiggle room and you don't have any Short-Term Savings or a balance in your chequing account right now, you'll need to save it up. This may push forward the start date of your strategic banking plan, but it's better to start off on the right foot.

Step 2: Spending Money

Since the money Jesse cannot spend ($1,137.50) is already taken care of in the Bills and Savings account, the money that he moves into his Spending account, his Hard Limit, is 100 percent guilt-free Spending Money. For Jesse we know that $1,137.50 from every paycheque must stay in his Bills and Savings account. So if his paycheque is $1,875, that means he has $737.50 left ($1,875 – $1,137.50) to blow to zero with every paycheque!

With every paycheque, Jesse should move $737.50 from his Bills and Savings account to his new Spending account. That way he isolates his Spending Money for the next 15 days, until the next paycheque.

Step 3: Automating the Bills and Savings account

Not only should Jesse automate as many of his Fixed Expenses as possible to be debited from his account, he should also automate the savings earmarked for various goals to ensure that they happen.

•

Four months after our meeting, Jesse and I checked in. He was very pleased. Not only had he met all his savings goals to date, he had been able to stop worrying about money each month.

"I feel like I won the time lottery," he said. "I didn't realize how much headspace money was taking up each month until I didn't have to worry about it anymore. Now I know that when it's payday, I have $737.50 for the next 15 days to eat, get around and enjoy life. Everything else happens behind the scenes and I don't even have to think about it."

Yes! I asked him if he felt that he had more control over his finances and a better grasp of what he could and could not afford.

"Definitely! It's so liberating to know when I can and can't afford something. I feel like someone opened the window and I can finally breathe."

I smiled. "Exactly."

CHAPTER 8

Can You Afford a Lifestyle Upgrade?

Wouldn't it be great if all our financial matters worked out easily? Well, that's not always—or usually—the case. Typically, as we get older our financial lives become more and more complex. More money, more problems, if you will.

The idea of affordability still applies when you're making lifestyle upgrades, which I define as financial choices that go beyond your daily Spending Money. These Lifestyle Upgrades are the types of financial choices that are relatively permanent and affect your Fixed Expenses. *Can I afford a bigger house? If so, how much? Can we afford daycare? If so, how much? Can I afford more rent? If so, how much? Can we afford this car? If so, how much?* When you have these conversations with yourself or family, it's really important to get the answer right, because what you're actually asking is *If I do this, will I be screwed?*

Wondering if you're going to screw yourself financially is common, and a direct reflection of uncertainty about what you can actually afford. *Will a $200 increase in rent mean I can never buy a home? Will a second car mess up my retirement savings? Will we be house-poor? Are we spread too thin?* The anxiety is twofold. Not only are you wondering how this new expense will affect your daily spending (*Am I going to feel broke?*), you're also worried that the choice may be truly irresponsible financially (*Will I have to reduce my Meaningful Savings? Or worse, will I start building up debt?*).

Lifestyle Upgrades aren't typically decisions that you make on a daily basis, but they certainly occupy a lot of headspace when you need to make a choice. Everyone understands that an increase in your Fixed Expenses will affect the ability to spend and save, but you need to ensure that you have all the information possible before making a big change. If you overspend on a Lifestyle Upgrade, reducing it down the road can be emotionally painful, involving downsizing, moving, selling the car, cancelling policies, moving back home. Lifestyle Upgrades aren't easily undone.

Once you sign on the dotted line for a Lifestyle Upgrade, you are committed, at least for a while and sometimes permanently. That's why you need to understand when you can and can't afford a Lifestyle Upgrade. In other words, when your Life Checklist is potentially out of whack.

Meet Sandy and Amit: A Tale of Two Trucks

Sandy and Amit

Ages: 42 and 38

Relationship status: married

Kids: 2, ages 12 and 14

Annual gross household income: $95,000
($45,000 + $50,000)

Assets: $5,000 in emergency savings; $85,000 and $100,000 in retirement accounts; house valued at $350,000

Liabilities: $4,500 home equity line of credit at 3%; $250,000 mortgage; $2,200 owing on Sandy's tax bill from last year; credit card debt fluctuating between $0 and $1,000 but typically paid off(ish)

Sandy and Amit lived in a rural town outside Calgary. For them, life in the country required two cars. Sandy was self-employed and needed a car all day for work, and Amit commuted daily. To visit a friend's house or drop the kids off at swimming was a 10-to-20-minute drive in either direction. There was no transit. "I think there is one taxi," they joked when we sat down. Two cars were a must.

One of their cars had been paid off for about eight years but was on its last legs. There had been a lot of changes over those past eight years. The kids had extracurricular activities that cost money, utility costs continued to climb, and they recently had to take out a home equity line of credit for some much-needed repairs on the house.

Now they needed a new car. The existing car was becoming a safety liability and a source of argument. Amit worried about driving it at night or in the winter. While the arguments might seem on the surface like they were about warranties and all-wheel drive, they actually had nothing to do with car colour or size and everything do with money and fear.

So Amit and Sandy needed a new vehicle. They agreed that they needed a truck. "It's a necessity where we live." Amit wanted a new (or no more than one year old) truck that would cost around $25,000.

"We need to get a used one," Sandy said to me. "We can't afford a new one."

"Yes, we can," Amit argued. "We have to."

Sandy thought they could get a reliable used truck for $18,000. Amit thought they should get a newer one so they wouldn't have to worry about warranty work and reliability and be right back in the same situation in five years.

Knowing they couldn't afford to buy either a new or used truck outright, they would have to borrow more on their home equity line of credit in order to purchase the vehicle. The line of credit had a lower interest rate than the traditional vehicle financing they were being offered. For a used truck, $18,000 borrowed at 3 percent meant an increase in monthly Fixed Expenses of $325 per month for five years. That was Sandy's preference. For a new truck, $25,000 borrowed at 3 percent meant an increase in monthly Fixed Expenses of $450 per month for five years. That was Amit's preference.

Amit pointed out that there was only a $125-a-month difference between the two payments. "I think that should be doable, no?"

This was a perfect example of how the Spending Vortex affects your ability to truly know whether you can or cannot afford something. Neither Sandy nor Amit actually knew if $125 a month was a big deal in the grand scheme of life. The only way to find out was to check how it would affect household cash flow and see if taking on the new expense was sustainable.

Working It Out

After looking at the numbers, I told Sandy and Amit that I'd like to keep their Fixed Expenses below 55 percent of their take-home income, if possible. If they added $325 or $450 to the $3,185 they were already spending on Fixed Expenses, the percentage of their Fixed Expenses would go up to 55.7 percent or 57.7 percent respectively. Both of those numbers were higher than I'd like, but they needed a new vehicle. The 55 percent Fixed Expenses rule-of-thumb didn't matter—this expense was going to happen. Telling them they couldn't afford a second vehicle would be useless because I'd be setting them up to feel like failures. The question was whether the increase would take them to 55.7 or 57.7 percent.

Joint monthly after-tax income	$6,300	
FIXED EXPENSES: Money You Cannot Spend		
Mortgage	$1,120	
Utilities	$350	
Home insurance	$150	
Property tax	$220	
Cable/Internet/subscriptions	$160	
Phone	$170	
Old car payment	$225	
New car payment	?	
Car insurance	$285	
Private life insurance	$200	
Line of credit minimum payment	$85	
Kids' activities	$200	
Bank fees	$20	
Total	$3,185	(51% of after-tax income)
MEANINGFUL SAVINGS: Money You Cannot Spend		
Line of credit above-minimum payment	$15	
Retirement savings for Amit	$500	
Retirement savings for Sandy	$500	
Total	$1,015	(16% of after-tax income)
SHORT-TERM SAVINGS: Money You Cannot Spend		
Vacation	$0	
Emergency savings	$200	
Total	$200	(3% of after-tax income)
SPENDING MONEY: Hard Limit	$1,900	(30% of after-tax income)

This is the thing about Lifestyle Upgrades. In order to make room for new expenses, you have to reduce elsewhere. You need to reduce other Fixed Expenses, Meaningful Savings, Short-Term Savings or Spending Money. The money has to come from somewhere to meet the goal. Sandy and Amit couldn't reduce any of their other Fixed Expenses to make room for $325 or $450. It was going to have to come from somewhere else. But where?

"I don't want to stop saving," Sandy said. "We are just now finally getting our savings back on track." Since neither of them had a pension or work retirement plan, they had to do all their retirement saving on their own. They now had $185,000 in retirement savings after inheriting some money the year before. However, they still wanted to ensure that they each invested $500 monthly in order to reach approximately $1 million in retirement savings in 25 years if they earned 4.5 percent net returns each year (see the Long-Term Savings Calculator in the Resource Library, page 306).

In addition, they wanted to keep paying $100 per month ($85 minimum payment + $15 from Meaningful Savings) into the line of credit in order to pay it off in four years (see the Debt-Payoff Calculator in the Resource Library, page 304). As a result, they couldn't reduce their Meaningful Savings to make room for the new truck. They had $5,000 in their emergency account but they planned to pay Sandy's $2,200 tax bill with that money, leaving $2,800.

Amit and Sandy had private health-care benefits, so they didn't feel that they needed to beef up their emergency account for health care. However, they did want to put aside approximately $3,000 per year for repairs and maintenance of both cars. As for job-loss protection, they estimated that they needed $4,685 per month for basic living: Fixed Expenses of $3,185 plus basic spending of $1,500 (groceries, gas and other basics). If Amit lost his job, he'd collect approximately $2,000 per month from Employment Insurance (EI). Sandy would still likely be working, bringing home $3,000 per month. So their minimum $4,685 would be covered by the $5,000 they brought in ($2,000 + $3,000).

However, if Sandy had a slow season or couldn't work, Amit's take-home income of $3,300 per month would not fully cover the $4,685. They would be short $1,385 ($4,685 – $3,300). They needed to set aside $6,925 ($1,385 × 5 months, because Sandy is self-employed and not eligible for EI). Therefore they should have $9,925 ($3,000 for the cars + $6,925 for a slow season for Sandy) in their emergency account. Since they would have only $2,800 in it, they needed to save another $7,125.

We all agreed that they needed to continue beefing up that emergency account over the next three years with $200 per month ($7,125/36 months, rounded up). As a result, there was no room to reduce Short-Term Savings without being financially irresponsible and leading to more money anxiety. Since they couldn't reduce Fixed Expenses, Meaningful Savings or Short-Term Savings, the new payments for the truck would be a direct hit on their Spending Money. It was the only other option—a reduction of either $325 or $450.

When it comes to a Lifestyle Upgrade that will increase your Fixed Expenses, you need to consider whether the related decrease in your Spending Money is sustainable over the long run. You cannot be on your best spending behaviour forever, so if it's not a realistic reduction in Spending Money, you're likely setting yourself up to fail by either going into debt or under-saving—a recipe for misery and continued worry. You'll feel broke.

"This new monthly payment will directly affect your Spending Money," I told them. "Let's see if a hit of $450 is realistic. If not, then you go with the used truck."

Adding $325 for the used truck to their Fixed Expenses reduced their Spending Money from $1,900 to $1,575, which was 25 percent

	New Truck	Used Truck
Monthly after-tax income	$6,300	$6,300
Previous Fixed Expenses	$3,185	$3,185
New car payment	$450	$325
Total increased Fixed Expenses	$3,635	$3,510
Total Meaningful Savings	$1,015	$1,015
Total Short-Term Savings	$200	$200
Total Spending Money: Hard Limit	$1,450	$1,575

of their after-tax income. This was a 5 percent reduction in their monthly Spending Money. Adding $450 for the new truck reduced their Spending Money from $1,900 to $1,450 per month, which was 23 percent of their after-tax income. This was a 7 percent reduction in Spending Money. Those may not seem like scary percentages, but it was clearly a significant drop in their cash flow when you looked at it in dollar amounts.

Within their current $1,900 Hard Limit (30 percent of their after-tax income), Sandy and Amit's spending broke down like this:

Groceries	$700
Toiletries	$100
Gas	$400
Everything else (gifts, clothes, entertainment, dining out/takeout, grooming, etc.)	$700

"We can't do much about the groceries, gas and toiletries," Sandy said. "We already watch spending there very closely. We have to eat and, as I've mentioned, we have to drive around a lot out here." So $1,200 (groceries, toiletries, gas) of their Hard Limit was non-negotiable, which didn't leave them with a lot of wiggle room.

	New Truck	Used Truck
Spending Money	$1,450	$1,575
Groceries	$700	$700
Toiletries	$100	$100
Gas	$400	$400
Everything else	$250	$375

"Whoa. That's not doable," Amit said.

"What's not?" I asked.

"Having only $250 for everything else we have to pay for each month. It's just not realistic."

Bingo. When you're assessing a change to your monthly cash flow, consider whether or not it will reduce your Spending Money by more than 5 percent. If it will, you could be setting yourself up to feel broke indefinitely and to ultimately fail at saving. Five percent as a percentage may not seem like a big deal, but when you really look at the numbers, you'll see whether it's completely unrealistic.

Sandy and Amit didn't live extravagantly as it was, and I explained to them that even the additional $125 (a new truck at $450 versus a used truck at $325) would feel really tough. I worried that they would eat into their emergency savings or take on more debt and lines of credit over time in order to survive, forgoing any equity that they were building in the house. Best to keep saving for emergencies and find a used truck for around $18,000 so they could pay their bills, continue saving and still have a life.

"I don't want to reduce our Spending Money further," Sandy said, "but we have to get the truck. So are we screwed?"

"No," I told them. "Even if increasing your Fixed Expenses means a decrease in your Spending Money by 5 percent or more, it doesn't mean you can't do it. It just means that you have to be mindful of the fact that you're going to feel this reduction in a big way. You are making a choice and acknowledging that you're going to have to reduce your spending to make room for this Lifestyle Upgrade. And now you know with absolute certainty how that will affect you on a daily basis." Used truck for the win.

New Hard-Limit Plan		
Fixed Expenses	$3,510	(includes used car payments of $325)
Meaningful Savings	$1,015	(holding steady)
Short-Term Savings	$200	(holding steady)
Spending Money	$1,575	(Hard Limit reduced by $325)

Sure, it would be awesome if Sandy and Amit could say no altogether to buying a new vehicle, but they can't. Instead they need to understand how the purchase will directly affect their daily life, and make the best financial decision before that happens. Your Hard Limit must represent a sustainable amount of Spending Money or else you will inevitably fail. You'll stop saving or potentially start taking on debt.

Saying yes to the used truck was now an empowered financial choice for Sandy and Amit. It was not an emotional decision, a default decision or one made out of fear, and that's why they felt more in control of their finances. Making empowered and mindful financial decisions becomes possible when you have the information and the tools to assess whether you can or cannot afford something, and are aware of the impact those decisions will have on your long-term finances.

•

You may be wondering how to apply this approach to your own life. Examples of Lifestyle Upgrades that require this type of assessment might include buying a house, doing a reno, getting a particular car, choosing a daycare or moving out. Sometimes the answer must be yes. Like Sandy and Amit, sometimes you don't truly have a choice. What you're really asking is "How much is this going to reduce my Spending Money, and is it sustainable?"

When debating a Lifestyle Upgrade, remember to think about how the decision, though it may seem small, will impact your overall finances. Figure out where the funds are going to come from in order to afford it. Will it be a reduction in Fixed Expenses? Meaningful Savings? Short-Term Savings? Spending Money? If you can't reduce your Fixed Expenses or your savings without being financially irresponsible, then it will be a direct hit on your Spending Money. You need to know if the increased expense of the Lifestyle Upgrade will reduce your Spending Money by more than 5 percent. If it will, you're going to feel that in a huge way. Things will be really tight. It's a red flag of unaffordability—proceed with caution!

Now that you know how to decipher whether something is affordable on a daily basis or in a bigger Lifestyle Upgrade scheme, you can move forward with confidence that you have the knowledge and the tools to make empowered financial decisions. No more Spending Vortex! Full control over your cash flow! Understanding when you can and can't afford something is crucial to Worry-Free Money. Now you know that when you're adhering to your Hard Limit, you're living within your means.

However, as the cost of living goes up, you may be forced to reduce your Spending Money more and more in order to live within your means and stick to your Hard Limit. *Ick.* It's not fun to reduce your Spending Money. But a reduction in Spending Money doesn't have to hurt as much as you may be worried it will. I have a way in which you can almost painlessly reduce your spending. It's called Happy Spending, and it's how you can live within your means without hating your life.

CHAPTER 9

Happy Spending

It may sound strange to think about your spending habits as happy or unhappy. But I assure you, there's a difference. Happy Spending is spending that you feel good about in the moment and, more importantly, afterwards. It's when you spend your money on things that are meaningful to *you*, not to your friends, parents, co-workers or financial experts. You spend your money on things and experiences that bring you satisfaction, so that living within your means doesn't have to be suffocating or restrictive. You can have a life that makes sense for you, not a budgeting template downloaded from the Internet. This is how you make living within your means feel good.

In a perfect world, all your Spending Money would be used for Happy Spending. But unless you're loaded, the reality is that you likely can't afford everything you want or need. Once you've siphoned off your Hard Limit and isolated the money you can spend to zero each month, you likely still have to make choices or trade-offs with that money in order to live within your means. If you don't, you will spend above your Hard Limit and end up right back in the overspending cycle, spinning your financial wheels.

We have already established that there are only four types of money:

- money for Fixed Expenses (predictable bills)
- money for Meaningful Savings (money that increases your net worth)

- money for Short-Term Savings (for spikes in spending and emergencies)
- Spending Money (for daily expenses)

You also know that your Hard Limit is the difference between the money you need to set aside for Fixed Expenses and Meaningful and Short-Term Savings and the money you use for day-to-day life—your Spending Money. The expenses that make up your Spending Money fluctuate and cannot be predicted. They include (but are not limited to) groceries, coffee, chocolate, magazines, beauty products, grooming, electronics, home decor, art, travel, transit, gas, weddings, showers, gifts, trainers, gym, pets, musical instruments, lessons—all the things that make up your life.

Disposable Income Is Not Disposable

You've likely heard financial experts and even family and friends refer to your Spending Money as "disposable income." But hold the phone! Think about the word *disposable*. If you look it up in a thesaurus, here are some synonyms you'll find: *throwaway*; *needless*; *unnecessary*; *trivial*; *nonessential*; *frivolous*. I'm sorry, what? Your disposable income is *not* disposable.

Do you really feel that any portion of your paycheque is "throwaway?" I definitely don't. Unless you can literally set your money on fire without a second thought, no part of your income is disposable. So let's agree to never use that term again to refer to the money that funds our daily lives. Okay?

When it comes to "How to Cut Expenses, Today" or "Five Best Ways to Save Money" articles and blog posts, they typically tell you to pay your bills and cut, cut, cut your spending where you can. I'm so tired of those pack-your-lunch and forgo-the-daily-latte tips. This type of frugality implies that you need to train yourself to buy only carefully budgeted and well-priced necessities such as groceries, gas and similar supplies. Anything beyond that is probably something you don't need, something that you simply *want*. If it's something you just want, as a motivated budgeter you should be able to cut back on it easily enough. If you can't reduce your wants and purchase only what you need, then you clearly suck at handling money. Why can't you control yourself? Are you weak-willed? Geez. It is exactly this type of mindset that makes you feel guilty or insecure every time you open your wallet.

If you're struggling financially right now, those preachy voices can be shrill and appear to be everywhere. But who really gets to decide what is a necessity and what isn't for you? Are new pants nonessential? A vacation with family trivial? A birthday dinner with your best friend unnecessary? Taking a taxi to get to a meeting on time because your kid puked on your outfit just before you left, needless? No. These are the kinds of expenses that make up our lives and say everything about who we are and how we show up in the world. My life is not frivolous and I know yours isn't either. If our Spending Money is a representation of our daily lives, then our Spending Money is as important as the money that goes towards paying for our Fixed Expenses and Meaningful Savings.

Unfortunately you have been trained to believe that your inability to resist spending money on things that aren't bills, milk or bread is the reason why debt levels continue to soar, when quite the opposite is true. After years in the trenches every day, dealing with real people surviving real life, I've realized that trying to live frugally is the problem. Instead of helping us to gain control of our finances and our lives, it perpetuates the guilt around spending on anything that makes us happy. Guilt inevitably leads to frustration and hopelessness. Eventually you simply give up and overspend or under-save, which only leaves you feeling broke. Cut spending, fail, repeat. Counterproductive? Absolutely. In order to break the cycle you need to look at your Spending Money in a whole new way.

Normally I hear things like "I spend so much on takeout, I should cut back" or "Is it okay that I spend $120 to cover my grey hair?" The answer is always "It's up to you." You can't simply point to the largest expenses in your monthly bank statement as areas to cut back. You need to be selective about where you choose to spend and where you choose not to spend.

When you invest your money in stocks or real estate, you choose very carefully. You hem and haw; you research and read; you meet with several financial advisors or house-hunt for months. Why? Because it's an investment. No one wants to make a rash decision. Your money is important and you want to invest it wisely.

You need to put the same kind of thought into your daily spending too. *Your Spending Money is an investment in how much you enjoy your life.* That's why cutting back can feel so hard and frustrating. It's not about how much money you make. Whether you earn $25,000 a year or $250,000, if you're cutting back on the wrong expenses it can feel like you're divesting from your happiness. It feels like none of the money you earn is for *you*.

Granted, you don't get a financial return on investment (ROI) from your Spending Money the way you do from investing in real estate or the stock market. That's because your money has gone to this store or that service provider. But you do get an Emotional Return on Investment (EROI) from your Spending Money—every single dollar.

Just like the returns on an investment, the EROI on your Spending can be positive or negative. It all depends on who you are and what's important to you. There is no right or wrong way to spend your money. But if you ensure that you spend on things with a high EROI and avoid those that give you a low EROI, you'll definitely enjoy your life more, even when cutting back. I call this Happy Spending.

Happy Spending

Think about where you spent money today or yesterday. Now think about which of those expenses made you feel proud, excited, joyful, unafraid, satisfied or happy. Any of your purchases that gave you these feelings are examples of Happy Spending. Those expenses had a high Emotional Return on Investment for you. You spent money and you felt good about it.

Now think about purchases you may have made that did not make you feel so good. Maybe they made you feel resentful, afraid, annoyed, regretful, ashamed or guilty. Purchases that make you feel blue are those with a low Emotional Return on Investment. I call this Unhappy Spending (so creative of me).

When you're trying to "cut back," it's simply not realistic to cut out things that give you a high EROI. Living within your means is not about isolating your needs versus your wants and simply cutting out the wants in order to live frugally. That is a recipe for disaster.

Remember your Life Checklist and the intense pressure to overspend? That pressure is real. It makes your wants feel like needs. Now put that intense pressure to spend against the frugal mindset that wanting is somehow a bad and shameful vice. It's no wonder you feel guilty when you spend money on things that aren't simply bills.

Enough already! You can't effectively reduce your expenses when you're trying to cut spending on things you love. Spending money should be pleasurable.

You only have so much money to spend within your Hard Limit each pay period. Don't you want to ensure that you're spending it on things that give you the biggest emotional bang for your buck? Don't you want to make those expenses count, big time? You should.

The goal is to reduce Unhappy Spending where you can to make more room for Happy Spending with the money that you have. By actively choosing to spend money on things that make you happy, you are more likely to stick to a financial plan, stop budgeting and get control over your money. Spending money without worrying about it—how wonderful!

How to Find Your Happy Spending

Step 1: Recall your Hard Limit from Chapter 6.

For example, let's say your monthly Hard Limit is $950 but you know you are spending more, since you are constantly dipping into savings or left with a credit card balance you can't pay off entirely each month. You know you need to make some reductions in your spending in order to live within your means. But you also want to ensure that you can live within your means without hating your life. Happy Spending to the rescue!

Step 2: Calculate your typical monthly Spending Money within your Hard Limit

Download your credit card (or debit) statements for the three months of the past year that are the most reflective of your normal life. Using the credit card bill from after the holidays just seems like cruel and unusual punishment—there's no need for that. Be sure not to include money that goes towards Fixed Expenses, Meaningful Savings or Short-Term Savings. Average out the expenses to a monthly amount. Let's look at our simple example:

	March	July	November	Average
Groceries	$300	$320	$280	$300
Toiletries	$20	$40	$30	$30
Gas	$150	$100	$50	$100
Entertainment	$200	$250	$300	$250
Self-care	$100	$120	$80	$100
Takeout	$60	$80	$70	$70
Shopping	$150	$150	$150	$150
Totals	$980	$1,060	$960	$1,000

In this case your average spending is $50 above your $950 Hard Limit.

Step 3: Rate your average spending for EROI

We talked about how your Spending Money provides you with an Emotional Return on Investment (EROI). Now I want you to think of your EROI on a scale of 1 to 5, then rate your spending as to how satisfied or fulfilled it made you feel. Score 1 for terrible, 2 for bad, 3 for indifferent, 4 for pretty happy and 5 for utmost happiness. A "must" (see the table on page 135) means that you can't get out of it and it's at the lowest it can possibly go.

Some spending within your Hard Limit is not really a matter of choice. Things like groceries, gas and toiletries (personal-care products, household cleaning supplies, toothpaste, toilet paper,

	Average	EROI
Groceries	$300	5
Toiletries	$30	MUST
Gas	$100	MUST
Entertainment	$250	5
Self-care	$100	3
Takeout	$70	1
Shopping	$150	4
Total	$1,000	

shampoo, conditioner, makeup and baby stuff like diapers and for-mula—anything you'd buy at a drugstore) are great examples of man-datory spending where there's not a lot of room to reduce. Groceries are interesting. There is a basic level of grocery shopping that is a must, that you can't get out of—everyone has to eat. However, a lot of times grocery stores can be a place where a lot of Happy or Unhappy Spending occurs.

For example, if you have a very high grocery bill from month to month because you're buying premade food at the deli (which makes you feel frustrated), then the total amount of your grocery bill is not a must and may even have a low EROI. Or perhaps eating organic food is really important to you and your high grocery bill rates a 5 out of 5 on the Happy Spending scale. Your grocery bill is part must, part choice. In order for something to qualify as a must, it must be non-negotiable and the lowest possible amount you can spend; in other words, it can't move any lower.

In our example, you spend $300 per month on groceries and get an extremely high EROI, a 5 out of 5. That signals that there are probably areas where you could reduce your grocery bill but you don't want to because that spending makes you happy. Additionally, the $30 on toiletries and $100 on gas are as low as they can go. Love it or hate it, you have to spend at least that much on those categories every month. There's no room for EROI because there's no wiggle room on these expenses.

Step 4: Reduce the Unhappy Spending first

In our example, you should not reduce groceries (5/5), entertainment (5/5) or shopping (4/5). If you try, you will be cutting back on the things you like the most, the expenses with a very high Emotional Return on Investment. Instead you should focus on reducing takeout (only 1/5) by $50. If you can do that, it's the only cutting you need to do!

Step 5: Set mindful goals to reduce Unhappy Spending

Now you know that you have to try to keep spending on takeout to $20 ($70 – $50) to keep your expenses within your Hard Limit. Perhaps you'll make it a new rule that you buy takeout only once a month instead of twice.

Essentially the goal is to identify areas within your Spending Money where you can reduce without making you feel frustrated. Happy Spending gives you permission to keep spending money on things that make you feel proud, excited or fulfilled, because you're reducing the expenses that don't make you happy. We will deep-dive into more complex examples—how to deal with Big Purchases, expenses that fall outside your daily Spending Money—later on, in Chapter 10.

Note that this is *not* a budget. You don't need to be checking in constantly with these categories to be sure you're on track. You may have one Happy Spending where you blow every dollar on groceries and then eat noodles while you pay for toothpaste the next time. It's up to you! Happy Spending is simply intended to make you mindful about where you're spending your money, and which types of expenses make you happy and which leave you feeling unfulfilled. The goal is to allow you more freedom to enjoy your money, not to constrain you.

Meet Jo

Jo
Age: 38
Relationship status: "It's complicated"
Kids: 0
Annual gross household income: $65,000
Assets: $45,000 in retirement accounts (part of a defined benefit pension plan to which she contributes 10% of her gross income a year, matched by her employer, which is amazing and rare; she has no plans to ever leave her job or pension plan); condo valued at $325,000
Liabilities: $250,000 mortgage (fixed rate of 3.4%); $3,250 credit card debt (promotional rate of 5%)

Jo, who is constantly being told "You spend too much," is a nurse who lives in a suburb of Vancouver. After reading through the documents she sent prior to our meeting, I didn't know what to expect from our first session, because I had been struck by a few of her answers to my questions. In response to "What do you want to get out of our financial planning session?" she had responded: "I need to suck less at finances and stop spending all my money. Not sure there's much you can do." Those are harsh words to use when talking about your finances. They show frustration and a lack of belief that anything will help.

Jo had failed at budgeting a bunch of times. Sitting down with me was a last-ditch effort to get control. It was interesting, because after looking over her finances, I realized that things really weren't so bad for her. Her situation definitely did not justify her goal to "suck less at money" and "stop spending all my money." What, then, was making her feel out of control and hopeless?

Sure she had some credit card debt, but it was manageable. "So, is the credit card balance consistently coming down, staying the same or going up?" I asked when we met.

"It's been slowly rising over the last 12 months," she told me. "Ever since I bought the condo. I dunno, I'm bad with money. Maybe it was stupid to buy the condo. But it is what it is, I guess." She laughed nervously, but I could tell that she was deflecting.

"You're not bad with money, and buying the condo wasn't stupid. You can afford it. You've just got a bit of Debt Creep going on."

She raised an eyebrow. "A bit of what?"

"Debt Creep," I explained. "It's when your credit card balance is slowly and steadily rising or your emergency or chequing account balance is slowly going down over time, even though you're actively trying not to spend money. It means you're overspending."

"Yes," she said. "That's it exactly. I feel like I'm so careful and budgeting all the time and yet my credit card balance is still going up. I just don't get it. I feel so irresponsible."

"You're not irresponsible," I assured her. "No one spends time and money on a financial session unless they seriously want to get their financial house in order. If you really sucked at money, you wouldn't care that you feel out of control and it wouldn't bother you that you have debt. The fact that you're here proves that you care about your finances and that you're not bad with money."

She smiled. "I guess that's true."

(Since you're reading this book, that goes for you too. The fact that you even picked it up and got this far means that you are not bad with money and that you genuinely care about your finances. Yay!)

I looked down at another document she had filled out for me. Her list of major financial goals read as follows:

1. Keep my condo.
2. Pay down my credit card this year.
3. Pay off mortgage by the time I'm 60.
4. Take one trip a year.
5. Live.

Here is my financial translation of those goals:

1. Keep the condo = Fixed Expenses. These must remain the same, so I needed to give her a plan that worked around them.
2. Pay down credit card before end of 5 percent promotion (12 months) = Meaningful Savings. Using the Debt-Repayment Calculator, we worked out that Jo needed to put an additional $180 per month (above the minimum payment) towards the credit card debt to pay down the $3,250 owing in 12 months.
3. Pay off mortgage by age 60 = Meaningful Savings. Jo had 22 years (264 months) to make this happen. So we did the math using the online Debt-Repayment Calculator and determined that she needed to put aside an additional $300 per month to go towards her mortgage.
4. One trip a year = Short-Term Savings. I asked her how much she realistically needed for a trip and she said $2,400 per year or $200 per month ($2,400/12 months).
5. Live. Basically Jo wanted a sustainable Hard Limit that didn't feel restrictive.

I smiled. "Let's dig in, shall we?"

Step 1: We calculated Jo's Hard Limit, taking into account her financial goals

Monthly after-tax income	$4,045	
FIXED EXPENSES: Money You Cannot Spend		
Mortgage	$1,050	
Condo fees	$450	
Utilities	$80	
Property tax	$200	
Phone	$50	
Subscription	$10	
Credit card minimum payment	$100	
Car insurance	$110	
Bank fees	$15	
Total	$2,065	(51% of after-tax income)
MEANINGFUL SAVINGS: Money You Cannot Spend		
Additional mortgage fund	$300	
Credit card above-minimum payment	$180	
Retirement savings in addition to pension	$0	
Total	$480	(12% of after-tax income)
SHORT-TERM SAVINGS: Money You Cannot Spend		
Travel fund	$200	
Total	$200	(5% of after-tax income)
SPENDING MONEY: Hard Limit	$1,300	(32% of after-tax income)

Step 2: We looked at Jo's typical spending

Here's how it shook out:

	February	August	October	Average (rounded)
Groceries	$420	$300	$420	$380
Toiletries	$40	$40	$70	$50
Gas	$150	$150	$150	$150
Work lunches and coffee shops	$80	$125	$100	$100
Takeout	$100	$120	$80	$100
Dinner out/outings with friends	$100	$350	$60	$170
Entertainment (books, movies, music)	$80	$150	$50	$95
Grooming	$50	$50	$50	$50
Clothes	$0	$50	$250	$100
Alcohol	$20	$100	$60	$60
Parking	$80	$10	$0	$30
Home decor	$120	$0	$0	$40
Gardening supplies	$0	$30	$0	$10
Yoga classes	$120	$0	$80	$65
Magazines	$10	$5	$30	$15
Taxis/Uber	$50	$0	$30	$25
Social events (weddings, showers, etc.)	$0	$100	$0	$35
Workout gear	$100	$0	$0	$35
Totals	$1,520	$1,580	$1,430	$1,510

So why was her credit card debt mounting? The problem was that Jo spent about $210 more a month than she could afford

($1,510 – $1,300) in order to reach her financial goals and deal with her daily spending. She needed to make some cuts.

"That makes sense," she said. Then she waved a hand as I started to speak. "I know what you're going to say, and trust me, I've already tried. I know what I am supposed to do but I can't seem to keep motivated with my plan."

"Okay," I said, "what is your current plan to reduce spending?"

"Limit groceries to only $50 a week. Take transit to work to save on gas. And only one restaurant meal a month." She rhymed them off so quickly it sounded like she had the list memorized.

"Wait a second," I said. "You're going to cut back on groceries and your lunchtime spending at the same time?"

Jo shrugged. "My parents think I live irresponsibly because I eat out so often. I don't know. My mom is an accountant. She worked out that if I stopped eating meals out and took public transit I could save $300 a month, which would save me something like $30,000 in interest on my mortgage."

These are all very normal ways to nip-and-tuck spending. And Jo's mom had made an amazing point about the interest on the mortgage. But here's the piece that Jo's mom was missing: "Has this plan worked?" I asked.

"No," she admitted. "I can never stick to it."

"And how do you feel when you fail?" I asked.

"Ugh, I feel so guilty every time I don't take my lunch or I drive to work. It's like, of course I want to save $30,000 in interest, but I also can't get up an hour earlier every morning to make lunch and take transit without hating my life."

I could feel her frustration. And here is where I got her to start changing the way she thought about her Spending Money. "You hate your life," I told her, "because you're trying not to spend money on the very things that you like the most. It's perfectly normal to spend money on things you want. In fact, you *need* to if you want to be happy and survive your daily life."

She raised an eyebrow.

"Let's look at your spending right now," I said. "You're typically spending the most on gas, groceries and dining out each month. Wanna know why? Because those are the things that you like to do the most. It's not an indication of where to cut. Most times, where you spend the most money is an indicator of where *not* to cut."

Now it was a just a matter of figuring out where Jo's Happy Spending stood versus her Unhappy Spending.

Step 3: We rated Jo's average spending for EROI

We went back to Jo's average monthly list and added a happiness-rating column. Then she went to work rating those expenses for EROI.

We looked at Jo's Happy Spending, starting with the 5s.

"Groceries," I said. "Why is this a 5 out of 5?"

"I love to cook," she told me. "And I don't want to buy crappy-quality food. It's important to me to buy organic."

"And gas?" I asked.

She laughed. "You know what? I hate taking public transit. It takes me twice as long to get to work because there isn't a good bus route. That's why I love driving. I know that taking public transit is financially smarter, but I end up driving all the time because I also love the extra hour of sleep that driving allows me."

We moved on to dinners out. "Dining out is what I do with my friends, family and partner," she explained. "It's what I do for fun. I

	Average Spending	EROI
(1 = Unhappy Spending, 3 = indifferent, 5 = utmost happiness)		
Groceries	$380	5
Toiletries	$50	MUST
Gas	$150	5
Work lunches and coffee shops	$100	4
Takeout	$100	2
Dinner out/outings with friends	$170	5
Entertainment (books, movies, music)	$95	5
Grooming	$50	4
Clothes	$100	4
Alcohol	$60	3
Parking	$30	1
Home decor	$40	2
Gardening supplies	$10	5
Yoga classes	$65	3
Magazines	$15	1
Taxis/Uber	$25	2
Social events (weddings, showers, etc.)	$35	4
Workout gear	$35	1
Total Spending	$1,510	

get excited about it and I'm always sad when I try not to do it." She shrugged. "FOMO, I guess."

Entertainment? "I love, love, love books and music. They are my hobby. Not being able to buy books or albums would make me really sad. They stay." She smiled. "I actually feel happy about that."

Finally, gardening supplies. "That only happens in the summer," she said. "I grow my own vegetables and herbs on the balcony and I'm obsessed with it. It brings me real joy. It stays."

After this exercise I pointed out that the very things she had been trying to cut back on before—groceries, driving and dining out—were the very things she valued the most. Every time she had budgeted in the past, she set herself up for failure because she was trying to reduce spending on things with the highest Emotional Return on Investment. Her budgets were literally a financial punishment for her. It's no wonder she failed.

However, Jo still needed to reduce her spending to fit comfortably within her Hard Limit, by at least $210 per month. We went back to her spending chart to examine the low-EROI expenses, starting with the 1s.

Step 4: We reduced Jo's Unhappy Spending

It was clear that Jo hated paying for parking (1/5 EROI), yet she had already said that she loved to drive. When I asked her about this, she said, "I hate paying for parking because it's usually totally avoidable and I'm just being lazy, or impatient on weekends. I can definitely get that down to once a month." Voila—$10 "saved."

I asked her about the magazines (1/5). "Ugh, yes. I pick them up when I'm on my lunch break and I'm bored. I feel irritated after I buy them. I can cut that completely. No problem." That's $15 "saved."

Last, the workout gear (1/5). She winced. "I bought that when I thought I was going to work out every day at home. They still have the price tags on. I regret them but I won't be buying anything else, because I'm out of the home gym scene for now. Yoga all the way." Another $35 "saved."

For Jo, these were the kinds of purchases she needed to be aware of in the future. Once you identify the spending trends in your life that give you low EROI, you can use that information to make mind-ful spending decisions in the future. That's how you reduce spending in a way that still feels good.

By starting with all the 1s in her list, we eliminated the pur-chases that actively created negative feelings. Jo found the whole process of cutting back her Spending Money way less painful than she had thought. She probably wouldn't be able to eliminate parking expenses completely, but the mindfulness was about reducing her spending exposure to those things.

Next we moved to the 2s in her list, starting with taxis. "Most times I don't like it when I've taken a taxi out of laziness," she admit-ted. "But when it's freezing or raining, I'm totally satisfied." The new mindfulness goal around this became "Only take taxis when it's raining or freezing and avoid otherwise" ($10 "saved").

The goal of the exercise, of course, was to end up with only the musts, 4s and 5s on her list, so we kept going with the 2s and the 3s and made trade-offs she felt comfortable with.

With more mindfulness in a few areas, Jo was able to reduce her spending by $210 per month. This meant that she could save that money and take a vacation without putting it on a credit card.

"See?" I said. "It's totally doable, without hating the plan. It's your money, Jo. You get to decide how it's spent. No one else. As long as you're not plunging into debt and you're meeting your goals, who cares where and how you spend your money? No one should. Period. Full stop."

I heard from Jo six months later. "So how is the new plan going? Are you living within your Hard Limit?" I asked.

"Yes!" Jo laughed. "At first it felt weird. Not cutting back on dining out as a way to save money felt totally wild, but I get it now. I

	Hard Limit	EROI
Groceries	$380	5
Toiletries	$50	MUST
Gas	$150	5
Work lunches and coffee shops	$100	4
Takeout	$50	2
Dinner out/outings with friends	$155	5
Entertainment (books, movies, music)	$100	5
Grooming	$50	4
Clothes	$100	4
Alcohol	$30	3
Parking	$10	1
Home decor	$0	2
Gardening supplies	$10	5
Yoga classes	$65	3
Magazines	$0	1
Taxis/Uber	$15	2
Social events (weddings, showers, etc.)	$35	4
Workout gear	$0	1
Total Spending	**$1,300**	

haven't had to dip into my travel account, I have $1,260 saved there, and I didn't even feel the cuts that we made. Plus I feel like I have way more of a say in how I spend my money, so I don't feel guilty anymore when I drive to work."

"That's wonderful."

"Yeah! I also told my mom, and it helped me communicate to her why I didn't want to give up dining out or driving to work. Now she gets it. It's not that I'm being financially irresponsible; I'm just spending in ways that she wouldn't. Now she's doing her own Happy Spending too!"

"Woo-hoo! I'm so proud of you. You are officially living within your means."

"Absolutely. And not hating my life."

•

Do not cut Happy Spending from your life. You need it! Happy Spending is how we stop budgeting and start living.

Remember, in order to move yourself forward financially, you need to live within your Hard Limit. That means there's a limit on how much you can spend. You need to ensure that you're spending money on things with a high Emotional Return on Investment so that you get the biggest emotional bang for your buck.

If you need to make reductions in your Spending Money so you can make room for other expenses or savings, here's what you need to do:

1. Rate your spending for how satisfied or fulfilled it makes you feel—this is Happy Spending. Rate 1 for terrible, 2 for bad, 3 for indifferent, 4 for pretty happy and 5 for utmost happiness, or "MUST," which means that you can't get out of it and the amount is the lowest it can possibly go.
2. Reduce the expenses with the lowest EROI—the Unhappy Spending—starting first with the 1s, 2s and 3s.
3. Make mindful spending goals around the reductions in Unhappy Spending. Like Jo, only take taxis when it's raining or freezing, and avoid otherwise.

When You Don't Agree on Happy Spending

If you're in a relationship or have a family or a roommate, it's probably not just your Happy Spending that matters. Other people's opinions matter too. How to divvy up joint money can often lead to big money arguments. No fun at all.

When we looked at Jo's spending and objectives, everything worked out just peachy because she didn't have to worry about anyone else's opinion. But things are not always so streamlined. Often when I go through this exercise with more than one person, there are disagreements on what is considered Happy Spending. "I think it's important to buy quality groceries" versus "I'd rather buy cheaply in bulk." Or "I want to splurge on a videographer for the wedding" versus "It's just a day. No!"

The problem is that no one is wrong and no one is right. While you may feel like your point of view is correct, when you take a step back, you can see that it is are mostly just personal preference.

Meet Pat and Lin: New Money in the House

Pat and Lin
Ages: 42 and 45 respectively
Relationship status: married
Kids: 3, ages 1, 3 and 5
Annual gross household income: $175,000 ($75,000 + $100,000)
Assets: $85,000 in retirement savings; house valued at $700,000
Liabilities: $425,000 mortgage; $40,000 line of credit at 4.7%

Pat and Lin came to my office to ensure that they were on track financially and being strategic about where they put their money. Their incomes were very strong but they hadn't been able to save much over the past eight years while their three children were in daycare. However, with their third child about to start school, the end of the daycare years had arrived. Woo-hoo! There will be more money available in the household budget on a monthly basis for the first time in years, but how should they allocate it?

"We don't want to waste it. We want to be strategic," Lin said. You may find yourself in a similar situation when you pay off debt or get a raise or return to work. It's a big question: How should you allocate new money coming into your household?

Let's start by looking at Pat and Lin's financials.

Pat and Lin didn't have credit card debt, which is great and very rare for daycare-years survivors. But for the past eight years they hadn't been able to save for a vacation or home repairs or their kids' education, because $2,000 a month was going towards daycare and they didn't have any wiggle room. It was a Fixed Expense.

Now that the $2,000 a month was about to free up, they needed to allocate it. It was a huge amount of money—a game-changer. First we needed to ensure that they had a plan in place to reach their Meaningful Savings goals.

- **Pay off their $40,000 line of credit in five years.**
  We used the Debt-Repayment Calculator (page 303) to figure out that they needed to put in an additional $585 per month above the minimum payment.
- **Get retirement savings to $700,000 over next 20 years.**
  Pat and Lin already had $85,000 in their retirement accounts.

Joint monthly after-tax income	$10,385	
FIXED EXPENSES: Money You Cannot Spend		
Mortgage	$2,250	
Utilities	$350	
Home insurance	$125	
Property tax	$350	
Cable/Internet/subscriptions	$160	
Phone	$275	
Car payment	$225	
Car insurance	$445	
Private life insurance	$270	
Line of credit minimum payment	$165	
Childcare (about to end!)	$2,000	
Gym memberships (recurring)	$90	
Bank fees	$30	
Charitable donations (recurring)	$50	
Total	$6,785	(65% of after-tax income)
MEANINGFUL SAVINGS: Money You Cannot Spend		
Line of credit above-minimum payment	$0	
Retirement savings for Pat	$200	
Retirement savings for Lin	$350	
Children's education fund	$0	
Total	$550	(5.5% of after-tax income)
SHORT-TERM SAVINGS: Money You Cannot Spend		
Vacation	$0	
Home renovation/repairs	$0	
Car repair ($600 per year)	$50	
Total	$50	(0.5% of after-tax income)
SPENDING MONEY: Hard Limit	**$3,000**	(29% of after-tax income)

Using the Long-Term Savings Calculator (page 306), we found that an additional $600 per month on top of what they were already saving would get them just over $700,000 in 20 years if they assumed a rate of return of approximately 5 percent.

- **Children's education fund at $32,000 per child ($96,000 in total) in 15 years.**
  To accomplish this, we used the Savings Goal Calculator and worked out that if they got a 4.2 percent net return, they needed to put in $131.21 per child each month. This would come to approximately $400 per month, rounded up.

When all the Meaningful Savings were subtracted from the $2,000, they ended up with $415 left over each month. So far so good, right? Everyone was stoked. But here's where things got a little dicey. A whole lot of Short-Term Savings goals were competing for this money.

What Pat wanted:

- A family vacation. The family hadn't taken a vacation in years. The kids were getting older, they could appreciate travel and Pat wanted to take them on a road trip. For all five of them it would cost about $5,000.
- Some heavy-duty sporting equipment. Pat had really got into triathlon since having the kids, and he wanted to be able to spend $700 (including tax) on a new bike in the next three months.

What Lin wanted:

- Nothing to do with triathlons. She thought it was an overly expensive sport and did not want household money to go towards such a one-sided goal.

- An update for the bathroom. Nothing crazy, but the tiles had cracks, the wallpaper was peeling and the fixtures were starting to wear out and looked dated. They were hosting a family reunion in 10 months and wanted the bathroom to be fixed up by then. This would cost $4,000.

This is a great example of what happens when people don't agree on what constitutes Happy Spending. So I asked them to rate their competing goals for spending happiness.

Happy Spending Assessment		
Goal	Pat's EROI	Lin's EROI
Family vacation	5	3 (if there's money, great)
Triathlon bike	5	1
Updated bathroom	3 (sure, but not important)	5

For Pat, vacations and triathlons got 5 out of 5 on the Happy Spending scale. For Lin, it was all about the bathroom. So what should they do? First, let's see if they could do all the things they wanted to.

If Pat and Lin were able to do everything in the next year, it would cost $9,700: $5,000 for the trip, $700 for the bike and $4,000 for the bathroom. In order to achieve this, they would need to put aside approximately $810 per month to get to $9,700 over the next year ($9,700/12 months). However, they had only $415 left each month to put towards Short-Term Savings. Therefore they were short $395 ($810 – $415) a month. Saving up for all those goals was not possible within the 12 months unless they cut back.

Since Pat and Lin had Fixed Expenses and Meaningful Savings that were nonnegotiable, their only other option was to look at their Spending Money ($3,000) and see if they could cut back somewhere within their Hard Limit to raise the extra $395 a month. I asked them to rate their spending on the happiness scale of 1 to 5.

	Pat	Lin	Joint	EROI (Pat, Lin)
Groceries			$1,000	4, 5
Dining out			$150	4, 4
Gas			$370	MUST
Budgie			$20	5, 5
Sports	$100			5, 3
Art class		$25		3, 5
Adults' self-care	$60	$25		3, 5
Kids' grooming			$40	5, 5
Cleaning service			$115	3, 4
Adult clothes	$60	$85		4, 5
Kids' clothes			$60	5, 5
Kids' activities			$600	5, 5
Outings with friends	$30	$50		5, 5
Babysitting			$120	5, 5
Family outings			$90	5, 5
Totals	$250	$185	$2,565	
SPENDING MONEY: Hard Limit			$3,000	

Since Pat and Lin had previously sat down with me for a financial session, they had already cut much of the Unhappy Spending from their lives. When we scanned the list, we saw that most of what remained was really Happy Spending for someone. There were no 1s or 2s to start with, so we examined the 3s (neutrals) on the list.

Lin was neutral about Pat's sporting hobbies, while they represented utmost happiness for Pat. Pat was neutral about Lin's art hobby, which was a 5 for her. So neither of those were up for a reduction. Pat seemed neutral about his grooming expenses and the household cleaning service.

Otherwise, everything was Happy Spending or nonnegotiable for the family. This was when the exercise got tough (or interesting).

Keep in mind that we could be talking about $100 per month or $50,000 per year in savings—the figures don't matter. The process is the same. There are bound to be times when families and partners encounter conflicting savings goals. How do you decide how to allocate money when there are conflicting financial goals? I'll show you.

Step 1: Ensure that none of the conflicting financial goals is putting Fixed Expenses, Meaningful Savings or emergency Short-Term Savings at risk

Happy Spending conflicts should be happening only after you ensure that your bills are paid (Fixed Expenses) and your financial butts are covered (meaningful and emergency savings). If that's not the case, then perhaps none of the conflicting goals is even on the table for discussion. Go back and ensure that enough money is being put aside each month to cover your Fixed Expenses, Meaningful Savings and emergency Short-Term Savings. For example, if there's a ton of household credit card debt and no plan to pay that down, and your partner wants to spend $400 of joint money on a weekend away, the answer should be no unless you (as a team) are willing to eat into your Spending Money to make room for it.

But Pat and Lin had their Fixed Expenses covered, they had siphoned off enough money to reach their retirement savings goals, and they had a realistic debt-repayment plan. Where the extra $415 per month ($4,980 a year) would go was truly a subjective matter, which was good. Since they'd covered their butt financially, this was not really a financial decision anymore. It was matter of opinion.

Remember, when it comes to how you spend your money, you're not solely right, nor is your partner. Everyone is right and everyone is wrong. That's what makes this so tough.

Step 2: First focus on goals that both of you benefit from

Even though Pat and Lin disagreed on the priority of the goals, they still had goals that would benefit both of them. The family vacation ($5,000)? Pat and Lin felt they would both benefit emotionally from that. The updated bathroom ($4,000)? They both felt they would benefit from that as well. As for Pat's new bike, it was a $700 expense that Lin didn't feel she would benefit from at all. So we shelved the bike . . . for the moment.

Step 3: Compromise, compromise, compromise on amount and timeline.

Recall that Pat and Lin had $415 per month to save, which would amount to $4,980 ($415 × 12 months) over the next year. With the shared goals of vacation and bathroom, there were only two ways to make them happen:

Option 1: Do both things for less money
I asked them about the vacation. "Can you do it for less than $5,000?"

Pat shook his head no. The plan was to do a cross-Canada road trip. He thought it would cost a minimum of $5,000. I checked in with Lin, and she agreed. The trip they both wanted would cost $5,000.

I brought up the bathroom. "Can it be done for under $4,000?"

Lin said, "Yes. The bathroom could be updated for about $3,000 if we do some of the work ourselves." I checked in with Pat. He agreed that they could definitely complete some of the work themselves to keep costs down.

Great. Now the shared goals had gone from $9,000 ($5,000 trip + $4,000 bathroom) to $8,000 ($5,000 trip + $3,000 bathroom). But they still had only $4,980, so we weren't finished yet.

Option 2: Adjust the timeline for either goal

We started with the vacation. "How far out can you guys push this goal?" I asked.

Pat said, "We can go on a trip this year or next. It would be best this year, but it doesn't have to be."

Then I turned to the bathroom. "Is the timeline flexible?"

Lin said, "Technically, yes. Nothing is broken yet, but I would really like to get it done before the reunion in 10 months."

I checked in with Pat. I asked him how he would feel about prioritizing the bathroom update over the trip. He was totally fine with it as long as the trip was in the works and they could book things to ensure that it actually happened.

Great! Progress.

Since they needed $8,000, I calculated that they could accomplish both the bathroom ($3,000) and the travel ($5,000) within approximately 20 months without making any cuts to their Spending Money. Twenty months × $415 = $8,300. They could do the bathroom in seven or eight months ($3,000/$415) and the trip 12 months after that ($5,000/$415) for a total of 20 months. And they'd have $300 extra to spend on the vacation.

"Deal?" I asked them.

"Deal," they both said.

Things don't always work out this well. Sometimes neither party feels that one goal has priority over the other. In those cases, the solution is to save equally for both and extend the timeline for both. If Pat and Lin had disagreed on the amounts or the timelines, I would have suggested that they save the $415 a month and create equal time horizons of 20 months for both goals. Bathroom and trip happen in 20 months—no one gets one first.

Step 4: Deal with non-shared goals

Could Pat have his bike (and ride it too)? Lin wasn't a miserly person who wanted to punish her partner, but she didn't see spending $700 on a bike as a shared household goal at all. In addition, Pat wanted the bike within the next six months for a big meet, which meant saving an additional $115 per month ($700/6 months, rounded down).

I asked Pat if he was willing to trade any of his personal Happy Spending to make room for the additional $115 per month towards the bike. Yes, I suggested he cut some of his Happy Spending, because that's all he had on his list. And if the bike was important enough, it would classify as Happy Spending as well.

We looked at their Happy Spending list again. Pat was willing to reduce his $60 self-care expense. He had been spending money on supplements for his training and it was getting expensive. He wanted to reduce spending by $30 by letting go of one specific supplement. He was also willing to reduce his clothing spending for the next six months. This would reduce his average clothing spending by half, raising another $30 a month to put towards the bike. The mindfulness goal became "No new clothes for the next six months." At that point there wasn't anything else he felt he could realistically reduce.

In order to make the bike happen, the couple needed to look at some of their joint expenses. I made it very clear that Lin had to agree to any cuts of joint expenses before they became part of the plan. First we turned to the cleaning service, since it was low on Pat's Happy Spending list. Lin had rated the bimonthly service at 4 on her Happy Spending scale. She enjoyed it but Pat was neutral. He suggested that for the next six months they forgo the service altogether.

Lin gave that a hard no. "It's a relationship-saver," she joked. She was, however, willing to compromise and have it only once a month, so long as Pat did more than his share of the household cleaning. He agreed. That would raise another $57.50 towards the bike each month. By trading out the lower EROI spending, Pat had raised $117.50 a month for the next six months to go towards the bike, which would more than cover the $700 ($117.50 × 6 months = $705).

I asked Pat and Lin how they felt about their new plan to distribute the freed-up daycare money.

Lin said, "I feel good. Excited. We've been so eager to get things back on track."

Pat agreed. "I know I'm overdoing it with the bike, but I promise, it's such unbelievably high Happy Spending for me that I will literally trade off almost everything else in the short run for it. I will do *all* the housework, I promise. It feels good to have a plan for all the things we want to do."

Lin smiled. "And it feels really good knowing that we laid all this out together beforehand so we won't end up arguing down the road. I'm relieved."

So was I!

•

When you and a partner disagree on where Spending Money should be allocated, follow these steps:

1. Ensure that none of the conflicting spending goals is putting Fixed Expenses or Meaningful Savings or emergency Short-Term Savings at risk. Otherwise they are a no.
2. Focus first on goals that both of you benefit from.
3. Compromise, compromise, compromise on amount and time-line. If you've only got so much money to spend, you need to make it count. Yes, everyone prioritizes spending differently, and there is nothing wrong with that as long as you compromise and make sure that everyone is getting something that is important to them.

Happy Spending makes sticking to a financial plan easier because reductions in spending don't hurt as much. Your Hard Limit is how you stop budgeting, and Happy Spending is permission to spend your money so you can start living. This combination will allow you to live within your means without resenting the financial plan.

Screening Out Unhappy Spending

Now you have your Hard Limit figured out and you've listed your Happy Spending. All that's left is to banish Unhappy Spending from your life and your finances will fall into place by themselves. Sounds easy, but not so fast! Unhappy Spending can be unconscious or, most of the time, habitual. It sometimes stems from obligations and often comes with guilt and fear attached, which makes it harder to cut than you may think. That's why it's important not only to recognize where your Unhappy Spending lies but also to understand what drives you to make those purchases with low EROI.

After years of asking clients to identify their Unhappy Spending, I have found that the following are usually the reasons behind the least gratifying purchases/expenditures of all:

- **Social Obligations:** maybe there's a shower, work party or annual event that everyone else in your social group is attending; not attending makes financial sense, but the guilt you feel for missing it is intense. You feel like a bad friend, a bad parent, a bad family member, a bad partner.

- **Inadequacy:** spending money under the Inadequacy Influence. You're feeling that you are not attractive, interesting, fit, smart, fun or exciting enough, so you spend money to feel better about yourself. Like the new work dress you bought because you felt like you'd been wearing the same thing every day and felt insecure around your co-workers.

- **F*ck-It Moments:** when you have no willpower left to say no and end up throwing money at a problem to make it go away. Maybe you're tired or hangry (so hungry you're angry) and retail therapy feels like the solution. This usually shows up as overspending on taxis, takeout, parking tickets, treats and sometimes major purchases that result in huge buyer's remorse.

It's not that all social gatherings are a waste of money and time, or that new clothes or health programs equal Unhappy Spending. Treating yourself to a taxi or takeout is not a sinful vice. That's not what I'm saying at all. I'm saying that you need to pay attention to the rationale behind the purchase. That's what will dictate how you feel about it later. It's not about the purchase itself.

Unhappy Spending may not feel like a big deal in the moment. And certainly an extra $40 splurge at the grocery store won't destroy your retirement or wreak havoc on household finances for years to come. The real concern comes when many of these transactions happen over time, again and again. A swipe of your credit card here, an ATM withdrawal there because you're stressed or overloaded or simply exhausted at the end of the day. The decisions you make on a daily basis may not be flagged as something you'll regret a few days later or when the credit card bill comes, and that's the problem. Unhappy Spending can so easily slip into your daily life and take over, swipe by swipe. That's why you need to learn to recognize it *before* it happens.

Pre-ashamed of My Spending

One really interesting perspective shift happened for me while I was doing the Real Selfies project. It alerted me to when I was about to make a purchase that was Unhappy Spending, *before* I spent the money.

I had been spending money and snapping photos of the bills, boldly displaying my spending habits on the Internet. I hadn't thought much about it until one evening when I was walking home from work, tired and hungry after a particularly crappy day. There in the window of one of my favourite clothing stores was a beautiful peacoat. A perfect peacoat that practically shone through the window. I had to have it.

I didn't actually need or even want a peacoat until right at that moment. In fact, I was already wearing a peacoat. Sure, it was three years old and not nearly as cute as the one in the window, but it got the job done. Truthfully, a new peacoat would have been completely redundant in my closet, but that didn't stop me from wanting it.

I wasn't always pleased that many of my clothes were a few years old, and in that moment my current coat felt ratty, old and ugly. I was under the Inadequacy Influence, and seeing that new peacoat made me feel that I needed to overspend to feel better about myself. Convinced that I "needed" a new coat, I popped into the store to take a better look.

"Want to try it on?" the saleswoman asked.

"Yes," I replied. "Absolutely."

I tossed aside my worn old peacoat and pulled on the beautiful new one. It fit like a dream and looked amazing. I loved it.

"Looks great," the saleslady said. "And it's on sale. Twenty percent off."

Ah, the power of a sale to give us instant FOMO (fear of missing out). Making us feel that the pressure is on, that stock won't last, that a deal is always a "good financial decision" regardless of the facts. My lucky day, right? I looked at the price tag—$350 before tax. With 20 percent off, $280.

"It's the last one in that size," she said as I admired it in the mirror. More FOMO.

Here's the thing: because I was in the middle of the Real Selfies project, I knew I had to post anything I bought that wasn't a regular purchase (like groceries and toilet paper) on the Internet for all to see. If I were to buy the new peacoat, I would have to take a photo of it and post the receipt as well. Most people don't have to do this and, until the project, I never had to either.

I was never really accountable to "future me" when I was about to buy something. However, in this unique scenario, I was forced to picture myself in the future (could be five minutes or five weeks from then) with this coat and photographic proof of my purchase on the Internet, to be judged by all, including—perhaps most crucially—myself. I didn't want to post it.

My tired brain was yelling *Buy this coat! You work really hard! It looks great! Your other coat is old, YOU DESERVE THIS!* But the knowledge that I would feel ashamed to admit to the Internet that I had spent $280 on a coat I didn't need was stronger. I was feeling "pre-ashamed" of my purchase, which was interesting to me. Knowing that I would have to post it on the Internet made me mindful of how I would feel about my purchase, *before* I swiped my card.

This pre-shame alerted me that buying the coat would be Unhappy Spending. I was about to lay down money for something with a low EROI because I was having a F*ck-It Moment and just wanted to feel good right then and there. I would have gone home, posted the picture with the receipt and felt ashamed and guilty and irritated with myself. And because it was on sale, I wouldn't have been able to return it.

I put the coat back on the rack and left the store. Huge.

The next day I was proud of my decision not to buy the peacoat. I had made the right call. And that was when it came to me: if you could find a way to identify your Happy versus Unhappy Spending triggers, then you could pre-screen for unhappy feelings or low EROI *before* you overspent. And as an added bonus, there is science to back up my theory.

A group of neuroscientists conducted a study about spending money that relates to what I experienced in that store. In this study, the scientists scanned people's brains while they were looking at a range of potential purchases. The first region of the brain to light up was the pleasure centre, of course. You see something in a store and you want it. *Ooh, that'd be nice.* Exactly like me with that peacoat in the window.

But here's the cool part. Once the study participants where shown the prices for the items, something called the prefrontal cortex lit up. The prefrontal cortex is where super-rational decision-making happens. So the study found that the pleasure centre kicks in first, followed by the more rational, logical part of the brain when the price tag appears. The price tag is like a reality check.

Here's the most nerdishly cool part. A third part of the brain also lit up when people were shown the price tag. Something called the insula (or insular cortex), which is implicated in processing pain. The insula is handy because it's how you learn not to hurt yourself. If you're a kid and you touch a hot burner on the stove even though your parents told you not to, it burns, causing you pain. That pain is registered with the insula so that the next time you go near the stove, your insula will be like, *Hey, don't touch that. Remember last time? You don't want to feel that pain again.* So you don't put your hand on the burner again.

What could this mean for you and your ability to avoid Unhappy Spending? Basically, those who have negative memories or experiences associated with overspending could be more likely to say no to a bad purchase *before it happens,* because they don't want to feel that way again. This is what happened to me in the store. As much as I wanted to purchase the coat in that moment, the part of my brain that remembered feeling ashamed of overspending was yelling *Girl, no! This coat is expensive, and if you buy it, you'll have to post it in the Real Selfies project. Then you'll feel ashamed and guilty. It's Unhappy Spending and you'll regret it.*

"Eureka!" I said to myself (seriously). "This is the answer." If you can learn to identify how you feel about a purchase before you buy it—perhaps by recalling how you felt the last time you went over budget (ashamed, frustrated, guilty, pissed, a.k.a. broke)—then you can train your brain to alert you when you're about to spend money on something that is Unhappy Spending, so you can avoid it.

That is why it is so important to rate your expenditures and make a list of your typically Unhappy Spending. You are literally training your brain to identify and remember what types of expenses and spending circumstances make you feel broke, guilty or afraid, so that the next time you are about to swipe your credit card, you can be like, *Ooh, that would be nice. But wait, it's going to cost me x dollars, which will put me over my Hard Limit. I always feel like crap when that happens because I end up putting off my other goals that have a higher EROI.* The message: "Do not buy. You will regret it."

A lot of times you are told to focus on positive savings goals in order to draw the strength to say no to overspending in the moment and to be motivated to live within your means. Tips like "Remember in the moment, before you swipe your card, that if you say no you'll be lying on a beach somewhere soon." That type of thing. Well, I'm saying, "F* that!"

Don't focus on the good; focus on the bad! Yes, I'm asking you to wallow in your past financial pain so you can identify your Unhappy Spending patterns. Why? Because just like the kid with the hot stove, I want your brain to be able to recall the pain of overspending and the feelings you had after spending money on things that made you unhappy. That way you can pre-screen your purchases and recognize Unhappy Spending *before* it happens.

When you understand what triggers Unhappy Spending versus Happy Spending, you can avoid feeling broke and spending money on things that don't fill you up emotionally.

This is how you learn to say no and make mindful spending decisions before they happen.

How to Pre-screen for Unhappy Spending

This is an exercise to remind your brain how icky it feels when you overspend. Basically it's an exercise to train yourself to recall how it felt when you put your hand on the hot burner—the financial burner, if you will. Get out your journals, people. Let's learn from your biggest spending blunders.

- What was the last spending mistake I made?
- What was the reason for spending money on that item?
- How did spending the money make me feel at the time?
- How did spending the money make me feel afterwards?
- Why do I want to avoid feeling like that again?
- How can I remember to avoid feeling like that in the future?

Remember, this can be something small, like taking an expensive taxi ride home, or something huge, like buying a timeshare you cannot afford. Be as descriptive as possible and be sure to do this exercise again and again, anytime you feel frustrated, resentful or ashamed of a purchase you made. This is an ongoing resource to help you really identify and pre-screen for Unhappy Spending that will lead to overspending. It will help you say no before the purchases that make you feel broke happen.

CHAPTER 10

Saying No to Overspending

For most of us there simply isn't enough money to do or have everything we want. Modern life puts heavy-duty pressure on us to overspend. Besides the big things like housing and transportation, there are everyday expenses like a data plan for your phone, a networking event for your career and, of course, the small things you barely think about, like subscriptions for online movies, music, news. Ten dollars here, fifteen dollars there. Eventually you have to say no to some things so you can say yes to others.

You've seen how the Hard Limit and Happy Spending give you the tools you need to gain control of your finances, a way to stop the Spending Vortex and live happily within your means, enjoyably, without worry for the future. But the key to using these tools is knowing when to say no to spending and when to say yes.

When to Say No

The Hard Limit lets you know what you can and cannot afford, alerting you to when you should say no, while Happy Spending ensures that you're spending money mindfully on purchases that will leave you feeling satisfied. Basically you're asking yourself two things before you spend money:

1. Can I afford this? (Is it safe to spend money?)
2. Does it make me happy? (Is it Happy Spending?)

These questions aren't mutually exclusive. Both must be considered at all times before you spend money. You have to be able to afford it (it's safe) and to be certain that your Emotional Return on Investment will be worth it (it's Happy Spending). If you cannot meet *both* of these criteria, you must say no to spending. This is the beautiful marriage of practicality and fun in your financial life.

There are three types of spending that you need to watch out for when deciding to say yes or no:

- **Spending Money:** your daily spending on clothes, coffee, gas, groceries, fun—within your Hard Limit.
- **Lifestyle Upgrades:** buying a house, rent increases, having kids, getting a car, home renovations paid on debt.
- **Big Purchases:** expenses that won't permanently affect your finances like Lifestyle Upgrades but are definitely outside the capacity of your daily spending.

Spending Money

Spending Money shouldn't be complicated now that you are living within your Hard Limit and have isolated your money for daily expenses in a separate chequing account (joint or individual). You know what you can and cannot afford on a daily basis. A quick look at the balance in your Spending account will let you know when you can and cannot afford something. If the answer to "Is this Happy Spending?" is yes, then the decision is easy. Go for it. Spend away!

"I spend $10 a day on lunches out," my client Randy told me. "And I'm 100 percent cool with it. For me, buying groceries is often a waste. I'm never home to cook and I'm throwing out mouldy broccoli all the time. Pretending I'll take my lunch every day is totally unrealistic for the way I live my life—it just won't happen. Going out for lunch is also social time with my co-workers. We vent about the day, bond, and try new places. It's fun."

Before she spends, Randy answers the two questions. Is it safe? Yes, lunches out are affordable within her Hard Limit. Is it happy? Hell, yes—lunch out gets a 4 out of 5 happiness rating. So she keeps going out for lunch without a second thought. No guilt. No fear.

On the other hand, we have Brad. "I'm so frustrated with myself," he confessed. "I can't believe I spend $10 a day on takeout lunch at the office. That's $50 a week! If I could just get it together and cook more I'd probably be way healthier, and I'd have so much more savings."

Now Brad answers the same questions. Is it safe? Yes, lunches are within his Hard Limit. Is it happy? No—it gets only a 1 out of 5 rating. Lunches out clearly don't bring Brad the same satisfaction that Randy enjoys. Cutting back on takeout was a no-brainer for Brad, while keeping the lunches out was a no-brainer for Randy.

Lifestyle Upgrades

For Lifestyle Upgrades, you also know that you need to say no or proceed with extreme caution if a new purchase will permanently increase your Fixed Expenses to more than 55 percent of your monthly after-tax income. If it will, the spending is not safe. You can't truly afford it.

Big Purchases

Life is messy and complex. A lot of our purchasing decisions fall somewhere between the categories of daily Spending Money and permanent Lifestyle Upgrades. These can be things like splurging on a designer couch or saying yes to a crib that costs more than the budget allows but matches the nursery. These are Big Purchases, which can't be decided simply by looking at your Spending account, because the amount required is likely larger than the balance that may be in there until the next pay period. However, such purchases also aren't Lifestyle Upgrades that will affect your Fixed Expenses permanently.

When a purchase is too big to fall within your Spending Money but is also not a Lifestyle Upgrade, you need to ensure that you are both safe and happy before you spend the money. Hopefully you've been using your Short-Term Savings to save up for Big Purchases. If it's a home repair, you've got it covered. If it's a trip, you've been saving for that too. That's the beauty of the plan so far—Short-Term Savings are designed to keep Big Purchases off your credit cards for good.

But what happens when you want to make a Big Purchase and it's something you haven't planned for in your Short-Term Savings? Typically such purchases will end up sitting on a credit card. So the question then becomes "Are you ever safe to spend on a credit card when you can't pay it off right away?" Before you swipe that card, use the Three-Question Check-In:

Check 1   Will this purchase permanently increase my Fixed Expenses to more than 55 percent of my after-tax income? Yes? Then don't spend. This is likely a Lifestyle Upgrade that you cannot afford. It's not safe.

Check 2 Will I need to eat into or reduce ongoing Meaningful Savings to accomplish this purchase? Yes? Then don't spend. Eating into your Meaningful Savings is not financially responsible. It's not safe.

Check 3 Will this decrease my Spending Money by more than 5 percent for longer than *six months*? Yes? Then don't spend. It's not safe.

So if you answer yes to *any* of the above, do not pass Go. Do not collect $200, and drop that idea like it's hot. You can't afford whatever you're looking at. It's not safe, regardless of how happy it makes you. Sorry.

Now you may be wondering why I set six months as the limit to how long you can safely carry a credit card balance for a Big Purchase. Isn't credit card debt the Big Evil? Yes, but I am realistic. If you can realistically pop a purchase onto your credit card and then reduce your other spending in order to pay off that debt within six months, I'm fine with it. As long as you don't put any more Big Purchases on the card until the initial purchase is paid off, there's a realistic and manageable plan of attack.

If it will take you longer than six months, it's out of your price range. You'll need to save up for at least part of it first. I know any credit-card-abstinence-preaching personal-finance junkies reading this will hate that I've just told you to go ahead and carry a balance. But I'm not going to sit here and demand that you never, ever again spend outside your Hard Limit. You're human, and so am I. I get it—I've been a bridesmaid; I've bought a bed frame; I've had to call an exterminator. You simply cannot plan for absolutely every Big Purchase you'll ever need. I've worked with enough individuals and families to know this to be true, and I don't want you to feel ashamed. But I do want you to know where that hard no is so you can use credit responsibly and safely.

How to Say Yes

Sometimes life demands that you spend outside your Hard Limit. So you need to have a plan of attack that's realistic. You must be mindful about unexpected Big Purchases, because that is how Debt Creep starts. Too many purchases outside your Hard Limit means that you can't realistically pay them all off and that you will be overspending and under-saving permanently. Your debt will rise or your emergency account will empty and you won't be moving forward.

Here's how my client Ray said yes to spending, even though it was a Big Purchase that he floated on his credit card.

Ray, a musician, wanted to purchase a new guitar. "It's $820, and it's amazing," he said.

The cost was clearly outside the realm of his monthly Hard Limit ($1,220). If he were to purchase the guitar with money from his Spending account, he'd have almost nothing left for the rest of the month. The guitar wasn't Spending Money; it was a Big Purchase, and one that he hadn't budgeted for. It would have to go on a credit card or he would have to eat into his vacation account.

"I really want this guitar," he said. "Can I afford it and still go on my vacation?"

I looked at the numbers. If Ray purchased the guitar and put the whole thing on a credit card charging 19 percent interest, his minimum payment on the credit card would be $17 per month. It was time for the Three-Question Check-In.

Monthly after-tax income	$3,200	
FIXED EXPENSES: Money You Cannot Spend		
Rent	$1,150	
Phone	$55	
Subscriptions	$20	
Bank fees	$5	
Total	$1,230	(38% of after-tax income)
MEANINGFUL SAVINGS: Money You Cannot Spend		
Down-payment fund	$450	
Total	$450	(14% of after-tax income)
SHORT-TERM SAVINGS: Money You Cannot Spend		
Vacation	$200	
Emergencies	$100	
Total	$300	(10% of after-tax income)
SPENDING MONEY: Hard Limit	$1,220	(38% of after-tax income)

Check 1   Will this purchase permanently increase my Fixed Expenses to more than 55 percent of my after-tax income? No. Even though his credit card minimum payment would increase his Fixed Expenses by $17, to 39 percent of his after-tax income, this was less than 55 percent and not permanent. Safe.

Check 2   Will I need to eat into or reduce ongoing Meaningful Savings to accomplish this purchase? No. Ray wouldn't need to decrease the $450 monthly contribution to his down-payment fund, which was a nonnegotiable. Safe.

Check 3   Will this decrease my Spending Money by more than 5 percent for longer than six months? No. Using the

Debt-Repayment Calculator, we figured out that Ray would need to contribute approximately $130 a month (in addition to the $17 minimum payment) in order to pay down the $820 within six months. Even though this repayment plan would decrease his Spending Money from 38 to 34 percent of after-tax income (a 4 percent drop), he could pay down the credit card debt over six

Monthly after-tax income	$3,200	
FIXED EXPENSES: Money You Cannot Spend		
Rent	$1,150	
Phone	$55	
Subscriptions	$20	
Bank fees	$5	
Credit card minimum payment	$17	
Total	$1,247	(39% of after-tax income)
MEANINGFUL SAVINGS: Money You Cannot Spend		
Down-payment fund	$450	
Credit card above-minimum payment	$130	
Total	$580	(18% of after-tax income)
SHORT-TERM SAVINGS: Money You Cannot Spend		
Vacation	$200	
Emergencies	$100	
Total	$300	(9% of after-tax income)
SPENDING MONEY: Hard Limit	$1,073	(34% of after-tax income)

months, as long as he didn't make any more unexpected Big Purchases over that period. Safe.

Was it safe? Yes, he passed the Three-Question Check-In. Was it happy? Yes—a 5 out of 5 happiness rating. Could Ray say yes to spending on the $820 guitar? Yes.

Ray was pumped. Great! He was stoked and I was satisfied that he had a realistic plan for repayment in place that wouldn't leave him paying down debt for an unsustainably long time. Over the six months, Ray would pay approximately $45 in interest as he paid down the debt. While I don't like anyone paying interest ever, he and I both agreed that $45 was worth the pain for the gain. Since it would be realistically paid off within six months, the expense was manageable. A great marriage of financial responsibility and happiness!

If, however, the guitar had cost $2,080, the answer would have been different. Let's see how that would have played out. Putting $2,080 on his credit card would drive up Ray's minimum payment to $35. Time for the Three-Question Check-In:

Check 1   Will this purchase permanently increase my Fixed Expenses to more than 55 percent of my after-tax income? No. Even though his credit card minimum payment would increase his Fixed Expenses by $35, to 40 percent of after-tax income, this wasn't over 55 percent and was not permanent. Safe.

Check 2   Will I need to eat into or reduce ongoing Meaningful Savings to accomplish this purchase? No. Ray wouldn't need to decrease the monthly $450 contribution to his down-payment fund, which was nonnegotiable. Safe.

Check 3   Will this decrease my Spending Money by more than
5 percent for longer than six months? Yes. In order to pay
back the $2,080 within six months, we calculated that
Ray would need to contribute $332 per month in addi-
tion to the $35 minimum payment. This would decrease
his Spending Money from 38 to 27 percent of after-tax
income—a significant 11 percent drop. Or, if he reduced
his Spending Money to a safe amount, as for the $800
guitar, and put a total of $147 on the card each month, it
would take him 17 months to pay off.

The problem was that life has a way of throwing curveballs. It was
unlikely that Ray would not have other unforeseen Big Purchases
over the course of the next 17 months. With only $853 left for
Spending Money, it's likely he would then have to overspend, outside his Hard Limit. Either way, it would be unsafe.

If this were the case, I would tell Ray to make a trade-off between
taking a vacation and purchasing the $2,080 guitar. He could take
the money earmarked for vacations and put it towards the guitar
so that he could pay it down realistically within six months. That
means he would need to put down $1,260 cash towards the guitar
and carry only the $820 on his credit card. This choice, while not
ideal, would keep him financially safe, and he would still get a say
in how his money was being spent.

If you buy something that requires you to reduce your Spending
Money for longer than six months or by too much (more than a
5 percent reduction), you are just asking for trouble. Not leaving
yourself with enough Spending Money to realistically survive daily
life for too long is a surefire way to reach the F*ck-It Moment and fail.

Monthly After-Tax Income	$3,200	
FIXED EXPENSES: Money You Cannot Spend		
Rent	$1,150	
Phone	$55	
Subscriptions	$20	
Bank fees	$5	
Credit card minimum payment	$35	
Total	$1,265	(40% of after-tax income)
MEANINGFUL SAVINGS: Money You Cannot Spend		
Down-payment fund	$450	
Credit card above-minimum payment	$332	
Total	$782	(24% of after-tax income)
SHORT-TERM SAVINGS: Money You Cannot Spend		
Vacation	$200	
Emergency	$100	
Total	$300	(9% of after-tax income)
SPENDING MONEY: Hard Limit	$853	(27% of after-tax income)

You likely won't ever pay off the credit card purchase, and eventually you will swipe the card, then swipe it again and yet again, while your financial goals slowly slip away.

When you are making financial decisions outside your Hard Limit, be sure you can safely afford them. Be sure they are safe purchases. While it may be irritating in the moment to say no, this will make you happy in the long run.

Long-Term vs. Short-Term Happy Spending: One Wedding, Two Guests

Avoiding Unhappy Spending is an important part of Worry-Free Money. Unfortunately, you can't just buy everything you want, so you need to ensure that you are enjoying the money you do have to spend. This makes you less likely to fall off the financial wagon and give up on the long-term plan. Before you spend, you need to be both safe and happy. But when it comes to Big Purchases, how will you recognize Long-Term Happy or Unhappy when you see it?

Ben is getting married. Guess where? The Caribbean. Here are the facts:

- The wedding will take place at a five-star all-inclusive resort. The minimum stay is one week, and you're guaranteed good food and even better drink.
- The wedding is 12 months away.
- The cost each guest will have to pay is $2,500 + airfare (so $3,000 to $3,500 per person).
- Ben is awesome and his partner, Gil, is also awesome. They are well loved.

Meet two of the invited guests, Dayna and John. They're not related but they both know Ben. Let's see how each of them viewed this wedding.

	Dayna	John
Relationship to Ben	good friend	cousin
Current Short-Term Savings balance	$28	$2,000
New savings over next 12 months	$1,200	$3,840

Dayna

Dayna really, really wanted to go. She has known Ben since high school and would also love a getaway from the crappy Canadian winter. She had been poring over the resort's website, envisioning her room and checking out the onsite restaurants.

I asked Dayna to pre-screen this Big Purchase and rate the wedding on a scale of 1 to 5 for Happy Spending. "Four out of five at least," she said. "All my friends are going. I wanna go!"

Was this wedding short-term Happy Spending? Yes, yes, yes! Great. We had part of the equation, but we needed more. We needed to know if this Big Purchase was safe. Could Dayna afford to go to the wedding? We looked at the numbers.

Including incidentals like a gift, a new outfit and potentially a new bathing suit, Dayna estimated the wedding would cost her $3,500

Dayna's Financial Picture

Monthly Income and Expenses		
After-tax income	$4,160	
Fixed Expenses	$2,280	(55% of after-tax income)
Meaningful Savings	$630	(15% of after-tax income)
Short-Term Savings	$50	(1% of after-tax income)
SPENDING MONEY: Hard Limit	$1,200	(29% of after-tax income)

Assets: $5,000 emergency account (enough for three months of Fixed Expenses and basic spending, less Employment Insurance, if she left her job); $65,000 in retirement accounts, with an ongoing $500 monthly contribution (10% of gross income)

Liabilities: $2,200 line of credit at 6 percent interest (being paid off at $130 per month over the next 18 months)

---

once all was said and done. The event was in 12 months, so she would need to bump up her Short-Term Savings to $290 ($3,500/12) in order to make it work, an increase of $240 per month ($290 – $50). Would increasing her Short-Term Savings by $240 per month be safe?

Monthly after-tax income	$4,160		
Fixed Expenses	$2,280	(55% of after-tax income)	hold
Meaningful Savings	$630	(15% of after-tax income)	hold
Short-Term Savings	$290	(7% of after-tax income)	$240 increase
SPENDING MONEY: Hard Limit	**$960**	(23% of after-tax income)	$240 decrease

The Three-Question Check-In

Check 1   Would this purchase increase Dayna's Fixed Expenses to more than 55 percent of her after-tax income? No, they could hold steady at 55 percent. Safe.

Check 2   Would she need to eat into or reduce ongoing Meaningful Savings to accomplish this purchase? No. She really wanted to pay off her debt in 18 months. Plus she had to continue putting away $500 per month for retirement to maintain her goal of saving 10 percent of her gross income towards her nest egg. Safe.

Check 3   Would this decrease her Spending Money by more than 5 percent for longer than six months? Yes. She would have to increase her Short-Term Savings by $240 per month for 12 months and reduce her Spending Money by $240, to $960 per month, to accommodate the trip.

This would be a reduction in Spending Money from 29 to 23 percent, which is greater than 5 percent. In addition, the 12 months was well beyond the six-month safety limit. Not safe.

Could Dayna afford this wedding? No. It was not safe.

Dayna agreed that reducing her Spending Money from $1,200 to $960 for a whole year would make things too tight. If the reduction in spending were needed for only six months, I might have said, "Go for it." Human beings are tough; we can do anything for six months if properly motivated. But a whole year? That's likely unsustainable. I've seen it too many times. A lot can happen over a year, and you can't know what other financial challenges (or windfalls) may lie ahead.

What we did know in the moment was that Dayna couldn't afford it. Naturally this wasn't what she wanted to hear, so we started trying some adjustments.

Dayna felt that she could comfortably save $100 per month to her Short-Term Savings (an extra $50) while still leaving enough Spending Money to survive the next year. While I agreed that a $50 reduction in her Spending Money was sustainable, her vacation fund would add up to only $1,228 ($1,200 new savings + $28 that was in there already) by the time the wedding came around, and she needed $3,500.

This meant that $2,272 ($3,500 – $1,228) would go straight onto a credit card, with the likely plan of adding it to the line of credit later. And therein lay the problem. Without this extra expense, in 12 months her existing line-of-credit debt would be almost gone. But now she'd be adding another $2,272, putting her right back into a cycle of debt. It wasn't safe.

While the payments Dayna would have to make to her line of credit might not screw up her retirement, they would keep her in a constant state of debt for another two years after the wedding! Her only other option was siphoning funds from her emergency account, which she knew was financially irresponsible and would cause her more anxiety. "I don't want to eat into my emergency account," she said. "Things are slow at work, and that makes me really nervous."

This is where the concept of long-term happiness comes into play. I asked Dayna a really important question: "Is this expense Happy Spending?"

"Yes, obviously. I really want to go."

"Okay, but how about a year from now, when you've got an extra $2,272 from this trip left on your line of credit? How will you feel a year from now?"

She paused. "I don't know. Not good, actually."

"Why?"

"Because I've been working so hard to save up for my other goals. I don't want to be in debt anymore."

"What do you think Future You would think about this purchase?" I asked.

"Future Me would probably say 'Don't do it' and call it Unhappy Spending, because I'll be resentful and frustrated about it down the road, rather than proud and excited."

As difficult as it was to admit, Dayna could not afford this wedding. It wasn't true Happy Spending. When it comes to spending, happiness and financial responsibility in the long run matter as much as happiness and financial responsibility now.

Was the wedding safe? No. Was the wedding happy? Yes, in the short term, but not in long run. This is when to say no.

John

Now let's have a look at cousin John.

John's Financial Picture		
Monthly Income and Expenses		
After-tax income	$3,200	
Fixed Expenses	$1,600	(50% of after-tax income)
Meaningful Savings	$320	(10% of after-tax income)
Short-Term Savings	$320	(10% of after-tax income)
SPENDING MONEY: Hard Limit	$960	(30% of after-tax income)

Assets: $8,000 emergency account (which is where it needs to be, since John owns a home); $2,000 in Short-Term Savings; $175,000 in retirement accounts (growing at 5 percent, with $320 monthly contributions in order to reach $600,000 in 30 years)

Liabilities: $0 (debt-free)

John had $2,000 in his Short-Term Savings account. In 12 months' time, if he continued to save $320 per month, he'd have $5,840 in that account. He could afford to spend $3,500 on the wedding.

The Three-Question Check-In

Check 1   Would this purchase increase John's Fixed Expenses to more than 55 percent of his after-tax income? No. There would be no changes to his Fixed Expenses.

Check 2   Would he need to eat into or reduce ongoing Meaningful
Savings to accomplish this purchase? No. John was ada-
mant about continuing his savings plan for retirement,
and so was I.

Check 3   Would this decrease his Spending Money by more than
5 percent for longer than six months? Nope. He could
easily take $3,500 from his Short-Term Savings fund
without reducing his spending.

Could John afford this wedding? Absolutely. It was safe.

But ensuring that John was living within his means was only
part of the equation. Safe *and* happy—both at the same time. We
needed to ascertain whether or not this wedding would also be
Happy Spending.

I asked John to identify how he felt about spending $3,500 on
the wedding.

"Not great. I mean, I love my cousin, but I got sick the last time
I went to a destination wedding. It's not really my thing either. Plus
I have no one to go with, and I've been saving up for a boat for like
a year." It was a used boat that was going to cost $4,000.

Now we had got to the heart of the matter. I asked John to rate
both of these goals for Happy Spending on a scale of 1 to 5.

Boat? "That's 5 out of 5. It's my passion. I think about fixing up
this boat literally 24/7. It's what I've been saving for." Wedding?
"Only 3 out of 5. I don't really want to go, but I don't want to be a
jerk either." This was a case of social-obligation spending, a major
cause of Unhappy Spending for John.

John had been saving for the boat for more than a year. Wanting
to enjoy some of his money in a way that made him happy did not

make him selfish. I repeat: it did not make him selfish. If John could afford both, he would go to the wedding and get his boat that year, as planned. But he couldn't. It was either the wedding or the boat. Not both.

If John allowed the pressure of guilt to make him say yes to the wedding, the approval of others would likely give him an initial feeling of satisfaction, and who doesn't like a trip somewhere warm? But that satisfaction would wear off quickly when he got home and settled into another year of saving for that boat.

"How would Future You rate the wedding a year from now if you didn't have enough for the boat?" I asked.

"Probably a 1 or 2. I would be really resentful that I had to wait even longer to reach a goal I've been working towards for so long."

Was the wedding safe spending? Yes. Was the wedding Happy Spending? Mildly in the short term, but not in the long run. This was also when to say no to spending. There would be no long-term happiness for John in that wedding.

John's highest Emotional Return on Investment was from the boat, in both the short run and the long run. Continuing to save his money for the boat was the best way to ensure that he didn't end up resenting his financial situation and feeling broke. In order to live within your means without hating your life, your purchases have to be both safe and happy. Not just one or the other.

Taking a moment to answer the Three-Question Check-In can help give you perspective. It's a black-and-white way to find out if something is safe spending. Is it within your means? If it's not, that alerts you to when you should say no to spending, regardless of how happy the purchase might make you.

Second, you must ensure that you've taken both short-term and long-term happiness into the equation. The question "Does it make you happy?" must focus on both short-term and anticipated long-term happiness in the future. If you are/will be happy in both the short and long run, then it is true Happy Spending.

Should You Spend Money? The Safe/Happy Check-In

Will this purchase leave you safe?

Check 1   Will this purchase increase your Fixed Expenses to more than 55 percent of your after-tax income? If yes, don't spend.

Check 2   Will you need to eat into or reduce ongoing Meaningful Savings to accomplish this purchase? If yes, don't spend.

Check 3   Will this decrease your Spending Money by more than 5 percent for longer than six months? If yes, don't spend.

Will this purchase make you happy?

Check 1   Does it make you happy right now? If it's a 4 or 5 on the EROI scale, that means yes.

Check 2   How will you feel about this purchase a year from now? If it's still a 4 or 5 on the EROI scale, that means yes.

Safe *and* happy. You must be both at the same time in order to live within your means without hating your life and to stop worrying about money once and for all.

CHAPTER 11

Saying No without Feeling Guilty

When it comes to your money, knowing when to say no to spending doesn't always translate into putting that knowledge into action. Over the years I've noticed that most people are okay with saying no to spending on themselves, but they are far less likely to utter that word if their decision negatively affects someone else or what someone else thinks of them.

It's not simply a matter of spoiling someone you love, either. Impossible spending decisions cover the gamut from once-in-a-lifetime events to routine day-to-day events. Things like going to a friend's bachelor party. You'll be happy to attend, but how much should you spend, and where will the money come from? Or heading to your niece's first birthday party. Of course you want to go, but it all adds up.

So the question remains: Why don't you say no sometimes when you know that you should? On a very basic level, you don't want to be a jerk. Who wants to be seen as cheap or broke? And who wants to risk hurting someone's feelings? I get it. And it's good that you don't want to be a jerk. But here's the thing: you're not a jerk for saying no to things you can't afford.

A lot of my clients report that they are okay with saying no to things that are clearly big expenses they can't afford, like a vacation with family or a weekend-long music festival with friends. "I can't afford to right now" seems like an acceptable response.

But what do you do when things *should* be doable? If, for example, your friends from work are all comfortable with going out for drinks, it's assumed that $30 or $40 should be affordable for you too. Well, sure, spending $40 won't likely mean you can't pay the rent or your property tax bill. But what if you shouldn't spend it, or what if you don't want to? Should you say yes anyway to avoid feeling like a jerk?

"I have to" is a line I hear over and over again about financial decisions my clients know aren't wise or that they know to be Unhappy Spending but which feel unavoidable. "I'll alienate my friends." "I'll hurt their feelings." "Everyone will think I'm cheap."

Here's the secret to saying no without the guilt—start talking about money.

Yep, that's right. Talking about money in a *real* way with family and friends will give you the strength and permission you need to say no without offending anyone. Talking realistically about money with your peers and family is one of the most important things you can do to end the cycle of overspending and save more money. It's critical to achieving Worry-Free Money.

Sadly, money is still the last taboo, a dirty little secret we keep to ourselves. It's time to break the silence. Time to be open and honest about when we can or cannot afford something. Knowing how our friends and family are faring financially will help us all save money. Trust me.

Yes, You Can Talk about Money

Years ago I had a life-altering night out with my girlfriends. Shortly after my IKEA meltdown, I was still actively afraid that I would never have enough money to keep up with my Life Checklist, which included things like buying a house and raising a family. I was so worried all the time. Then I received a text message from my friend Renee: "My bday dinner out on Wednesday. You in?"

Renee is a good friend. She was turning 30 and wanted to go somewhere special, somewhere really nice. Read: expensive.

I responded immediately. "Yup! Count me in."

Interesting. This was likely going to be an $80-plus night for sure. I was feeling broke and worried about my financial future and yet I had agreed to go without even batting an eye. What was I thinking?

Going out for dinner didn't mean I wouldn't be able to buy groceries that week, but I definitely felt guilty and frustrated about it. I shouldn't be spending money on dinner out. Or should I? Was it safe spending? I wasn't sure. Was it Happy Spending? I wasn't sure.

My husband and I had just got married and we were desperately trying to save up for a down payment on a house. An $80 night out would mean that I either had to cut back my regular Spending Money or eat into my Short-Term Savings that month, which I didn't want to do, since I was going to be a bridesmaid at three weddings that summer (legit) and had been saving up.

For purely financial reasons I wanted to cancel my RSVP. I knew I shouldn't go, but I also knew that if I didn't go I'd be riddled with guilt that I'd missed Renee's special birthday. Of course, if I went, I'd feel equally guilty about spending money I shouldn't have on an expensive night out. Not to mention the frustration I'd feel knowing I had to make unrealistic cuts to my spending that week to make up for it.

Now, my friend is important to me and I didn't want to miss her birthday, so I didn't cancel that RSVP. But I was bothered by the fact that it was going to be such an expensive night. Excitement, resentment, frustration, guilt, happiness—so many complex and ugly feelings over a simple RSVP. I love my girlfriends and I love having a social life, but I hated how social outings kept me feeling broke, perpetuating my financial worries. Because I wanted to save more money for other goals, every social outing decision felt complex and fraught with danger.

But that's just it, isn't it? Every financial decision we make *is* complex, and we make those decisions every day. No wonder it's hard to say no. Hosting friends for the hockey game. Heading out for a Mother's Day brunch. A housewarming gift for my best friend.

In an ideal world I would have texted Renee and said: *Hey, Renee, I'm saving up right now. Any chance we can choose a less expensive restaurant?* It would have been such a relief to be honest. To tell her I wanted to celebrate her birthday but shouldn't spend $80 right now. Ask if there was something we could do to keep the cost down. But I didn't.

Why didn't I talk openly about the money? A few reasons:

- I didn't want hurt her feelings. I didn't want to make her feel as though she wasn't important to me or that she was a jerk for picking an expensive restaurant.
- Technically I *could* afford it. I could fit this dinner into my Hard Limit and it wasn't going to make or break our overall money plan or sit on my credit card for more than six months.
- I was afraid my friends would judge me. If I said I couldn't afford it, maybe they'd think that we were hard up (this was my insecurity over quitting my Bay Street job to head out on my own), or that I was being cheap, which felt worse.
- FOMO. I didn't want to miss out on the fun! I love these women and enjoy their company.

Like I said, I didn't cancel, but on the way to the party I did something I normally wouldn't have. I broached the subject of money with a friend who was taking the subway with me. "I wish we were going somewhere a bit cheaper," I said.

She immediately agreed. "Oh my god, I feel the same way!" Which I understood, as she had just bought a house.

Another girlfriend met us as we are walking into the restaurant. I brought up the subject again. "I wish we were going somewhere a bit cheaper," I said. "I'm really trying to save."

She was a little taken aback by my bluntness, but then she said, "Oh man, me too. We have two weddings this month. Ugh, life is so expensive."

Now this was interesting; so far I was batting three for three. While we were all stoked for Renee and wanted to go out for her birthday, we all wished we were spending less money. Yet no one had said anything about it.

I decided to conduct an experiment. For the record, I've known these women for a while, some of them for more than 18 years, and we hang out a lot. Everyone at the table was between the ages of 28 and 45. We laughed, ordered food and had a great time. Then, when we'd ordered another bottle of wine for the table, I asked if anyone was feeling worried or guilty about the money they knew they'd be spending on the dinner. (That's what you get for hanging out with a financial planner.)

Everyone was kind of awkward at first, as people usually are when we get real about money. No one said anything, so I opened up about my own situation. I explained that I loved going out and said what a great time I was having. Then I admitted that I should have said no because I was trying to save, but I was afraid of missing out and

I wanted to celebrate Renee's birthday. So instead of being honest from the start, there I was about to spend more than $80 on dinner and wine, knowing that I'd either have to say no to something else important that week or forget about saving money—again.

"Are you upset that you came?" Renee asked tentatively.

"No, not at all," I said and squeezed her hand. "I'm just wondering if I'm the only one feeling this way." I told them I felt like I was in a vicious spending cycle that I couldn't stop. Like there was always something coming up. I explained that I was frustrated because my personal goals kept getting pushed farther and farther away but I couldn't say no when important things, like that dinner, came up.

Once I had opened up and showed my own vulnerability, they all started sharing. Brené Brown would have been so proud of us. It was like the floodgates had opened, and it was amazing. *Everyone* was feeling frustrated and guilty, even the birthday girl, and they felt a lot of relief talking openly about it. I took a chance and asked if I could record the conversation. With everyone willing, I plunked my phone in the middle of the table and let the conversation unfold. It was wild.

Turns out that we were *all* afraid of not having enough money. Some of us owned a house, some paid rent. Some were single, some married, and some had kids. Some were barely scraping by and others had well-paying jobs. But we agreed on one point: we were all worried about money.

There we were, eight women out for dinner, spending too much money on wine and beautiful food, and talking about how frustrated we were that there was never enough money. Oh, the irony. Why was that? Because we still don't like talking about money with our people.

Clients lay out the details of their finances for me day in and day out, but those same clients don't share that information with the people closest to them, because they don't want to be judged. Where we spend our money shows how we prioritize our values. If you tell someone how much you spend on rent and they say it's too much, they've just called you financially irresponsible. If you admit how big your mortgage is and you can see in their face that they think you over-spent, you'll feel like an ass. And if you tell someone how much money you make, you risk making your peer feel inadequate, or you could end up feeling inadequate because perhaps it's not as much as they earn.

When we talk about money, the emotional stakes are high. So we don't. We prefer to keep things private. That's why it remains the final taboo and the cycle of guilt and fear keeps going round and round. It perpetuates feeling broke.

We're fine with general comments like "Oh man, that's expen-sive" or "Yeah, we spent too much," and the old catchall "They make good money"—vague references to our finances that evoke nothing more than a nod of agreement from whomever you're talking to—when what we need is real money talk. The nitty-gritty numerical details that I have the privilege of seeing every day in my job as a financial planner. Exactly the kind of earnest and honest discussion we had at the birthday dinner that night.

That discussion was groundbreaking and had all of us very excited. "Bring another bottle of wine!" we called, and my friend Kristy laughed, saying that now she would have to wait till her next paycheque to buy a toilet for her new house. We all died laughing. It was funny because it was true.

I took another chance and asked the women to fess up about how much they really made a year. We went around the table one by one, admitting how much money we made and, for those who were in rela-tionships, how much their partners made. It felt great to get it all out.

When I said how much I made, Renee was surprised. She had thought I made a lot more, an assumption she'd made because I worked in finance.

"Yeah, but I work for myself now," I said. "It's different. I don't make as much as I used to." It was wonderful to be able to set the record straight. If only we had done that a long time ago! Then I could have said *I love you but I don't want to spend $80 on Wednesday. Can we go somewhere else?* without hurting her feelings. Being open about what I earned, complete with the numerical details, would have allowed me to suggest a change of plan without guilt, because she wouldn't think I was sitting there earning megabucks and nit-picking about her dinner venue. Once she knew what I made, she got it. I could say no without being judged.

The profound effect that night had on our lives is still evident to this day. These many years later, we still make plans differently. When birthday parties, get-togethers, weddings, even our kids' birthdays come up, my girlfriends can say "I shouldn't be spending that money right now since I'm saving for _____. Can we make another plan?" or "Congrats on the house. I didn't get you a house-warming gift because I'm trying to save for my own house" without feeling guilty, cheap or judged. We can sit things out without feeling shame. We have permission to say no to overspending. And, most important, the person hosting the event or receiving that information doesn't take it personally. Everyone wins.

In addition, knowing how much each of us earns allows us to celebrate raises and new jobs without comparing ourselves to one another or assuming that some people really have it going on when truly they don't. It sets realistic expectations for the entire group. Talking about money has made it possible for us to say no to spending that isn't safe and happy at the same time, which means we can live within our means without hating our lives. It's helped us all worry much less about money.

Spreading the Word

After seeing the profound effect that money honesty had on my own group of friends, I made up my mind to share this strategy with my clients too. I started with Beena.

Beena was frustrated. She and her husband had been trying to save up for a family vacation for two years, yet they kept dipping into their savings to cover the cost of daily life and putting off the holiday.

After going through their finances, here's where Beena and her husband stood:

Monthly after-tax income	$7,915	
Fixed Expenses: Money You Cannot Spend	$4,800	(61% of after-tax income; too high!)
Meaningful Savings: Money You Cannot Spend	$800	(10% of after-tax income)
Short-Term Savings: Money You Cannot Spend	$315	(4% of after-tax income)
SPENDING MONEY: Hard Limit	$2,000	(25% of after-tax income)

Their Short-Term Savings broke down as follows:

	Per Year	Per Month
Vacation fund	$1,980	$165
Gifts and birthdays	$1,200	$100
Car repairs	$600	$50
Totals	$3,780	$315

One of the key problem spots Beena identified was the spike in spending for birthday parties for her kids and their friends. You'll note that the amount they set aside was $1,200 per year.

"These parties are relentless," she said. "My kids are invited to so many. And we end up shelling out $25 a pop for the gift and card and wrapping paper. It adds up!"

"What about the parties for your own kids?" I asked.

"We try to keep the costs down, but by the time you add in the cake, a gift and an activity for everyone to take part in, you're looking at $350 per kid. And our parties are considered low-key." She shook her head. "I feel like a bad parent for not renting blow-up castles or video game systems. It's wild." (Here's the Inadequacy Influence rearing its ugly head.)

Beena's annual spending on birthday parties for her kids and their friends looked like this on the Happy Spending spectrum:

	Cost per Year	EROI	
Birthday parties for her kids	$700 ($350 each)	4	(Will try to reduce)
Gifts for other kids	$500 ($25 each)	2	(It's too much)

Beena and her partner could technically afford this. But spending money on these parties ate directly into the money she wanted to use for purchases with a much higher Emotional Return on Investment. For Beena, the parties were Unhappy Spending. Was the expense safe? Yes. Was it happy? No, neither in the short term or the long term.

Beena should have said no to these parties. But that was not so easy. It was a matter of social obligation and fear that her kids would be shunned if they went to a birthday party without a gift. So she and her partner continued to shell out $500 a year on Unhappy Spending and resented it when they couldn't take a family vacation, making them feel broke.

After identifying the problem, I suggested that she try talking with the other parents about the money spent on these parties. "Just try it," I told her. "I bet you're not the only parent who feels like this. I hear this complaint a lot."

After a bit of thought, Beena was willing to try. That year she resolved to prioritize her family vacation (true Happy Spending) over other kids' birthday parties and have the guts to explain to the other parents what she was doing—a birthday-gift boycott. "If they don't like it, too bad. My family comes first," she said. We high-fived (literally).

A few months later, Beena touched base by email to let me know what had happened with the birthday-gift boycott.

Thank you *so much* for suggesting that I talk about money with the parents of my kids' friends. It's been a game-changer. I was terrified at first, but the next time my daughter was invited to a party, I bit the bullet. I called her friend's mom and told her that Nina was really excited to go to Olivia's party, and while she might kill me for this, I was calling to see if there was something we could do about gift expectations.

Olivia's mom, Nancy, asked me what I meant, and I told her honestly that we have been trying to save for a family vacation for some time but we keep dipping into our short-term savings for social events—things like birthdays, showers, etc.—and I just had to draw a line in the sand. I told her I'd like to brainstorm some creative ideas so that Olivia would have a great party and Nina wouldn't show up empty-handed and Nancy wouldn't end up thinking I'm a jerk.

Once I'd opened up about it, Nancy was all over it. She said she felt the same way and was even feeling guilty about throwing the party, because she so gets it. "It's $25 here, $40 there," she said, "plus the time spent shopping and wrapping. It's exhausting." She was so excited to discuss alternatives. We came up with a plan that each parent would contribute $10 and Olivia would get one awesome gift that came from everyone.

All the parents were so into it. Shannon, it's a birthday-gift revolution. Now all of us do it. Everyone is saving time and money, plus the kids get something really special, so they don't feel hard done by (First World problem). Some parents are even using the $10 gifts towards their kid's education fund! It's become the norm within the group. We like to think we are fighting the consumerism mentality with our kids, but really we are just trying not to go broke one-upping each other with more crap to give our kids. This will save us hundreds a year, as well as so much anxiety and worry. Thank you!

At our financial check-in a year later, I found out that Beena had implemented the birthday-gift boycott with as many of her children's friends as possible. "Ninety-five percent of them are so excited about it," she told me. "Those who aren't are judging me for sure, but hey, I know this is the right decision for my family and my finances."

I asked her why she thought that talking about money was directly linked to the success of the boycott. "Because everyone knows we aren't trying to be cheap or jerks. We don't want to hurt feelings, but we are also so tired of spending so much. The big thing is that every family who implemented this idea is relieved to be spending less money and having more breathing room."

I asked her if she ever felt guilty about asking a parent to participate. "Not at all. I just tell them that we aren't able to afford things that are important to us as a family if we keep shelling out hundreds each year for birthday gifts. The fact that I'm so honest about it makes it impossible to call me a jerk. Who would?"

Amazing, I thought. *This is how we start change. This is how we make change. If more of us were honest and open about our finances, it would become the norm.* It's all about being willing to be vulnerable.

The key is not just to say "I can't afford this." The key is to explain the effect that spending money has on your overall finances and what's not happening because of it, and then to suggest that there might be an alternative. That's how you say no effectively without hurting the other person's feelings.

If you ask what's possible, it also leaves room for discussion and new possible solutions. Rather than bailing at the last minute (which does hurt feelings) or spending and resenting it (which makes you feel broke), there is a solution that works for everyone.

Try it. Next time you have to say no to a bachelor party or a reunion or a Father's Day event because of the cost, try talking about your finances in a real way so that you can explain why you're saying no, without hurting anyone's feelings or feeling guilty about it yourself.

How to Say No without Guilt (How to Talk about Money)

1. Take a big breath.
2. Explain the negative effect that spending money on this particular item/event will have on your overall finances.
3. Outline what is *not* happening because of it.
4. Ask if other alternatives are possible so that everyone wins.
5. Accept that someone may not agree.

Talking about Money: A Family Affair

Talking about money is important not only when dealing with your peers but also with your own family—parents, siblings and especially children.

Kids cost money. There's no two ways about it. I used to make the joke that my job was the best form of birth control in the world after I'd seen just how much children can mess with the household finances.

While parents love their kids and wouldn't change a thing about them, there's no denying the fact that children heighten the financial fears and pressure to overspend that modern life has brought us, because we care so much about them. Raising a human is an expensive adventure that comes with so much social and cultural pressure. The most broke-feeling clients I have are parents or those who want to be parents one day.

The parents I meet want to give their kids what they believe is their best shot at life and raise them the way they were raised, or preferably better. Now, if you're reading this and thinking, *I don't have kids. Why should I read on?* I urge you to. If you do want kids one day, this will help. If you don't want kids one day, perhaps you can relate because there's someone in your life who depends on you financially, someone you love fiercely who requires you to spend money. When you love someone like that, it makes it very hard to say no.

There's a lot of pressure to spend money on your kids: class trips, hot-lunch programs, a new phone, back-to-school shopping—the list goes on. Modern life has made what's considered "normal" more expensive than ever. I remember when only drug dealers and Zack Morris had mobile phones or pagers (ahh, the good old days). But now a personal cellphone is considered normal for an 11-year-old.

Yet even as all this pressure to spend mounts, wages are being squeezed and the cost of housing continues to rise for so many of us. These days I'm meeting more and more parents who are literally going broke trying to keep up with their kids. The problem is that the kids don't know what's happening financially behind the scenes, because there's still a lot of stigma around talking openly and honestly about money with our kids. I don't want them to worry. I don't want them to think we're unsuccessful. I don't want them to tell other kids' parents.

Getting real about money with your kids is scary. The very person who's costing you money is the exact person you're trying to protect from knowing there is a problem. It's complex. But too often I see parents throwing themselves into financial peril in order to support their kids' lifestyle expectations. That's not okay.

Parents need to get financially real with their kids in order to stop overspending and feeling broke. Saying no does not make you a bad parent. You need to learn how to say no without feeling guilty. The only way to do this is by talking about money and making your kids part of the household financial discussions.

Meet Andy and Max

Andy and Max

Ages: 45 and 48

Relationship status: married

Kids: 1, age 14

Annual gross household income: $120,000 ($70,000 + $50,000)

Assets: house valued at $650,000

Liabilities: $25,000 line of credit; $515,000 mortgage

My clients Andy and Max are a perfect example of this. They have a daughter, Chloe, who is involved in competitive dance. Chloe is a gifted athlete. Her dance career began when she was young and it wasn't long before she excelled far beyond her peers. This girl has it. She loves to dance. It makes her happy, it keeps her active and, because she's so dedicated, it takes up most of her time. As a result, her dance teammates are her best friends, her community. Without them her entire social network would collapse. The problem: Chloe's dance training and competitions cost $12,000 a year.

Max and Andy were in my office because they were sinking. They were using their home equity line of credit like an ATM and had nothing going towards retirement savings. They kept on borrowing an average of $5,000 every year with plans to roll it into the mortgage at renewal. They felt like they were going broke—because they were.

"Our finances are a house of cards," Andy said. "At any moment the whole thing could come down. One significant rise in interest rates or a job loss would devastate us financially."

Here's a shakedown of their finances:

Monthly after-tax income	**$7,920**	
FIXED EXPENSES: Money You Cannot Spend		
Mortgage	$2,400	
Utilities	$300	
Cable/Internet	$100	
Phone	$160	
Subscriptions	$20	
Property tax	$350	
Home insurance	$100	
Line of credit minimum payment	$175	
Car payment	$275	
Car insurance	$120	
Total	**$4,000**	(51% of after-tax income)

MEANINGFUL SAVINGS: Money You Cannot Spend		
Retirement savings	$0	
Line of credit above-minimum payment	$0	
Total	$0	(0% of after-tax income)
SHORT-TERM SAVINGS: Money You Cannot Spend		
Home repair fund	$0	
Car repairs	$0	
Total	$0	(0% of after-tax income)
SPENDING MONEY: Hard Limit	**$3,920**	**(49% of after-tax income)**
Spending Money	Per Year	Monthly Average
Andy and Max		
Groceries		$930
Dining out/lunch out/coffees		$600
Gas		$300
Dog		$70
Grooming ($600 + $360)	$960	$80
Clothes ($720 each)	$1,440	$120
Family outings/entertainment ($100/week)		$400
Total Andy and Max		**$2,500**
Chloe		
Phone		$100
Dance	$12,000	$1,000
Christmas	$600	$50
Summer camps	$480	$40
Clothes	$1,020	$85
Grooming	$240	$20
Birthday	$300	$25
Outings/vacations with friends (4 × $225)	$900	$75

Sleepovers	$300	$25
Total Chloe		$1,420
Total Spending Money		$3,920

As we looked over the numbers, the most glaringly obvious thing for me to ask was "Are you willing to give up dance?" But Max beat me to the punch. "Dance is nonnegotiable. We know it's too expensive, but it's her life."

I asked them to rate dance for Happy Spending. "It's a 5 out of 5 for us both," Andy said.

"And like a 6 out of 5 for Chloe."

As you can see, there was not a whole lot of wiggle room there. Dance would cost them $12,000 a year for another three years. Something had to give. The first thing to do was stop the bleeding. That was Step 1.

"The first goal this year," I told them, "is to stop going into debt by $5,000 every year and using the line of credit. If you can get through the year without using the line of credit, you'll be winning."

Now, you may be judging me for not telling them to sell their house, or rip their kid out of dance, but why would I waste their time and money on a plan they wouldn't put into action? It would be shame-y and gross and wouldn't move them forward at all. I wanted to design a plan that made sense for *them,* one that was realistic and that they would actually embrace. I'd rather they agreed to save $100 and then did it than have them agree to save $1,000 and just give up because it was so far-fetched, given their financial reality and Life Checklist.

They needed a way to reduce annual spending by about $5,000 (the amount they kept borrowing on the line of credit) so that they stopped going into debt. They told me that they usually dipped into the line of credit to pay for unexpected things, like $1,000 on car repairs and usually about $4,000 on home repairs. Therefore they needed to build up a Short-Term Savings account with about $5,000 per year ($416 per month) to stop the cycle of debt.

We went through their monthly Spending Money to identify possible places where they could realistically cut back.

Most of the things were already Happy Spending. The only things Max and Andy were willing to reduce were excessive convenience groceries and their takeout lunches, which were lower on the EROI spectrum at 3 out of 5. Cutting anything else would be unrealistic, they thought. As far as they could tell, there was no more room for reductions.

The new mindful spending goals were to go out for lunch only twice a week and to buy a premade dinner once a week. By reducing this spending they had raised approximately $210 per month. This would mean annual savings of $2,520 ($210 × 12 months), but that wasn't enough. They still needed to come up with $2,480 ($5,000 – $2,520) a year to hit their goal of $5,000.

You'll note that the $2,520 they were willing to reduce by were all things that affected only Max and Andy, not Chloe—a perfect example of how they were sacrificing their own happiness to keep from having to adjust their spending on their daughter. But at this point it had to happen. Something had to give.

"Do you think Chloe would be open to reducing any of her expenses?" I asked.

"She's 14. Probably not," Andy joked.

"Well, do you see any other places to reduce besides her expenses?"

"No, I actually don't," Andy replied.

	Monthly	EROI	New Goal
Andy and Max			
Groceries	$930	3	$900
Dining out/lunch out/coffees	$600	3	$420
Gas	$300	MUST	$300
Dog	$70	5	$70
Grooming ($600 + $360 per year)	$80	5	$80
Clothing ($720 each per year)	$120	5	$120
Family outings/entertainment ($100/week)	$400	5	$400
Total Andy and Max	**$2,500**		**$2,290**
Chloe			
Phone	$100	?	
Dance ($12,000/year)	$1,000	?	
Christmas ($600/year)	$50	?	
Summer camps ($480/year)	$40	?	
Clothes ($1,020/year)	$85	?	
Grooming ($240/year)	$20	?	
Birthday ($300/year)	$25	?	
Outings/vacations with friends ($900/year)	$75	?	
Sleepovers ($300/year)	$25	?	
Total Chloe	**$1,420**		
Total Spending	**$3,920**		

"Me neither," I said. "I think it's time we brought Chloe into the conversation." I could see that this comment made both Max and Andy uncomfortable. So I said, "You don't want to. Why is that?"

"I don't want her to worry or feel guilty about the things she wants to do. It's not her fault that we don't make enough money," Andy said, holding back tears.

"Whoa, whoa, whoa," I said. "This is not a personal failure. You both have solid incomes; you are not bad parents. The expectations you are putting on yourselves are unrealistic. That's the problem." (Sounded like a Life Checklist item to me.)

They stared at me but said nothing, so I pushed on. "Chloe's expenses are $17,040 a year. That's $1,420 a month—18 percent of your take-home income! That's very high. Do you think she would relish the idea of her parents being in tears and sacrificing their retirement in order to pay for her dancing?"

"Of course not. She'd be devastated," Andy said.

"Exactly. Right now she has no idea that you can't afford this, so of course she wants everything. We need to try to reduce her annual spending by $2,480, to $14,560 a year, so you can hit your financial goal of saving $5,000 to Short-Term Savings. We'll find out if we can reduce her spending in a way that feels good for everyone. No guilt, no shame."

I gave them an activity to do at home:

1. Sit down with Chloe, letting her know in advance that it's a talk about money and finances and that it's a family meeting, so she knows it's a serious conversation. Blame it on me.
2. Show her the list of her expenses.
3. Explain that her expenses come to 18 percent of the family budget.
4. Explain what's being given up in order to continue spending so much, that you're not putting away enough for retirement.
5. Explain that she has to get her annual spending down from $17,040 to $14,560—her Hard Limit.
6. Explain what Happy Spending is.
7. Have her rate her spending happiness on a scale of 1 to 5.

8. Then ask if she would be willing to reduce the expenditures that have a lower happiness rating. Go through the list of her expenses line by line and ask what she thinks is possible. Every decision should be hers.

9. Add up the total costs and promise that every year she'll get to decide what her Happy Spending is. Her life will change as she grows, and the demands will change.

Andy and Max did exactly that. Here was Chloe's Happy Spending list:

	Annual Cost	EROI	What's Possible
Phone	$1,200	5	$1,200
Dance	$12,000	5	$12,000
Christmas	$600	3	$100
Summer camps	$480	1	$0
Clothes	$1,020	4	$410
Grooming	$240	4	$50
Birthday	$300	1	$50
Outings/vacations with friends	$900	3	$450
Sleepovers	$300	5	$300
Total Chloe	$17,040		$14,560

For the next two years, Chloe would have $2,560 above the $12,000 for dance ($14,560 total) to spend however she'd like. So the plan was to sit down as a team and Chloe would map out how she wanted to spend the money that year. By doing this, her parents managed her expectations. She was involved and understood the reasons for the cuts. As a plus, she was able to make her own financial choices. She was part of the discussion.

One year later, Max and Andy came for their check-in. "How did it all play out?" I asked.

"Brilliant! Chloe is the coolest. We talk about finances now in a way we never did before. She is so mindful of the cost of things, and it's helped make us more mindful too. Back-to-school shopping was such a breeze because she knew she had $210 to work with, so it wasn't really a stressful thing for us. And the holidays were totally changed. We didn't have a credit card hangover after Christmas because we had set a limit and Chloe's expectations were managed. We all just worked within the plan."

"Did you feel guilty about the reductions?"

"No, because I would never have made those cuts for her, but she made them for herself. Her Christmas budget was so low and she didn't care at all. I could never have made that decision before without feeling tremendous guilt," Max said.

"I thought that maybe it would be awkward," Andy said. "And I worried that maybe she'd feel bad about dance, but that didn't happen. Because she understands why there are boundaries and gets to choose how she spends her portion, she's satisfied. She totally gets it."

Financially, Max and Andy were getting back on track. They hadn't tapped the line of credit once in a whole year, so the payments they were making were actually going towards the principal. They felt empowered and excited again, full of hope. Their goal for the next year was to use the additional money coming in from their expected raises towards the line of credit. Slowly they would get to where they needed to be financially.

"Only two more years of dance," Max said. "Then we will be able to live life like kings."

"Not so fast," I said. "Once the dancing is over, all that money is earmarked for retirement. We have to make up for lost time."

"We know," Andy said. "Maybe Chloe will use some of her student loan to take us on a trip?"

I laughed with them. "Tell her to come in for an appointment when she's finished school. I'll help work that in," I joked.

Empowering your kids to be part of the financial discussion is crucial if you don't want to go broke trying to keep up with their lifestyle. Not only will you be improving your own financial life, you'll also be teaching your kids that they can't have everything and empowering them to make trade-offs themselves. This will not only help you live within your means, it will also help your kids become financially responsible adults.

Introducing Hard Limits and Happy Spending to your kids is the best way to help them feel like they have control over their own finances. And they still get to enjoy life, so you don't have to feel guilty about saying no to them and reducing spending. Remember, when the plane is going down, you have to put the oxygen mask on yourself first and then you help the babies. It's the same with your money.

How to Say No to Your Kids about Spending Money Beyond Your Means

1. Have a family meeting.
2. Show them a list of annual expenses.
3. Explain what's not happening in the family finances because of overspending. Is it a vacation? Is it repairs for the house? Is it retirement? What's at stake?
4. Outline the reduced annual goal for their spending.
5. Explain what Happy Spending is.

6. Have them rate their spending on a scale of 1 to 5.

7. Ask them to reduce their Unhappy (or less Happy) Spending so that their annual spending is in line with their own Hard Limit.

8. Allow them to decide each year how their annual Hard Limit is spent.

Part Three

The Future Is Financially Friendly (I Promise)

Between those nagging feelings of financial inadequacy and the intense pressure to overspend, modern life can be tough to navigate. But with Hard Limits and Happy Spending, you know a way to survive that allows you to stop budgeting and start living and doesn't make you want to give up on being financially responsible.

Now come the final pieces of the puzzle: implementing the plan and making it stick. For good. This is all about strategy.

Implementing new financial plans can be fun at first, especially when you're excited about making changes. The hard part is making those changes stick after the initial rush of motivation fades. That's why it's important to design your new financial plan around your real life. Your plan has to be doable and, more importantly, it has to inspire confidence that you're going to be okay financially in the long run.

I'm not saying it will be easy. Real life is tough and unpredictable, and dealing with money can sometimes be more aggravating than fun, even if you love spreadsheets. I guarantee you'll have moments when you come close to saying "F*ck it." You might even fall off the financial wagon completely and overspend on your credit card more than a few times. Frustration and failure are part of the financial journey. No one is perfect. The key is to get back on the financially awesome wagon, especially when it's hard. Confidence in your financial plan and abilities and the knowledge that your goals are realistic make it easier to dust off after the lapses and climb on again.

Staying motivated to stick with your financial plan is how you find your way to Worry-Free Money once and for all. That "stick with" is important and will lead to amazing results. Once you see the debt going down, emergency savings rising and your nest egg growing, you'll be pumped. You'll know that your new financial plan feels a whole lot better than getting caught in the Spending Vortex and feeling broke.

CHAPTER 12

Making Change Happen:
You've Got Levers—Pull 'Em!

There's a line from *The Simpsons* that I love and hate. When Marge mentions that she'd like to try a new career path, Homer says, "I don't know, Marge. Trying is the first step towards failure." It's funny because it's true. Depressingly so. You can't fail if you don't try, right?

Unfortunately, that kind of thinking can creep into your finances as well. If you attempt a change and fall short of your expectations, you risk feeling like a financial failure. After a few false starts it's easy to give up and stop trying altogether, to just close your eyes to reality and hope that everything will turn out okay.

But here's the thing: change—real change—is what gives you real hope. Seeing the debt melt away, watching your retirement savings rise and not feeling guilty about the money you spend on a vacation are examples of real change that pump hope back into your finances, even if you stumble a couple of times.

Past financial-plan failures mean nothing. They're simply an indication that whatever you tried didn't work for you. It's like dating. Should you never go on another date because the last one didn't work out? Hell, no. Dating helps you figure out who meshes with you and who doesn't. Trying a new financial plan is like dating your money. You just need to find the right fit—one that makes you feel good, one that doesn't make you worry.

Homer Simpson was wrong. Trying is the first step towards getting what you want for yourself, your family and your future, and it all begins with change. But keep in mind that change does not look the same for everyone. What works for someone else may not work for you.

Small Changes Create Big Waves

When people first come to my office, they usually expect me to tell them what to do. Certainly I can give them a list of things they should start doing with their finances:

- Pay off debts.
- Save up an emergency account.
- Put aside at least 10 to 20 percent of gross income for retirement.
- Pay off your mortgage in 15 to 20 years (if applicable).

It's a good solid list, but most people can't possibly achieve everything at the same time. There is only so much money coming in, and the last thing I want is for you to look at a list of financial goals and feel discouraged before you even start. It's best to think of it as a financial wish list and start by prioritizing which parts are most important to you right now. As I've said before, I'd rather you made a plan to save $100 a month and actually do it than make a plan to save $1,000 and fall short of your own (self-defeating) expectations.

You can tackle the rest of the list over time. As long as you're motivated and are implementing changes, even small ones, eventually you will get there. You *will* win. Who knows, maybe once you get going on this, you'll be motivated to make more and more changes. It may even turn into a financial snowball that just keeps getting bigger and better. Never underestimate the power of that first small change.

Meet Dylan

Dylan

Age: 27

Relationship status: newly single

Kids: 0

Annual gross household income: $40,000

Assets: $1,000 in emergency account; $8,000 retirement savings

Liabilities: $6,600 credit card debt at 19% (a hangover from two bachelor parties and two months' unemployment)

Dylan had been my client for a while. When he last came to see me, I was surprised to learn that he was in the middle of a nasty breakup. Not only was it rough emotionally, the split was completely messing with his finances and his plans.

Dylan had been living with his long-time partner for five years. His ex, Maria, earned $82,000 a year as a brand manager, which was significantly more than the $40,000 Dylan earned as a designer. Together they were renting a beautiful two-bedroom apartment in a great neighbourhood in Vancouver. The rent was $2,200 per month. Maria was paying $1,562 and Dylan $762 of their shared expenses ($2,200 rent + $24 renters' insurance + $100 for cable/Internet), an equitable split, given that Maria earned more than double Dylan's salary. He would never have been able to afford that apartment on his own.

After five years, Dylan had grown accustomed to the lifestyle afforded by having a two-income household. They lived near parks and their favourite coffee shops, and many of their friends were within a 20-minute bike ride. The previous year, when I had seen

Dylan and Maria together, they were saving for a wedding and a down payment. Having kids was on their three-to-five-year plan.

Dylan was not expecting the breakup. Not only was he emotionally unprepared, he was also financially unprepared for the added expenses of being single. So we sat down to work on a new financial plan. Here's how his pre-breakup finances played out:

Dylan's pre-breakup financial goals had been to—

- Pay off his credit card in one year. Using the Debt-Repayment Calculator, Dylan had worked out that he needed to put $612 per month ($400 Meaningful Savings + $212 minimum payment) towards the credit card to accomplish this goal.
- Rebuild his emergency account to $3,000 over the next 15 months. This meant he would have to save $200 per month for the next 15 months ($3,000/15).

His Hard Limit before the breakup was $1,016 per month. Having that much Spending Money for daily life was doable. Yes, he had to be mindful every now and then, but it was enough to allow him to enjoy life and still sleep at night. Post-breakup, not only was he heartbroken, but without a partner to split the monthly bills he was also about to face some tough financial decisions.

"I want to live relatively close to my friends," he told me. He paused a moment, as though what was coming next was hard to say. "What I want is a one-bedroom apartment. I think I can get one for $1,500. I need to know how screwed I'll be if I take that on."

As I mentioned earlier, Dylan had become accustomed to a certain standard of living. I needed to brace him for impact. "Your spending money is going to take a big hit here."

Monthly after-tax income	$2,800	
FIXED EXPENSES: Money You Cannot Spend		
Rent (shared)	$700	
Utilities (shared)	$0	
Renters' insurance (shared)	$12	
Cable/Internet (shared)	$50	
Phone	$59	
Credit card minimum payment	$212	
Life and disability insurance	$141	
Bank fees	$10	
Total	$1,184	(42% of after-tax income)
MEANINGFUL SAVINGS: Money You Cannot Spend		
Credit card above-minimum payment	$400	
Retirement savings	$0	
Total	$400	(14% of after-tax income)
SHORT-TERM SAVINGS: Money You Cannot Spend		
Vacation	$0	
Emergency savings	$200	
Total	$200	(7% of after-tax income)
SPENDING MONEY: Hard Limit	$1,016	(37% of after-tax income)

The real issue? How low we could take his Spending Money without being totally unrealistic. I wanted to solve this problem first before we tested different rent costs so that the Spending Money he would be left with was realistic. I worried that if I started off by testing the $1,500 rent, Dylan would just agree that he could live within the confines of whatever Spending Money was left over, just to ensure that he could (on paper) afford it. By looking first at how much he could realistically reduce his Spending Money, I would know how low he could go in a sustainable manner.

	Average Spending	EROI	Change	New Amount
Groceries (single)	$270	5	+ $30	$300
Toiletries	$30	3	– $10	$20
Work lunches/coffee	$100	2	– $50	$50
Takeout dinners	$116	3	– $116	$0
Dinners out/outings with friends	$170	5		$170
Entertainment (books, movies, music)	$80	4	– $50	$30
Grooming	$20	5		$20
Clothes	$50	5		$50
Alcohol	$80	3	– $16	$64
Fitness	$50	3	– $50	$0
Social outings/tickets	$50	5		$50
Total Spending	$1,016		– $262	$754

After going through Dylan's numbers, we reduced any Unhappy Spending where we could. This meant the following mindful goals: no more takeout dinners (Dylan loved to cook; Maria was the take-out person); reducing the morning coffee to every other day; no more movies out (that had been a date-night thing twice a month); reducing alcohol purchases to $15 a week; and quitting the gym and working out at home.

That left him with a Hard Limit of $754 per month. This pushed the boundaries of what I would consider sustainable for him, given his former lifestyle. But at least now I knew that if the rents we tested pushed his Spending Money lower than $754, we'd be creating the perfect environment for worry, frustration, frequent F*ck-It Moments and likely quickly mounting credit card debt. I didn't want to set him up for financial failure.

Dylan was set on a one-bedroom apartment close to friends and community. "Especially now that I'm single," he said, "I need to be near people." I got it. So we looked at how his finances would shake down if he rented the place for $1,500.

By renting a new place on his own for $1,500, Dylan would set himself up for a lot of frustrating things to happen with his finances:

- an increase in Fixed Expenses to a whopping 73 percent of after-tax income—well over the recommended 55 percent
- zero money going towards paying down his credit card, so no Meaningful Savings
- zero money going towards his emergency fund, so no Short-Term Savings
- Spending Money reduced to 27 percent of after-tax income, which is a 10 percent drop from his previous 36 percent

Not only would he literally be living from paycheque to paycheque, but when we crunched the numbers using the Debt-Payoff Calculator, we discovered that, without the $400 additional going towards his credit card balance each month, his credit card debt wouldn't be paid off for 44 months (3 years, 8 months). As a result, unless Dylan received a massive raise or made income adjustments, it would be more than three years before he could put any savings (the $212 that would be freed up after the credit card was paid off) towards his emergency fund. And it would

	Pre-breakup	Post-breakup
After-tax income	$2,800	$2,800
FIXED EXPENSES: Money You Cannot Spend		
Rent	$700	$1,500
Utilities	$0	$0
Renters' insurance	$12	$24
Cable/Internet	$50	$100
Phone	$59	$59
Credit card minimum payment	$212	$212
Life and disability insurance	$141	$141
Bank fees	$10	$10
Totals	$1,184	$2,046
MEANINGFUL SAVINGS: Money You Cannot Spend		
Credit card above-minimum payment	$400	$0
Retirement savings	$0	$0
Totals	$400	$0
SHORT-TERM SAVINGS: Money You Cannot Spend		
Vacation	$0	$0
Emergency savings	$200	$0
Totals	$200	$0
MONTHLY SPENDING: Hard Limit	$1,016	$754

take an additional nine and a half months to build it up to $3,000 ($212 × 9.5 months = $2,000, plus $1,000 in there already). Essentially, a $1,500 rent meant it would take 54 months (4 years, 6 months) to reach his original financial goals.

I asked him about moving into a cheaper basement apartment for $1,200 instead. His Fixed Expenses would still be above 55 percent but not nearly as high as for the $1,500 apartment. Dylan shook his head. "I lived in a basement apartment when I first moved here and it wasn't good for me. I know it's cheaper, but it feels like a huge step backwards. Not good for my emotional well-being."

Realizing that his emotional and mental health were as important as Dylan's financial health, we dropped the basement idea and instead crunched the numbers for an apartment farther away. But once we added an extra $250 for his likely commuting costs, his Fixed Expenses came in at more than 73 percent of his net income. Again, no win.

Because his family lived in Nova Scotia, moving back home with Mom and Dad for a while was out of the question. That was when Dylan started to lose hope. "So I'm f*cked," he said.

"No," I told him. "We just need to delay some of your financial plans. Extend the time horizon." As his financial planner, it was important for me to show Dylan that there was still hope, even when everything felt so broken.

No matter how basic or fancy your planning tools may be, when it comes to managing your finances, you only have two levers: Earn More or Spend Less. There is no third lever, no magical unicorn solution that will allow you to spend more, earn less and still save. It's mathematically impossible.

Sure, Dylan could quit his job and move to Nova Scotia, but was that a practical solution? Could he find a job? What about friends? A community? Happiness? No dice. Dylan's job and his community were in Vancouver. Moving to Nova Scotia was totally unrealistic. No matter which way we sliced it, the breakup meant that Dylan would be forced to live beyond his means for the next five years. Welcome to real life.

But all was not lost. There was still hope, still a way to make it better. For Dylan, we could reach "better" by adding $100 per month in income or subtracting $100 per month in expenses. Just $100.

I started with the first lever: Earn More. "Do you think you could bring home an additional $25 a week after tax?" I asked. "That way you could rent the $1,500 apartment and still maintain $754 as your Spending Money while saving $100 per month."

He thought for a moment, then said no. "My work isn't always nine-to-five. Projects have strict deadlines and I'm often working 12- to 16-hour days plus weekends as it is. I don't see how I can be reliable for another job."

"Okay, no problem." I said. I tried the second lever. "Do you think you could find a place to rent for $1,400?"

"Hmm, probably. I think I could crash at my friend's place until I find a rental for $1,400. But how big a difference would $100 make in the grand scheme of life?"

"You'd be surprised," I told him. "If you can find a rental for $100 less per month, I think we can get your finances back on track in two and a half years instead of four and a half." Enter: Hope.

Using that extra $100, we came up with Dylan's realistic financial survival plan:

- Call the bank and try to negotiate a lower interest rate on your credit card.
- Pay $312 per month towards the credit card ($212 minimum + extra $100 saved).
- Don't take on new debt. Live within your Hard Limit.

I didn't want to move the $1,000 that Dylan had in his emergency account to the credit card, because he wasn't sure about his job security. Yes, mathematically that was probably the best bang for his buck, but I didn't want to make him feel even more broke and risk putting

Monthly after-tax income	$2,800	
FIXED EXPENSES: Money You Cannot Spend		
Rent	$1,400	
Utilities	$0	
Renters' insurance	$24	
Cable/Internet	$100	
Phone	$59	
Credit card minimum payment	$212	
Life and disability insurance	$141	
Bank fees	$10	
Total	$1,946	(69.5% of after-tax income)
MEANINGFUL SAVINGS: Money You Cannot Spend		
Credit card above-minimum payment	$100	
Total	$100	(3.5% of after-tax income)
SHORT-TERM SAVINGS: Money You Cannot Spend $0		
SPENDING MONEY: Hard Limit	$754	(27% of after-tax income)

him into scarcity mode by emptying all his accounts. In addition, taking money from his retirement account didn't make sense because much of it would be taxed at a higher rate than the interest he was paying on his credit card.

Dylan called his bank from my office. It wouldn't reduce his credit card interest rate and he couldn't consolidate the debt, leaving him to pay it off at 19 percent. Such is life. But the good news was that, with our $100 plan, he would pay off that credit card in 26 months (just over two years). That would free up $312 that could then go towards his Short-Term Savings for the next seven months ($2,000/$312), which would add another $2,000 to his emergency account, bringing the total to $3,000.

In just over two and a half years—33 months—Dylan would have paid off his credit card and rebuilt his emergency savings, thanks to the $100 per month he thought wouldn't accomplish much. "Whoa, seriously?" he said. He still didn't quite believe that $100 could make such a difference.

"Take a look," I said and showed him the graphs. "You'll shave two years off your debt-repayment plan and save about $1,065 in interest on the credit card." It was a big win.

I reminded Dylan that this three-year plan was based only on what we could see now. "Your life is going to change so much in the next three years," I told him. "With potential tax refunds, windfalls, new jobs, raises and such, this could all happen a whole lot sooner. We can't know what's down the road, but we do know that this plan is sustainable for now. Never discount the power of $100 a month. It goes a very long way."

He looked relieved. "Okay, I'm definitely going to wait until I find a place for $1,400. And any windfall like a tax refund will go towards the credit card."

I smiled. "Oh yes."

Two and a half years later, Dylan and I sat down again. He seemed pleased. His credit card was paid off and he was starting to rebuild the emergency savings.

"Things look like they're right on track," I said.

"Better than on track. After our meeting I started to do a bit of freelance graphic design on the side. That money has been paying for things like travel, a friend's wedding, even a couch—things I couldn't fit into my Hard Limit."

"That's fabulous!" I said. "But the last time we met, you didn't think you could earn more. What happened?"

"When you first asked about it, I shot down the idea because I was already stretched so thin at work and exhausted. Freelancing seemed daunting and terrifying on top of my regular job. But when I thought about it in terms of $100 a month or $25 a week, I realized that was only about six or seven logo designs over an entire year. I could realistically do that for some of my friends and acquaintances who run their own businesses. It felt doable, you know? Really manageable. I started putting the word out and the work came in! It works out to $1,700 before tax each year. The $1,300-ish I keep after taxes has been enough to give me some extra fun money while still sticking to the credit card and emergency account plan." (For more on this, see "Side-Hustle Money" in the Resource Library, page 308.)

"That's wonderful! I'm so happy you found a way to pull the income lever."

He nodded. "Framing it as only $100 a month or $25 a week helped make it feel doable. Plus, being able to use it for fun things kept it super-motivating."

I was so pleased. We rejigged things again and updated his plan. His income had increased to $41,616 a year and his Fixed Expenses had remained the same, despite an increase in transit costs. "I got rid of cable," he explained.

Once he had finished rebuilding his emergency savings, he planned to reallocate the $312 per month to retirement savings and tack on an additional $50 per month, bringing the amount going towards retirement up to $362 per month (10 percent of his gross income, including the freelance work).

"Keep using freelance income to fund Short-Term Savings," I told him. "No freelance, no trips. Try to match your spikes in income with spikes in spending, and use the steady income to get the heavy financial work done."

As impossible as it had seemed to him during our initial meeting, Dylan was happy and hopeful again. By being both realistic and kind to himself, he prioritized his needs and determined what was most important to his happiness. Once we knew that staying in Vancouver mattered most, we designed a plan that he could live with. It was one that put him back in control again, knowing he could still move forward financially even though the path would be different and perhaps a bit slower than he wanted.

•

Life happens. Breakups, divorces, job losses, bad financial calls. Things may start to go off track and hopelessness can creep up on you. But here's the thing: there is always hope. There is always a reason to try.

When the unforeseen happens, remember:

- Your goals may take a little longer to achieve, but that doesn't mean that won't happen.
- Even $100 a month goes a long way.
- There are always two levers to pull: Earn More and Spend Less.

Don't be afraid to try both levers. The amounts don't have to be dramatic to be effective. Small changes make big waves.

You've seen that $100 can go a very long way. But what if that isn't enough to keep all your financial balls in the air while moving you forward at the same time? How do you make realistic changes and stay motivated when you're sinking, despite your best intentions?

Meet Drew and Kelly

Drew and Kelly

Ages: 36 and 34

Relationship status: married

Kids: 2, ages 1½ months and 4

Annual gross household income: $150,000 ($75,000 + $75,000)

Assets: house valued at $750,000; $50,000 in retirement savings (plus Drew has a defined benefit pension—yay!)

Liabilities: $475,000 mortgage at 2.7%; $45,000 line of credit at 7% interest

Drew and Kelly came in for an emergency financial meeting. "Every time it rains, I have anxiety because I'm sure that will be the one," Kelly said. "The basement wall will finally give, and I already know we can't afford to fix it. We just don't have the money."

I hadn't seen them in four years. Kelly's eyes started to fill as she gave me the lowdown on what was going on at home. "We just keep taking on more credit card debt, though I don't feel like we live extravagantly. We budget every single dollar." She wiped away the tears. "I feel like we've done everything we're supposed to. We make good money, but I feel so screwed every day. I don't know what we're doing wrong."

They both looked at me for an answer and my heart broke for them, because they hadn't done anything wrong. I jokingly asked if they wanted to go out for a glass of wine instead of finishing our financial session.

They laughed. "Ha, that would be great. We haven't been able to afford fun in a long time," Drew said.

Drew and Kelly were married five years ago. They both earn $75,000 a year, which amounts to approximately $8,000 per month after taxes and deductions. Drew has 10 percent pension deductions coming directly off his paycheque and they are matched up to 5 percent, which is great. It means that 15 percent of his income is going towards retirement savings.

In their first year of marriage they bought a $650,000 house with a down payment of $175,000 (27 percent). They were debt-free at the time, with no kids. To a lender looking just at their incomes, their sizable down payment and their lack of debt, the conclusion was easy: Drew and Kelly could definitely afford that house.

Monthly Housing Costs ($34,260 per year)	
Mortgage	$2,175
Utilities and insurance	$380
Property tax	$300
Total	$2,855

However, when they came to see me before buying the house, I had told them they should pay no more than $500,000. They wanted kids and needed to think beyond mortgage, utilities and taxes. They needed to baby-proof their finances and make room for the pending costs of raising another human.

But they fell in love with the $650K house. The bank said it was affordable, friends and family said it was affordable; all signs pointed to Go, so they bought it. Like so many people, they assumed their incomes would go up over time and they would grow into the house when they had kids. They moved in, did about $30,000 worth of basic renovations and popped that right onto a line of credit (cheap debt). During the renovations, they got pregnant with baby number one.

Their total monthly costs for housing were $34,260 a year, only 22.8 percent of their gross annual household income. By most standards, housing shouldn't come to more than 30 to 35 percent of your gross income, so at 22.8 percent they should have been laughing, right? What went wrong? Why was Kelly back in my office feeling like they'd made a huge mistake? Like they were house-poor, with no hope for their financial future.

Here's the thing: Drew and Kelly weren't house-poor. After two kids, they were baby-poor. When they were crunching the numbers on that house four years earlier, they didn't think to add in the Fixed Expenses that were waiting down the road.

Before kids, they were able to put $900 towards Meaningful Savings. Of that, $700 per month ($8,400/year) went towards Kelly's retirement savings and $200 went to their then $30,000 line of credit above the minimum payment of $850. At that rate of savings, they were on track to pay off their $30,000 line of credit in 2.6 years (see the Debt-Payoff Calculator on page 304) and Kelly was able to put away 11.2 percent of her total gross income for retirement. Everything looked great. In addition, before children they had a $3,000 annual vacation fund, a $3,000 annual home-repair fund and a $1,200 annual holiday/gift fund in their Short-Term Savings.

Then came maternity leave. And after that, the daycare years. The cost of having kids blindsided them, utterly and completely. Kelly and Drew hadn't baby-proofed their finances, which means they didn't take the future cost of raising kids into account when they were assessing how much they could afford for a Lifestyle Upgrade like buying a $650,000 house. When you buy a house or take on some other expensive Lifestyle Upgrade based on numbers that don't reflect future childcare expenses or potential minivan payments, it might look like you can afford all those things. However, if you haven't planned for diapers, daycare and maybe swimming lessons, affordability can go out the window.

In the past four years Drew and Kelly had tacked an additional $15,000 onto their line of credit, bringing the total up and over the original $30,000 to $45,000, and had emptied their trip and home-repair funds. On average, they were overspending by about $8,000 a year. Here's a comparison of their monthly cash flows.

After kids, their Spending Money was reduced to $1,695 per month. This was a 4 percent decrease (25 percent – 21 percent). The worst part, however, was that life with kids left no room for Meaningful Savings, let alone Short-Term Savings.

Kelly and Drew were clearly strapped, living from paycheque to paycheque and taking on more and more credit card debt. That's why Kelly was always anxious when it rained. They truly couldn't afford the repair, and in this case an extra $100 per month wouldn't cut it. I felt for them.

"We can't sell the house," Drew said. "We have kids, they're in good daycares. I don't even know where we'd move to."

"But we can't afford the house," Kelly countered.

"Oh, you can afford your house," I said. "You just can't afford daycare plus the house. But here's the good news: the daycare years are temporary. We just have to find a way to hang on and not sink financially until they're both in school."

Drew and Kelly's financial pain would last another four years. But once daycare was totally done with, they could start a new financial plan. Hope is always there.

Some people would be quick to judge them. "Hey, sell your house," they'd say. "Downsize and stop whining." (Hey now, watch

	Before Kids	After Kids
Monthly after-tax income	$8,000	$8,000
FIXED EXPENSES: Money You Cannot Spend		
Mortgage	$2,175	$2,175
Utilities	$280	$280
Home insurance	$100	$100
Property tax	$300	$300
Cable/Internet	$120	$120
Phone	$200	$200
Car insurance	$200	$200
Car payment	$280	$280
Line of credit minimum payment	$850	$850
Daycare	$0	$1,800
Totals (% of after-tax income)	$4,505 (56%)	$6,305 (79%)
MEANINGFUL SAVINGS: Money You Cannot Spend		
Line of credit above-minimum payment	$200	$0
Retirement savings	$700	$0
Totals (% of after-tax income)	$900 (11%)	$0 (0%)
SHORT-TERM SAVINGS: Money You Cannot Spend		
Vacation fund	$250	$0
House-repair fund	$250	$0
Holidays/gift fund	$100	$0
Totals (% of after-tax income)	$600 (8%)	$0 (0%)
SPENDING MONEY: Hard Limit	$1,995 (25%)	$1,695 (21%)

that Money Hate.) They might even criticize me for not advising them to sell. But Drew and Kelly did not want to move; they'd already made that clear. Designing a financial plan that asked them to downsize was a nonstarter, and totally unrealistic for how they would continue to live their life.

Instead we turned all their financial goals for the mat leave/daycare years into one simple one: stay afloat. Avoid sinking further into debt while trying to brace for spikes in spending and household emergencies. Forget retirement savings for Kelly in the short run (Drew's pension would still be happening in the background). Right now they had much bigger financial fish to fry, and 25 years in which to catch up later. The new plan gave them permission to not worry about retirement savings in order to focus on the true financial danger in front of them—debt.

After crunching the numbers, we arrived at their real-life, barebones minimum financial goals:

- Live within the $1,695 Hard Limit and stop going into debt during the daycare years.
- Try to put aside $1,000 a year for Short-Term Savings to keep out of debt.
- Try to pay down the line of credit to make room for future home repairs (approximately $5,000/year).

This is a great example of when $100 per month just isn't enough to help. As motivating and helpful as that extra $100 can be, in this case we needed a bigger overhaul to get them out of financial trouble during the daycare years. But we started by looking at those same two levers: Spend Less and Earn More.

The First Lever: Spend Less

Drew and Kelly's Fixed Expenses were just that: fixed. The only option they had was to reduce their Spending Money to live within their Hard Limit of $1,695 without taking on any new debt. How to do that? Reduce their Unhappy Spending by $300 ($1,995 – $1,695).

	Average Spending	EROI	Change	New Amount
Groceries	$700	MUST		$700
Dining/lunch/coffees out	$60	4	– $40	$20
Gas	$200	2	– $100	$100
Toiletries/diapers, etc.	$250	MUST		$250
Adult grooming/drycleaning	$70	MUST		$70
Family clothes ($1,000 each)	$160	4	– $50	$110
Outings/entertainment ($75/week)	$300	5	– $25	$275
Date night	$100	5	– $25	$75
Gifts	$50	4	– $35	$15
House stuff	$55	MUST		$55
Kid stuff	$50	4	– $25	$25
Total Hard Limit	**$1,995**		**– $300**	**$1,695**

This was a bit painful, since most things were a must or rated 4 and 5 for Happy Spending. However, they had to make trade-offs in order to live within their means. The $300 had to come from somewhere. Their new mindful spending goals for living within the $1,695 Hard Limit:

- Only get takeout coffee on weekends, saving $40 per month.
- Cut down on gas by walking more and biking to work. Only drive two days a week max, saving $100 per month.
- Shop more at second-hand stores for clothing for them and the kids, saving $600 per year (approximately $50 per month).

- Reduce family outing costs by keeping them under $70 per week, saving $25 per month.
- No gifts unless handmade or under $15. They vowed to tell the family that Christmas would be all about the love and presence (rather than presents), saving $420 per year ($35 per month).
- Reduce toy and kids' stuff shopping to once a month, saving $25 per month.
- No trips for the next four years.
- Take the children to Disneyland in five years to celebrate the end of the daycare years.
- No home renos except emergency repairs, which would have to go on the line of credit. "If you need to repair the basement or do any emergency house repairs over the next four years, it must go on the line of credit," I explained. "There is no other option."

Living within their Hard Limit of $1,695 wouldn't keep them out of debt if there were any spikes in spending or home emergencies. That was a big problem. But with no more wiggle room in expenses, the only other lever they had was to bring in more money.

I was giving them permission to spend outside their means in the case of an emergency. Even though that's not "financially responsible," it's realistic. Financial plans *must* be realistic in order for people to follow them and stay hopeful for the future.

The Second Lever: Earn More

Every summer, Drew and Kelly went to their parents' cottage on weekends and for one two-week stretch in the summer (lucky!). Because they lived in a relatively desirable neighbourhood and owned their home, it was possible for them to offer their house for rent on an online B&B site to bring in more money annually. They typically went to the cottage for one week over March Break (7 nights), two full weeks in August (14 nights) and six weekends over the summer (12 nights). The house was empty and available for rental during those times. Thirty-three days per year—only 9 percent of the entire year—and during prime tourist season in their city. Huzzah!

Given their location, they discovered they could rent out their house for $182 per night, which would bring in approximately $6,000 per year ($182 × 33 nights) before tax. That $6,000 was taxable, but their daycare bill, which was well over $6,000 a year, counted as a tax deduction. That would completely offset the taxes payable on the extra income as long as they had receipts that qualified for the daycare deduction (see "Daycare Life" in the Resource Library, page 309).

Drew was hesitant at first, but I was able to show him how we could use that $6,000 wisely. Under Meaningful Savings, $5,000 would go towards the line of credit each year, in addition to the $850 they had to pay each month. The additional $1,000 would go towards Short-Term Savings for the holidays, large purchases and unexpected life expenses, safeguarding them against more debt.

The extra $5,000 against the line of credit each year meant their debt would be paid off in under four years (see the Debt-Payoff Calculator, page 304). What's more, if a housing emergency were to occur, they would have paid down enough on the line of credit to leave room for emergency repairs. We weren't talking decorating or renovations. Strictly emergencies, like leaking walls. Bringing in this extra money was a great way for them to protect themselves against large spikes in spending while holding on for their dear financial life over the next four years.

"Why wouldn't we just put the $1,000 onto the line of credit for emergencies or spikes in spending, instead of into a savings account where it will earn only 1 percent interest?" Kelly asked.

"Great point, but it's important for you both to see where the money for large purchases or spikes in spending is sitting. There is something comforting about knowing you have money available, not simply more credit, and that you can spend that money if you need to. It helps take away the guilt about spending and is way more motivating than putting it against the line of credit."

Drew and Kelly left my office encouraged. Sure, the new plan wasn't the kind you usually think about when it comes to finances. But they valued staying in their home above everything else and were willing to rent it out in order to bring in more money. (Never underestimate the power of the side hustle to bring in more money.)

Four years later, Drew and Kelly were back in my office. They had only $10,000 left on the line of credit. A few home-repair emergencies had kept them from paying it off completely (the basement did flood), but they had taken on no new credit card debt. Daycare costs had been reduced to $800 per month, since the kids still required afterschool care, but this reduced monthly Fixed Expenses by $1,000 per month ($1,800 – $800).

Renting out their place when they were away had worked out really well. "It's been our lifeline. I can't believe we didn't think of it before," Drew said.

Now it was time for a new plan. I started with the extra $1,000 per month now available to them. "If you take that $1,000 per month you're saving on daycare and add it to the $850 you're paying towards the line of credit, you'll have the whole thing paid off in six months! Then you'll have freed up $1,850 a month that can go towards retirement savings and make up for lost time."

"Do we still need to rent our place out?" Kelly asked.

"You should. You still have to rebuild your home-repair, vacation and emergency funds. Once those are topped up and retirement savings are back on track, you can stop."

"I have a feeling we'll be renting it out forever," Drew said. "What would happen if we put an extra $6,000 towards the mortgage over the next three years?"

Swoon! I opened up the online mortgage calculator. "Your mortgage is at $418,685 right now, with 21 years to go. If you put in an additional $6,000 per year on top of your regular mortgage payments, you'll pay it off in 16.2 years, 4.8 years earlier than without. You'd be mortgage-free by 60 instead of 65."

"I'm in," Kelly said.

"It just makes sense," Drew agreed.

Our original plan had not only given Drew and Kelly hope when all seemed lost, it had also motivated them to keep making positive changes once they were out of the financial dark. You can see the empowerment and motivation that come from getting the financial ball rolling.

Drew and Kelly are a great example of how getting creative with your finances and thinking of ways to either bring in more money or reduce expenses can help move your finances forward. It takes effort and time but it's doable, and it feels wonderful once you start seeing financial progress.

Remember, you have only two levers: Spend Less and Earn More. But there are plenty of ways to make those levers work for you! The key is to make your plan realistic and doable in the short run so that it will be sustainable over the long haul.

CHAPTER 13

Making Financial Lemonade: Opting Out of the Life Checklist

When life gives you financial lemons, make lemonade.

Sure, it's an old cliché, lemons to lemonade, but when it comes to your finances there are enough lemons out there to sour even the best-laid plans. Things like the ever-increasing cost of living, wage stagnation and the steady erosion of full-time jobs with benefits. It's easy to feel like you're falling behind, failing to tick the boxes on your Life Checklist fast enough, or perhaps not at all. Those perceived failures can leave you feeling worried, inadequate and overwhelmed, paving the way for those financially destructive F*ck-It Moments. But a little sweetness—a spoonful of sugar, if you will—can make all the difference.

When it comes to your finances, the sugar I'm talking about is a reality check. I know that's not as exciting as a quick-fix solution and may seem less than sweet at first, but trust me, a reality check is like a big financial hug. One that delivers a swift kick in the pants to your Life Checklist, a list that may have been leading you down an unrealistic financial path for years.

Realizing that your Life Checklist may need a few tweaks, or maybe a complete overhaul, doesn't mean you've failed at life. It's not lowering your expectations or settling. It's merely a perspective shift, clearing out old ways of thinking to allow newer, more realistic ones to take root. It's throwing yourself a financial life jacket so you can get yourself out of the deep end and breathe.

Symptoms of an unsustainable Life Checklist can include—

- feeling resentful towards others' financial success
- staying in a job that makes you utterly miserable in order to afford a lifestyle
- feeling like a failure, like you can't win and there is no hope
- no forward momentum in your finances for years because of overspending and/or under-saving

If any of these symptoms seem familiar, your Life Checklist may not only be unrealistic, it's likely setting you up for a lifetime of golden handcuffs, stress or fear.

The good news is that there is a way out. I know, because people who are tired of treading water come to my office every day, searching for a solution. That solution starts with a reality check and a close examination of their Life Checklist. They bring in their lemons and, together, we make financial lemonade.

If you can manage to make financial lemonade, you'll survive modern life without feeling resentful. Sometimes you have to redefine what success looks like for you, and that may mean opting out of some of the items on your Life Checklist. It means you're choosing to live differently from how you thought you would. It means that you're choosing happiness.

Like Donovan and Jamie, a couple who always talked about owning a home and living in the country. After years and years of trying, they realized that it just wasn't realistic. They simply could not afford it. There was no work for either of them in a rural area, no way to earn a living. Because they weren't independently wealthy, the solution was to opt out of that idea on their Life Checklist, examine what was truly important to them, and write a new list. Turned out that living close to their jobs was actually more important to them than they had originally thought. With no long commute, they had more time to spend with their adult kids, and that is what mattered most to them both. While they couldn't afford to buy a house near their jobs, they were happily renting an apartment near work and their kids and ticking other boxes on their Life Checklist instead.

And then there was Donna, who planned to move in with college friends after school. Her Life Checklist dictated that this was the true measure of success, the only way of proving her independence and accomplishment after completing her education. A quick reality check meant pushing that goal a little farther down the road, and taking advantage of the lucky offer to move back home with her parents so she could pay off her student loans faster.

Things didn't work out the way Donovan, Jamie and Donna had planned. But opting out of their existing Life Checklists and embracing new directions with realistic expectations meant that none of them resented the change. And therein lies the key to true Worry-Free Money and financial success. If you don't resent your realistic situation, living a life that doesn't look like the one you've always envisioned won't feel like a compromise. It will feel like a perfect fit.

That's what opting out of the Life Checklist gives you. Not necessarily what you thought you wanted, but 100 percent what you need, as my client Anne discovered when more than a few financial lemons dropped into her lap.

Meet Anne: Living Like a Golden Girl

When Anne was 33, her Life Checklist vision of retirement looked something like this:

- happily retired at 65
- mortgage-free home
- living near her kids and, with any luck, grandkids
- travelling somewhere warm once a year with her partner

Sounds great, right? Here's what actually happened:

- messy, financially crippling divorce at 42
- single mom of two with little or no child support
- at 58, not nearly enough money saved for the retirement she had planned

Life didn't work out the way Anne thought it would. Financial lemons.

Anne
Age: 58
Relationship status: single
Kids: 2, ages 26 and 28
Annual gross household income: $65,000
Assets: $269,397 in retirement savings
Liabilities: 0

Being a single parent is one of the most difficult financial gigs out there. Anne had to start her financial life over again at age 42, using her $120,000 profit from the sale of the matrimonial home as a nest egg. Child support was low and barely offset the costs of housing, transportation and groceries.

Despite the lemons, Anne had worked hard to be financially responsible. She hadn't overextended herself with housing costs, strove to live within her Hard Limit and kept socking away $25 a month towards her retirement. (Remember, small changes can make big waves.)

"My kids were great," she said. "They knew where we stood financially. As a single parent, you have to be honest about finances with your kids. There's no way to survive otherwise."

Seven years ago her youngest child moved out. Anne kept living within her Hard Limit and didn't have any debt. She wanted to retire but wasn't sure she could ever stop working, and that was keeping her up at night.

When we first met, she had seven years to go until retirement. "Is it too late to start saving?" she asked.

"Hell, no," I told her. "It's never ever, ever too late."

Anne had managed to keep the $120,000 from the divorce invested at an average annual rate of return of 5 percent, and she had added $25 per month without fail ever since the divorce 16 years earlier. She currently had approximately $270,000 in retirement savings (see the Long-Term Savings Calculator, page 306). Would it be enough?

Seven years ago, here's how her finances flushed out.

"Now that the kids have both moved out, it frees up about $415 a month from my Hard Limit that I can add to savings," Anne said. Perfect. We could reduce her Hard Limit Spending Money to $1,200 per month ($1,615 – $415) and increase her retirement savings to $440 per month ($415 + $25).

Monthly after-tax income	$4,300	
FIXED EXPENSES: Money You Cannot Spend		
Rent	$1,950	
Utilities	$200	
Renters' insurance	$25	
Cable/Internet	$100	
Phone	$80	
Bank fees	$5	
Total	$2,360	(55% of after-tax income)
MEANINGFUL SAVINGS: Money You Cannot Spend		
Retirement savings	$25	
Total	$25	(1% of after-tax income)
SHORT-TERM SAVINGS: Money You Cannot Spend		
Vacation	$200	
Emergency savings	$100	
Total	$300	(7% of after-tax income)
SPENDING MONEY: Hard Limit	$1,615	(37% of after-tax income)

I busted out the Long-Term Savings Calculator. "If we assume an average rate of return of 5 percent over the next seven years, your retirement portfolio will be approximately $425,000 when you turn 65."

Seven years later, Anne was about to retire. She had done everything I suggested. Her expenses had remained relatively steady over the past seven years even though her cost of living had risen with inflation. Luckily her income had kept pace with regular cost-of-living increases, so she was able to save the same amounts.

When we sat down again, she let me know how she saw her retirement plans shaping up. "I know that I'd like to spend more

	Average Spending	EROI
Groceries	$400	5
Toiletries	$60	5
Work lunches/coffee	$30	5
Takeout dinners	$50	5
Dinner out/social outings	$200	5
Entertainment (books, movies, music)	$60	5
Grooming	$100	5
Clothes and misc. shopping	$200	5
Health	$100	MUST
Kids (while at home)	$415	5
Total	$1,615	

than $3,000 a year on travel once I retire. I really want to live near my kids, so moving farther away for cheaper rent is something I'd like to avoid at all costs."

We fleshed out a retirement budget to test if it was doable. Anne figured she would need the same after-tax income that she had while working—$4,300 per month (in current dollars) or $51,600 per year ($4,300 × 12 months)—in retirement. Her Canada Pension Plan statement indicated that she would receive $10,033 per year in CPP, and she also qualified for the maximum amount of Old Age Security, which was estimated at $6,942.36 at the time. She planned to withdraw the rest from her registered assets and wanted her portfolio to last until she was 90. Using the Long-Term Savings Calculator, we calculated that she could use the equivalent of $24,000 (pre-tax, in current dollars) every year from her registered accounts until she turned 90.

Using an online tax estimator, we calculated that her total after-tax retirement income would be $36,141 per year in current dollars.

This worked out to $3,011.75 per month, approximately $3,000 per month after tax. (Note that these are approximations and were used to estimate cash flow specifically for Anne. Everyone's retirement cash-flow projections will look different.)

With $3,000 in after-tax income, Anne would be $1,300 short each month ($4,300 needed – $3,000 sustainable Spending Money). To give her a retirement where she could live close to her kids, travel, and stay healthy and safe, we needed to find a way to either reduce monthly spending by $1,300 per month ($4,300 – $3,000) or bring in an additional $1,300 per month in current dollars.

"Oh, I think reducing my expenses by $1,300 is doable," Anne said. "With the Golden Girls plan."

"What do you mean?" I asked.

"Well, three of my friends and I are thinking about moving in together once we retire, *Golden Girls* style. One couple and one other single friend. We've been chatting about this for years, since none of us is going to be able to retire securely otherwise."

Anne, Thomas and Sheena, and Lily had talked about moving in together in their "golden years" if things didn't pan out the way they all planned. Thomas and Sheena had lost a lot of money in the 2008–09 stock market crash and had never fully recovered financially. Lily had been a freelancer her whole life, and while she had saved, there wasn't enough to support her even on a reduced retirement income.

"Retiring single is too expensive for us," Anne said.

They all wanted to stay in town; that was nonnegotiable. None of them owned property or a home, so their plan was to rent a three-bedroom house and all move in together. They would split the costs of rent, utilities and household maintenance among the four of them.

"Golden Girls" House Rental Plan		
Category	Per Month	Per Person
Rent	$3,760	$940
Utilities	$320	$80
Cable/Internet	$100	$25
General household fund	$100	$25
Renters' insurance	$100	$25
Total shared expenses	$4,380	$1,095

Here is Anne's projected retirement Hard Limit spending based on $3,000 per month after tax (in current dollars):

Monthly after-tax income	$3,000	
FIXED EXPENSES: Money You Cannot Spend		
Shared household account	$1,095	
Utilities (shared)	$0	
Renters' insurance (shared)	$0	
Cable/Internet (shared)	$0	
Phone	$80	
Bank fees	$5	
Total	$1,180	(39% of after-tax income)
MEANINGFUL SAVINGS: Money You Cannot Spend		
Retirement Savings	$0	
Total	$0	(0% of after-tax income)
SHORT-TERM SAVINGS: Money You Cannot Spend		
Vacation	$250	
Emergency savings and health care	$250	
Total	$500	(17% of after-tax income)
SPENDING MONEY: Hard Limit	$1,320	(44% of after-tax income)

"This is brilliant," I said.

She beamed. "It's the only way we can all stay here and still have a life. Plus, on my own I'd never be able to afford a place like the one we are planning to get. It will feel like a Lifestyle Upgrade."

Living together with roommates would allow all of them to have a great retirement at a fraction of the cost. "It's obviously not where I thought I'd be at 65," Anne said. "But life throws us all curveballs. I've learned to roll with them. This is what I can do, so why complain about it?"

She was so right! I wish more people had this attitude. Anne was taking her personal financial lemons and making some fabulous lemonade. Sure, she'd have three roommates in retirement, and that wasn't on her original Life Checklist. But by opting out of her fantasy retirement into a much more realistic one, she could do the things that were important to her without worrying about money. She knew she could afford this. She would be safe and happy.

"Because we want this to work, we talked to a bunch of people who have already retired to shared accommodation. Their feedback has been so helpful. They told us to have noise rules in place before we move in, set up a shared household-repair fund, address what happens if someone wants to move out or passes away, and get a lawyer involved to put it all in writing.

"We've done all that," she added, "and I think we're ready to go. I just wanted to make sure it's financially feasible."

"It is totally feasible," I told her. "Please let me know how it all works out."

•

A year later, I checked in with Anne.

"Now that we are all moved in," she said, "I can't imagine retiring to a place by myself. I would have gone from seeing people every day at work to seeing no one at all. I don't want to eat every meal alone and only get together with people when I make plans to see them. For me, the community aspect is so important—an added bonus of a financially sound plan."

I couldn't help smiling.

"It's kind of like being in a university dorm," she joked. "Only the house is beautiful and we don't have constant keg parties going on next door. And it gets better! Lily and I are thinking about starting a business from the house so we don't get bored. 'Grannies Who Garden.' Green thumbs at your service."

"That's hilarious, and awesome. What are you going to use the extra income for?"

"More travel. That's our big goal. We're heading to Iceland next year!"

No one in the Golden Girls house was failing at life. In fact, they were winning. Their financial security was locked down and their individual quality of life was way up. By opting out of their unrealistic Life Checklist expectations, they had all won.

Meet Sam and Dani: A Tale of Two Downsizers

Unfortunately, not everyone is as flexible financially as Anne, and my job often means telling people that things are *not* going to be okay if they stay on their current trajectory. It sucks, and sometimes their Life Checklist won't allow them to hear or believe the truth. Like Sam and Dani, who were already in trouble when they came to see me the first time.

Sam and Dani

Ages: 55 and 43

Relationship status: married

Kids: 3, ages 10, 12 and 14

Annual gross household income: $150,000

Assets: house valued at $1.3 million; $180,000 in retirement savings

Liabilities: $750,000 mortgage; $100,000 home equity line of credit; $13,000 credit card debt; $30,000 car loan; $20,000 car loan

---

I had met Sam and Dani four years earlier, when they came in for a household financial planning session. They had been rolling their massive monthly credit card bills into a home equity line of credit once a year, and then rolling that into their mortgage every three to five years at renewal. They fought about money all the time and both were losing sleep. Equity-rich and cash-strapped—the classic definition of house-poor. Sam and Dani didn't want to live like that anymore. They wanted a change.

Being house-poor is terrifying. Even if you don't own a home, being rent-poor is just as bad. Your Fixed Expenses for housing are way too high, eating up all your money. (Perhaps a better term would be *dwelling-poor* or *home-poor*, but for the purposes of this section I'll stick with *house-poor*.)

The symptoms are typically the same:

- Your monthly housing bills and repairs add up annually to 40 percent or more of your household after-tax income.
- You are carrying large balances on credit cards that cannot be paid off except with a line of credit, robbing Peter to pay Paul.
- You've had very little or no money going towards retirement or additional mortgage payments for three or more years.

- You've tried three times to stick to a hardcore budget that would lower your discretionary spending and increase debt repayment and emergency/retirement savings, without success.
- Your mortgage is more than three times your gross salary (that is, if you make $80,000, the mortgage is greater than $240,000).
- You have rolled ever-increasing lines of credit into your mortgage for two or more refinances in a row.
- You are ignoring major repairs year after year. These are not updates or decorative renos but serious issues like a leaky roof, a mouldy basement or electrical and plumbing problems.

How do people end up in this situation? The biggest single cause of becoming house-poor is the way in which affordability was calculated before the purchase was made or lease signed. Chances are that everything looked fine on paper at the time, and perhaps for a while it was. Then real life happened and there was no plan in place.

I usually hear the following: "We just assumed that we'd spend less money once we were in the place, but we didn't. It was a totally unrealistic expectation." "We didn't factor enough emergency or retirement savings into our cash-flow calculations." "We didn't factor in new commuting costs, rising interest rates, increasing utility bills." And perhaps the most dangerous comment I hear in today's economy: "I assumed I'd make more money and that things would be better down the road." Whatever the reason, the home was likely purchased or leased on the assumption that incomes would go up and real life wouldn't happen.

Here's the thing: I've seen hundreds of house-poor individuals and families over the years and only nine of them were willing to sell and downsize. So there you go. If you're house-poor and you own your home and the idea of downsizing makes you want to shut this book and never speak of it again, you're not alone.

For Sam and Dani, house-poor was their reality. Both had been raised in houses with backyards and two-car garages. That was their normal, the life they expected to have for their own kids one day. A house with two cars and a backyard was high on both of their Life Checklists.

Ten years ago they bought their dream home, a beautiful four-bedroom house in the burbs, smack dab between their places of work. They paid $550,000, and yes, the value has appreciated considerably since they bought it. But that didn't solve their daily cash-flow problems. On paper they have equity, but in reality they couldn't afford that house.

When I gently broached the idea of downsizing at our first meeting, I think Dani wanted to rip out my throat for even suggesting it. She immediately got tears in her eyes and said, "Out of the question," so we moved on. I know when something is unrealistic.

Together we worked on their Happy Spending list, cutting out anything that gave them low Emotional Return on Investment. We managed to create a tight but sustainable Hard Limit. They left happy, motivated and excited.

Two years after that, they were back in my office with more debt, much less hope and way more fighting. When I asked what had happened, they admitted that they simply couldn't reduce their spending. The house had needed major repairs, and as hard as they tried, they couldn't stick to their Hard Limit the way they thought they could.

Their combined $160,000 household income was high, which is why they felt like they could afford the four-bedroom house way back when. But that $10,600 per month was quickly spent on a family of five in a big house.

Two of their kids had intense food allergies, so the grocery bill was

Monthly after-tax income	$10,600	
FIXED EXPENSES: Money You Cannot Spend		
Mortgage	$3,360	
Utilities	$480	
Home insurance	$151	
Property tax	$620	
Cable/Internet	$120	
Phone	$320	
Car insurance	$325	
Car loan 1 minimum payment	$390	
Car loan 2 minimum payment	$450	
Line of credit minimum payment	$550	
Credit card minimum payment	$350	
Total	$7,116	(67% of after-tax income)
MEANINGFUL SAVINGS: Money You Cannot Spend		
Line of credit above-minimum payment	$0	
Additional mortgage payment	$0	
Children's education fund	$0	
Retirement savings	$0	
Total	$0	(0% of after-tax income)
SHORT-TERM SAVINGS: Money You Cannot Spend		
Vacations	$0	
House-repair fund	$0	
Holidays/gifts	$0	
Total	$0	(0% of after-tax income)
SPENDING MONEY: Hard Limit	$3,484	(33% of after-tax income)

high and making cuts was not an option (extremely high Emotional Return on Investment there). Sam and Dani drove in opposite directions to work every day, so two cars were needed. In addition, the kids were in a number of extracurricular activities. Driving around on weekends to games, sleepovers or competitions was the norm.

For Sam and Dani, $3,484 was simply not enough Spending Money for them, even without any Short-Term or Meaningful Savings. They had tried and tried to reduce spending and save money, but they obviously loved their lifestyle.

When we went over their Spending Money again, here was how things broke down:

	Amount	EROI
Groceries	$1,500	5
Pet food/supplies	$100	MUST
Toiletries/supplements	$200	MUST
Gas	$660	MUST
Car repair ($1,200/year)	$100	MUST
Work lunches/coffees	$260	4
Kids' hot-lunch program	$150	5
Takeout (pizza night twice a month)	$70	5
Kids' activities		
Ballet ($3,168/year)	$264	5
Karate ($1,140/year)	$95	5
Swimming ($1,200/year)	$100	5
Gifts for other kids' birthdays	$40	2
Entertainment (books, movies, music, tickets)	$150	4
Haircuts ($1,200/year)	$100	MUST
Clothes for kids ($500/year each)	$125	4
Clothes for adults ($1,200/year each)	$200	4
Alcohol ($20/week)	$80	3
Holidays and birthdays ($1,000 + $450)	$120	4
Misc. shopping	$40	2
Total	**$4,354**	

The total was $870 more than their Hard Limit of $3,484 (with no savings whatsoever). Even if they cut down Unhappy Spending (miscellaneous shopping and gifts for other kids), that only amounted to an $80 per month reduction in Spending Money, which still left them going into debt an additional $790 ($870 – $80) every month. This meant that they would continue to go into debt by $9,480 ($790 × 12 months) every year just to keep up with their daily life.

The scarier thing was that we hadn't yet included large unforeseen emergencies. In the past year Dani and Sam had spent $6,500 on home repairs, and they usually spent $5,000. In addition, they were likely to spend $3,000 a year on travel, because they rented a cottage every year for a family vacation.

The first time they came in to see me, we set them up with a plan, but they couldn't make it work. Dani experienced a salary freeze, termites invaded the house and the couple realized that eliminating family vacations was nonnegotiable. Between home repairs, groceries, kids' activities and daily spending, they had taken on $13,500 worth of debt in the past year alone. This had been the cycle since they bought the house 10 years before.

Not only were they constantly taking on debt, Sam was now 55 years old. Retiring in 10 years would be nearly impossible on their current trajectory. All their eggs were in the real estate basket, with an ever-increasing mortgage. Something had to give.

Looking at their budget again, I knew I could find places they might cut. But that's not what this whole thing was about. It's never about what I *think* people can do, it's about what *they can* do. And, more importantly, what they will do. Every person and every family is different.

Sam and Dani had tried to stick to a Hard Limit that reduced their monthly spending to $3,000 per month so they could start paying down the debt, but every time they were unsuccessful. Which meant they could not afford to stay in the house and maintain their lifestyle. Reality. Lemons.

In this second meeting, I again lovingly brought up the idea of downsizing. Sam was totally in agreement. Dani again looked at me with tears welling up, but this time she said, "I don't think there's another way. We can't live with this stress anymore. It's affecting our entire family." Even though their egos felt crushed, they knew it was time. And right then and there, they made a huge leap. They opted out of their Life Checklist and changed direction from what they expected to what was realistic.

They decided to sell their dream home and purchase a small three-bedroom townhouse in the same school district, so their kids could stay in the same schools and still be near their friends. Staying in their current neighbourhood was essential to their emotional well-being, so moving farther away for something larger was not a good idea. They were willing to make the lifestyle adjustments necessary to stay in the neighbourhood.

Here's how it played out:

- When the mortgage came up for renewal, they put their house on the market, taking advantage of skyrocketing housing prices. The house sold for $1.3 million ($1,235,000 after 5 percent fees were deducted).
- They paid off all their debts, a total of $913,000. This included the $750,000 mortgage, the $100,000 home equity line of credit, $50,000 for both car loans and $13,000 worth of credit card debt.
- They used the $322,000 left over ($1,235,000 − $913,000) to purchase a smaller three-bedroom condominium townhouse

in the same neighbourhood for $650,000, paying $22,000 for closing and moving costs and making a $300,000 down payment. Their new mortgage was for $350,000 at 2.9 percent over 25 years.

Here is Sam and Dani's new Hard Limit plan:

Monthly after-tax income	$10,600	
FIXED EXPENSES: Money You Cannot Spend		
Mortgage	$1,650	
Utilities and condo fees	$500	
Home insurance	$100	
Property tax	$370	
Cable/Internet	$120	
Phone	$320	
Car insurance	$325	
Car payment 1	$0	
Car payment 2	$0	
Line of credit minimum payment	$0	
Credit card minimum payment	$0	
Total	$3,385	(32% of after-tax income)
MEANINGFUL SAVINGS: Money You Cannot Spend		
Line of credit above-minimum payment	$0	
Additional mortgage payment	$725	
Children's education fund	$225	
Retirement savings	$1,325	
Total	$2,275	(22% of after-tax income)
SHORT-TERM SAVINGS: Money You Cannot Spend		
Vacations	$250	
House-repair fund	$400	
Total	$650	(6% of after-tax income)
SPENDING MONEY: Hard Limit	**$4,290**	(40% of after-tax income)

Their new housing costs were only 25 percent of their monthly after-tax income, and best of all, they were debt-free. This had freed up so much cash flow! Here is how they used it:

Meaningful Savings

- $725 extra per month towards the mortgage ($8,700/year) so that the balance would be approximately $140,000 by the time Sam retired in 10 years and they could afford the monthly costs on Dani's income alone. This ensured they would be mortgage-free by the time Dani retired. (See the Online Mortgage-Repayment Calculator, page 304.)
- $1,325 to retirement savings, approximately 10 percent of their gross income. Dani would still need to keep saving once Sam retired, but we used the Long-Term Savings Calculator to find that if they managed a 6 percent net rate of return on their $180,000 plus the new contributions, they should have approximately $544,500 in their portfolio when Sam retired in 10 years.
- $225 to the kids' education fund, something they never thought they'd be able to accomplish. It wouldn't be enough to pay for all the kids' schooling, but it would help offset the cost, something that was really important for them.

Short-Term Savings

- $250 for vacations ($3,000 per year) so that they could continue to have family time.
- $400 for a home-repair fund and emergencies ($4,800 per year). Home-repair costs would likely be lower in the townhouse, but large purchases and emergencies were bound to come up, so

we all agreed to set up a home-repair and emergency account to cover these.

The best news was that they could accomplish all this forward momentum and still have $4,290 left over for Spending Money! This was an amount that was realistic and sustainable for them.

	Amount	EROI
Groceries	$1,500	5
Pet food/supplies	$100	MUST
Toiletries/supplements	$200	MUST
Gas	$660	MUST
Car repair ($1,200/year)	$100	MUST
Work lunches/coffees	$260	4
Kids' hot-lunch program/lunch money	$150	5
Takeout (pizza night twice a month)	$70	5
Kids' activities		
Ballet ($3,168/year)	$264	5
Karate ($1,140/year)	$95	5
Swimming ($1,200/year)	$100	5
Gifts for other kids' birthdays	$0 (cut)	2
Entertainment (books, movies, music, tickets)	$150	4
Haircuts ($1,200/year)	$100	MUST
Clothes for kids ($500/year each)	$125	4
Clothes for adults ($1,200/year each)	$200	4
Alcohol ($20/week)	$80	3
Holidays and birthdays ($1,000 + $450)	$120	4
Misc. shopping	$16 (reduced)	2
Total	$4,290	

•

A year later they came back to see me. Everyone was sleeping well and their quality of life had risen dramatically, because every dollar spent didn't feel terrifying. They were prepared for emergencies, job losses and the like and were finally able to put money away for their future.

Dani said that she and Sam were better parents because they didn't spend their evenings fretting and fighting over money. "I thought the kids would care about moving to live in a townhome," she said. "I kept waiting for them to yell, 'I hate this place!' You know, the way teens can rip you to shreds with a single sentence. But they didn't." She paused. "I think it's because life is genuinely happier than before. The kids can sense that. Plus we were really honest with them."

I asked her how she felt about the move overall. "In retrospect, it was the smartest decision we've ever made. I wish I'd had the courage to do it four years ago."

"I think we needed to fail again and again in order to believe that it was the only option," Sam said.

"The hardest part was getting over the fact that we will never have grandkids in the old house," Dani admitted. "At first I felt as though downsizing was an admission of our financial failures, but I don't resent it at all now. Now I know it's actually proof of our bravery and financial smarts." Later, Dani told me something I hadn't expected. They had heeded my advice to be honest with friends and family about their financial situation. "Tell them what's happening," I had urged her. "What kind of friends will judge you for selling because the house costs too much? No one you should want to know, that's for sure."

So Dani had taken a chance. She told her people that the house was eating money and that raising three kids was expensive. She even admitted that they weren't building retirement portfolios and had taken on over $200,000 in debt since buying the house. The wonderful thing was, once she'd opened up to their friends and family about her finances, those friends felt safe and free to do the same. Dani discovered that many of them were living the same way she had been—always on the edge, always worried. They also wondered all the time about downsizing, but they too were emotionally attached to their home and lifestyle and didn't want to disrupt the kids. Her friends didn't judge her at all. In fact, they levelled with her. They thought she was brave.

Moving day was not the shameful event she had anticipated. All their friends and family came to help out, the way they do when you're 20 and moving into your first apartment—beer, pizza, tears of sadness and tears of relief. Moving day was the first time Sam and Dani had been debt-free (besides a mortgage) in more than 10 years.

Dani told me that her friends now checked in with her on a regular basis to see how it was playing out and if she regretted the move. Her answer was always the same: "Moving was the hardest thing I ever had to do and I will miss that house forever, but I can't put a price tag on my sanity." Dani and Sam still drove by the house now and then. Although the pangs of nostalgia and loss were still there, in the grand scheme of life, they didn't regret downsizing.

Dani felt that two of her pals would eventually follow suit because they were in the same cycle of debt and stress that she and Sam had been in for years. "We are so downsizing again, to an apartment once the kids move out, so we can travel in retirement," she said. "The kids can sleep on air mattresses in the living room when they come to visit. I never want to feel that afraid or be that broke again."

Sam and Dani had taken what felt like financial lemons and made lemonade. They opted out of their own Life Checklist, got back on track and were revelling in their new-found financial freedom. They had found Worry-Free Money.

Sometimes life doesn't work out the way that we planned, and I suspect this will be the case more and more as we navigate the murky waters of modern life. It's different out there now, and the cards that many of us have been dealt simply can't provide the hand we want to play. Instead of feeling resentful or miserable and constantly over-spending to keep up with a Life Checklist that is unsustainable, why not just opt out altogether? Say "No, thanks, that's not realistic for me right now," and then get creative. Find another way to be happy, even if it means not having all the things you thought you'd want when you were younger.

It doesn't mean you've lost the game. It means you've created new rules. And that lemonade will taste sweeter than you ever thought possible.

CHAPTER 14

Uncertainty = Real Life: It's Different Out There Now

This chapter is a real kick in the pants. I'm still hugging you, but I'm also hoping to give you a hard dose of reality so that you can survive modern financial life without worrying.

With the rise of precarious employment, stagnating wages, corporate cutbacks and robots that could take over your job, there's no denying that a lot has changed over the past 10 years. Without a financial plan that reflects this new economic reality, you can find yourself wide awake in the middle of the night, worrying about what you'll do if you get laid off or the furnace breaks down or interest rates rise. If you're not financially prepared to roll with the punches, you're going to be constantly living in scarcity mode, which breeds more and more frequent F*ck-It Moments.

With this new reality in mind, I began testing a theory with clients that I'm now convinced is an important antidote to worrying about money. You might want to write this down: *Have an emergency account.* Revolutionary, right?

Defeating the Scarcity Mindset Once and for All

Having an emergency account is one of the most common financial tips out there, but more often than not it's dead last on my clients' lists of financial goals. That's why I want to take a moment to stress the importance of emergency savings, especially in these "interesting" times.

I know there are plenty of reasons to avoid emergency savings. Paying down debt feels good because you're getting it off your plate and saving the interest. Saving for a home, school, business, renovations or a wedding also feels good, because you're saving up for something big, tangible, financially responsible. Add in the pressure from banks, financial experts and family telling you to make your money "work for you" and warning you that you shouldn't have money "sitting around doing nothing," and it's no wonder emergency accounts get no love. Well, I love, love, love emergency accounts.

An emergency account is not a waste of resources. Think of your emergency account like having parents at a high school party. You resent them when the party is going well, but if party-crashers show up, you realize very quickly how grateful you are that they're there to contain the damage.

Here's what I've been noticing over the past five years: clients who have money stashed in their emergency accounts feel broke less often than those who don't, and they don't overspend as much either. Maybe you're thinking, *Well, duh.* Of course my clients with emergency accounts don't overspend. They're obviously good with money. But for many of them, it wasn't always so.

Emergency Accounts: A Warm Blanket of Calm

For years Daryl suffered from yo-yo budgeting and general money anxiety. During that time, whenever he came in for a financial checkup, my advice was always the same: "Prioritize emergency savings. Keep the money in a high-interest savings account. Do not touch it unless it's an emergency."

He always agreed at the time and then months later would admit that he had taken all his emergency savings and thrown the money at the mortgage, or into his retirement account on the last day of the year, or at a trip on a whim. All very reactive financial decisions.

"I know, I know," he would say to me. "But the Bank of Canada announced that they might raise interest rates, so I panicked and threw it on the mortgage. Then, during tax season, the bank kept reminding me to invest, so I threw some into my retirement account." While these may not sound like bad financial decisions on the surface, the problem was that none had been made with purpose or planning. They were knee-jerk reactions, driven by outside pressure and by his own fears about the future. He was worried all the time and losing sleep, even though his long-term savings were on track.

"I just don't see why I'd keep money in a savings account when my investments are getting 6 percent and my savings account is getting 1 percent," he finally confessed to me. "Plus I have my line of credit for emergencies."

I understood his thinking. Looking only at the math, the argument definitely favours investing the money or paying down the mortgage over keeping that money on the sidelines in a high-interest savings account. But over the years I've seen the positive psychological effects of having an emergency account. There's something very powerful about opening up your banking app or statement and seeing a big chunk of money sitting there. It's like a warm blanket of money calm.

Loads of people want to use their line of credit as their emergency account. But here's the thing: you still need to pay it back over time. If you use your line of credit for an emergency, you're going into debt to bail yourself out of a financial emergency situation. This compounds your fear and anxiety that you're not going to be okay. Borrowing to dig yourself out of financial emergencies only makes you feel more out of control. You didn't have enough money to bail yourself out, so now you're making your financial situation worse to solve the problem. It's like kicking yourself while you're already financially down.

But with an emergency account in place, you won't be left with a financial hangover when things get back to normal. You'll feel more in control over what's happening because you were prepared. This will make it easier to stick to your plan over the long haul.

But still Daryl could not resist the siren song of "make your money work for you." When he came back to see me again, he was two months into an unexpected job loss and his situation had worsened. "You never think a layoff is going to happen to you until it does," he said.

With no emergency account to get him through the layoff, he had racked up $8,000 in additional debt on his line of credit just to survive, leaving him feeling defeated, frustrated and broke. That was the tipping point for him. He understood at last that even though leaving money in a lower-interest emergency account might irritate him sometimes, it was more important to have it within reach when he needed it. So once he found a new job, he made it a priority to rebuild his emergency savings account and keep it for emergencies, regardless of the investment returns he could potentially earn or the interest he could save on the mortgage.

In Daryl's case we needed to put aside money for unexpected repairs and job loss. He had great private health insurance, so he felt covered on that front. Here is how his plan looked:

Daryl's monthly Fixed Expenses totalled $3,000, and he figured he needed $1,400 per month to pay for groceries and gas so he and his son could get by if he lost his job again. That came to $4,400 per month after tax ($3,000 for Fixed Expenses + $1,400 for basic spending).

Daryl received $800 per month in child support from his ex. Because Daryl was an employee, in the event of another job loss he would likely qualify for approximately $2,000 per month in Employment Insurance benefits. That would give him $2,800 per month ($800 + $2,000), but he needed $4,400 per month just to get by. Without an emergency account, he would be short $1,600 ($4,400 – $2,800) each month.

Daryl had already seen what would happen if he had to turn to his line of credit for this money, and he never wanted to be in that situation again. He was ready to set aside enough to fund three months' worth of basic living expenses. In his case, that meant $4,800 ($1,600 × 3). Based on his historical spending patterns, his emergency savings would need to also include $3,000 for average annual home repairs, $1,600 for car repairs and the $4,800 for unforeseen job loss, for a total of $9,400. If he took two years to rebuild his emergency account to $9,400, he would need to deposit $391 per month to that account for 24 months ($9,400/24).

•

A year later, Daryl and I checked in again. His emergency fund was at $10,000 (he had received an unexpected tax refund), he had stopped fretting about the money "doing nothing" and he was sleeping much better.

"How's it going?" I asked.

"Good. It's funny, before I had the emergency savings account on the sidelines, things used to really freak me out. If I had a bad day at work or my boss was acting weird, I'd internalize that and worry about it for days, convinced I was going to lose my job. I realized I was terrified of being fired or let go because I didn't have a safety net, and the littlest thing in the office could send me into a tizzy." Now that he had an established emergency savings account in place, he didn't lie awake at night analyzing something his boss had said and worrying about layoffs that he couldn't control.

"I've survived one layoff and now I know I'm prepared if it happens again. And I'm not scared of my house anymore. I used to see it as a money pit and was really resentful every time I had to drive to Home Depot or hire a contractor to fix something. I knew that was part of home ownership and that stuff was going to happen, so it never should have felt like a surprise. But because I wasn't financially ready, it always did. Now a water mark on the ceiling doesn't feel like the end of the world. I know I've got money set aside to deal with it."

This has been the outcome for so many of my clients. Fears and anxieties about money can be reduced by having an emergency account that you can see every time you log into your online banking. There is something innately satisfying about seeing your safety cushion. It's reassuring on a deep level. "Sometimes," Daryl admitted, "when I'm starting to feel anxious at work or anxious about the house, I open up my online banking app and just look at the emergency account. It honestly makes me feel better."

Believe me when I say that your money *is* working for you in an emergency account. Not in a hit-you-on-the-head-with-financial-returns way, but on a deeper, emotional level. Always attack high-interest debt (like credit cards) first and then put in the effort to build your emergency fund over time. Make it a priority. It's as important as your other savings goals. It's the key to Worry-Free Money in these interesting times.

The Unknown Future of Work

Robots are real and technology is advancing faster than ever before, touching every aspect of our lives. Who doesn't like advances in medical technology that can save lives or an app that can have your coffee ready for pickup every day at the time and place you like? But on the buzz-kill side of things, the uncertainty of future work is a reality. Experts are predicting more short-term temporary jobs and more major shifts to come.

The future of work is uncertain, and many of my clients are worried about whether they will have a job in 15 years. I share their fear—the words *robo financial planner* can cause a sleepless night for me. Sure I tell myself that I embrace technology and that I'll find a way to adapt my business and continue to add value, but I can't always get that kind of perspective. That's because I don't know what adapting will look like or if it will work in the future. It's scary.

I'm not writing a manifesto on how technological advancement is going to throw us into a post-work economy, but not addressing the robotic elephant in the room will not make it go away. Counting on the financial assumptions that we planners used in the past is unrealistic and even naive. The new economic landscape likely means fewer jobs and lower wages on the horizon. Financial advice given even five years ago doesn't hold water in the face of this new reality. We need to adjust our ideas of what being okay financially means, so we can thrive.

Meet Kirsten and Jocelyn

> ### Kirsten and Jocelyn
>
> **Ages:** 34 and 46
>
> **Relationship status:** married
>
> **Kids:** 2, ages 2 and 5
>
> **Annual gross household income:** $115,000 ($55,000 + $60,000)
>
> **Assets:** house valued at $385,000; $55,000 in retirement savings (Jocelyn has a defined-benefit pension plan)
>
> **Liabilities:** $200,000 mortgage at 2.5% interest

Kirsten lived in a townhouse with her partner and their two kids. "We've outgrown the house," she told me at our first meeting. "We'd like to sell it and get a bigger place but I'm afraid to."

Kirsten and her partner had a combined household income of $115,000 ($7,000 per month after taxes and deductions), which was great. Jocelyn worked an administrative job. She wasn't sure what the future of academia looked like and was worried that her job might not exist in 15 years. "I will probably lose my job to a robot," she said.

Kirsten and Jocelyn's goal was to purchase a bigger home in the same town. Their friends, family and communities were all there, giving them the advantage of free daycare four days a week (score!). They wanted a $650,000 house and had been pre-approved for the $465,000 mortgage they would need. But could they afford it in light of a changing workforce?

"We want to ensure that we'll be okay if neither of us has a solid income or a job 15 years from now," Kristen said when we sat down.

As much as I hated to validate her worry about the future of work, given the stark realities of modern life, I agreed with her. To ensure that they would be okay, we needed to come up with a plan that would meet the following goals:

- Be mortgage-free in 15 years.
- Save 12 percent of Kirsten's gross income for retirement, in addition to Jocelyn's defined-benefit pension ($550 per month).
- Travel for $7,200 every three years ($7,200/36 months = $200 per month to Short-Term Savings).
- Put aside $3,600 per year for home repairs and emergencies ($3,600/12 months = $300 per month).
- Maintain a similar amount of Spending Money ($2,500 per month) so they wouldn't feel broke in order to make the plan sustainable.

It's important to note that we were diversifying their risk between real estate and stock market investments, not choosing one or the other, to prepare for retirement. If you have decided that renting versus owning is best for you, be sure to take advantage of the fact that you don't have to worry about paying for repairs and maintenance or interest on a big mortgage, and put that extra money away! You're not building equity on something you could potentially sell one day, so you should be aiming to over-save towards your retirement. Aim to save 20 percent of your gross income if you're renting, which is double the minimum 10 percent savings rule-of-thumb.

On the next page, you'll find a snapshot of the couple's finances before we figured out how big a mortgage they could realistically afford.

In order to meet these other goals and maintain their spending level, Kirsten and Jocelyn needed to keep their mortgage payment

Monthly after-tax income	$7,000
FIXED EXPENSES: Money You Cannot Spend	
Mortgage	?
Utilities and condo fees	$245
Home insurance	$90
Property tax	$300
Cable/Internet	$100
Phone	$200
Car insurance	$150
Part-time daycare	$600
Total	$1,685
MEANINGFUL SAVINGS: Money You Cannot Spend	
Retirement savings	$550
Total	$550
SHORT-TERM SAVINGS: Money You Cannot Spend	
Vacations ($2,400/year)	$200
Emergency fund ($3,600/year)	$300
Total	$500
SPENDING MONEY: Hard Limit	**$2,500**

to $1,765 or less in order to still be able to afford all their other Fixed Expenses ($1,685), Meaningful Savings ($550), Short-Term Savings ($500) and Spending Money ($2,500). Using the online mortgage calculator, we found that a $265,000 mortgage at 2.5 percent with a five-year term would result in payments of $1,765 per month if it was to be paid off over 15 years.

Our plan—with a $265,000 mortgage—didn't look much like the one they had been approved for, with good reason. On paper they could afford a $465,000 mortgage amortized over 30 years, assuming that low interest rates lasted forever. But when we took real life into consideration, we realized they couldn't rely on that assumption going forward. A mortgage of $265,000 was what they could truly afford if they wanted to stick to their plan without worrying about their financial future.

If the approximate equity in their current home was $185,000, they could afford a house costing approximately $450,000 ($265,000 mortgage + $185,000 down payment), assuming that closing costs, realtor fees and so forth were dealt with outside this equation. This was $200,000 less ($650,000 − $450,000) than the house they wanted to be able to afford. A sacrifice to be sure, but here's the thing: saddling themselves with a $465,000 mortgage that wouldn't be paid off for 30 years would put Kirsten and Jocelyn in deep trouble if they had to take a pay cut or lost their jobs altogether in the next 15 years. Plus, overextending themselves would just lead to sleepless nights.

Kirsten and Jocelyn left with a plan that wasn't exactly what they wanted, but it felt good and safe and freed them from worry. They wouldn't be overstretching themselves and could deal with the uncertainty of the future. They were willing to make those sacrifices in the short run because the fear of being jobless and feeling scared every time they spent money was worse than the disappointment of living in a smaller place without a backyard big enough to implement the plans they had been daydreaming about. This was a direct opt-out of the expectations on their Life Checklist.

•

I know the whole uncertainty-of-work thing is hard to hear, but I believe it's naive to ignore it. For anyone out there who is worried about whether they will be okay financially in the future, making changes now is critical. I like to call it "robot-proofing your life."

- Always attack high-interest debt (like credit cards) first, and then put in the effort to build your emergency fund over time. Keep the emergency money in a safe, liquid account that you can easily access, and don't get tempted to spend it on a vacation. Make it a priority.
- Don't overextend yourself. If you have a mortgage or you're thinking about buying a home with a mortgage, try to match your amortization period with a realistic time horizon for stable and steady income. Could be 15 years, could be 25 years, but ensure that you've thought about this and what is realistic for your industry.
- Diversify your long-term savings. Ensure that you're putting aside money to pay down your mortgage as well as investing in your retirement portfolio. If you're renting, aim to save 20 percent of your gross income for retirement.
- Ensure that you're saving enough for retirement and the future of uncertain work. Given that the job market may change drastically for all of us in 10 or 20 years, if you know that you've got a plan of attack, you can stop being afraid, because you know there is enough money in the long run.

Robot-proofing is like a Boy Scout motto for financial planning: Hope for the best, prepare for the worst. And if the worst never happens? You'll be debt-free sooner, with money to spend. Win-win all around!

CHAPTER 15

No Regrets:
There's More to Life Than Money

When it comes to money, sometimes it's hard not to imagine *What if . . .*

What if I'd taken that unionized job with a pension? What if I'd bought Apple stock in 1980? What if I'd bought a house downtown 20 years ago? What if I won the lottery? These types of what-ifs are harmless fantasies, the kind of daydreams we all have, and there's nothing wrong with that. The problem comes when *what if* really means *I can't believe I did (or didn't do) that*—when we believe that a financial choice we made years ago has negatively impacted our finances ever since.

I had a chance to buy Apple stock in 1980 but I went for safe instead. I'm such an idiot. The vendor of that house signed back for $1,000 more and I walked away. I'm such an idiot. Financial regret. Shoulda, woulda, coulda. Didn't. And you can't stop beating yourself up for a decision that made perfect sense at the time.

This kind of regret can destroy your confidence in the financial future, making it impossible to trust your financial decisions, to go with your gut anymore. It eats away at your happiness and appreciation of your circumstances, reminding you how little you have compared to what you could have had, how bad you are with money. This regret can keep you up at night and makes you second-guess every financial move you make into the future.

Below is an email from a client who had deep financial regret over a house purchase he didn't make, a purchase that would have put him on the same financial footing as his friends who were cashing in big. Have a read.

Meet Daniel

Daniel

Age: 50

Relationship status: married

Kids: 0

Annual gross household income: $105,000

Assets: $500,000 in retirement accounts; condo valued at $450,000

Liabilities: $0

Dear Shannon,

When I met with you last time, you did a great job convincing me that I'm doing well [which he was]. However, with each passing day I feel like my wife and I made a mistake buying the condo when we got married.

Real estate is in the news every single day. I just read an article about how the average price of a single detached home in the city is appreciating by $100,000 every year. That's a 15 to 20 percent increase every year. The average price of those homes is now $1.2 million, and in the suburbs the prices are closing in on $1 million.

A friend who is only a few years older than me told me his house is now worth $2 million. He bought it for $500,000 20 years ago. To be honest, I don't know if he said $2 million or $1.2 million because I almost fainted from disbelief and envy when he said it. I had no idea his house was worth so much.

> Conversely, last time I checked the value of our condo, it was worth around $467,000. That means it's appreciating by around 3 to 5 percent a year [which is still great]. Nowhere near the 15 to 20 percent of a single-family home.
>
> I know we're in good shape financially, but those kinds of prices and rates of appreciation can make a rational person like me become very irrational. I feel like we're missing out on so much money because we made the wrong choice. I've even thought about moving to a different city or even a different province just to escape the hype.
>
> Any advice?
>
> All best,
>
> Daniel

You can see the themes of missing out, of comparison with others, and overall financial frustration. Trust me, Daniel was in good shape financially. Great, actually. But financial regret has taken hold and plagued him constantly, stealing his peace of mind and perpetuating the feelings of being broke, inadequate and ultimately disappointed in his financial future.

I went through something similar myself a while back. After I'd been working on Bay Street for some time during my early career, my then boyfriend (now husband) and I had managed to save $25,000. At 25 years old, that was a ton of money for us.

During the stock market crash of 2008–09, interest rates plummeted and chat around the office, the dinner table and everywhere I went confirmed what I had been thinking: we had a down payment; we should buy something. Debt was cheap. Being an overachieving Capricorn and hell-bent for leather towards financial security, I headed straight to the Internet and started researching places for sale.

Armed with a mortgage pre-approval, we started going to open houses. We found a townhouse listed at $343,000. We had just enough to put down 5 percent, including closing costs. All we had to do was pull the trigger and put in an offer. We were 25 years old and about to jump into a deal that looked great on paper.

It was a ridiculous night. We stress-ate pizza, called my parents a hundred times, discussed, agonized and discussed again. I cried twice. But here's the thing: while we had been approved for the mortgage, we couldn't really afford that townhouse. Not really. When I looked at what we'd have left over to spend each month after paying condo fees, mortgage, utilities and property tax, it wasn't much. We would have been house-poor for sure. No trips, no extras, no life.

We just weren't sure. Something felt off.

Ever since graduation we had been on a hardcore debt-reduction and saving plan (that's what happens when you date a financial planner), leaving us with very little cash in our pockets every month, a very low Hard Limit. Our student debt had just been paid off, so we had savings and finally some financial breathing room. We had talked about taking a trip for so long, eating meatballs and fantasizing about going to Europe once we'd paid off our loans.

Buying that townhouse would mean the austerity would continue. No fun and definitely no trips for a long time. Was that what we really wanted? The answer, after more discussions and even more pizza, was no. We passed on the townhouse and went to Europe instead, using $6,000 of what could have been our down payment. We also bought a bed frame. And eight months later I quit my Bay Street job. Eep!

The day Daniel's email arrived, I checked to see what townhouses were selling for in the complex we had been considering.

Interestingly, a unit similar to the one we would have paid $343,000 for seven years earlier had just sold for $609,000. According to the online mortgage calculator, our mortgage would have been approximately $250,000 by now, which means we would have been sitting on a nest egg worth $359,000 ($609,000 – $250,000) of tax-free equity. Damn. That would have been nice. Woulda, coulda, shoulda. Didn't.

Financial regret could be hounding me to this day. *What if we'd bought that townhouse?* morphing into *I can't believe we didn't buy that townhouse*, giving me plenty to beat myself up over. But you see, I quit my Bay Street job that year to launch the Barter Babes project— a one-year project in which I traded unbiased financial planning advice with more than 300 women in exchange for goods or services. No money changed hands. Smartest/stupidest thing I ever did.

While I dislike the term *stupid*, if you'd looked at the finances, you'd have wondered what I was thinking. To support my project, $15,000 of our down-payment savings went towards subsidizing rent and a cellphone for a year, plus $35 a week for my Spending Money (which, by the way, was not enough). To add to the fun, my husband was laid off the same year and we ended up taking on credit card debt. We had our share of lemons that year and were definitely not winning at life. To be completely honest, it was brutal. I had to take money out of my retirement savings to survive.

But here's another thing: the Barter Babes project allowed me to do things differently, to work with ordinary people, not just the high-net-worth clients I'd been dealing with in my Bay Street job. I saw the impact that solid, unbiased, affordable financial advice had on the lives and well-being of the 310 women I bartered with. That smart/stupid project changed my life—I was hooked. When it ended, I couldn't go back to Bay Street. I was a totally different person. My Life Checklist had morphed. So I struck out on my own, launching the New School of Finance, my fee-only practice that keeps financial advice affordable. Six years later we have offices, an amazing team and a client waiting list.

As an added bonus, my husband and I have travelled abroad and now I'm writing this book. None of this would have happened if we had bought that townhouse. I would never have quit my job. I would never have started the Barter Babes project, which propelled me into my career and future business. I would never have travelled to Europe or South America. I would never have started the New School of Finance and you wouldn't be reading this book. Everything would be different, and not in a good way for me.

Whenever I have those moments when I think *I can't believe we didn't buy the townhouse,* I remember that we made the best decision for our life and our journey at the time. Not someone else's journey. Ours.

When I wrote back to Daniel, I gave him the same advice I give myself. Here's what I said:

Hi Daniel,

Thank you so much for sending this email. I understand what you're feeling and ask you to consider the following:

1. Fifteen years ago, you couldn't have predicted this extreme rise in house prices. You bought a home that was perfect for you and your wife and the life you wanted at the time. Your mortgage is fully paid, which is fabulous. But more importantly, you have been happy in that home. Would you be able to say that if you'd been carrying crushing debt all that time? Maybe not.

2. Never compare yourself to anyone else, because you have no idea what their financial situation is. The friend in the $1.2 million (or $2 million)

---

house could be swimming in debt. Things might look great on the out-side, but they could be living in a pressure cooker on the inside. So stop thinking about them and focus on you. You have what you need in order to do the things you want, and that's more than enough to be happy.

3. There's no denying that luck plays a part in all our lives. Sometimes people get lucky in real estate and stock markets, and sometimes people win the lottery. None of that means they're better with money than you are. Luck played a role, and resenting luck is like resenting rain when you've planned a picnic. You can't control the weather, but you can spread your blanket on the rug indoors and hold that picnic anyway. Think of all the bugs you won't be swatting while you fill your plate!

Cheers,

Shannon

Daniel thanked me for the response and said it was good advice. When I heard from him again close to a year later, he admitted that at first it had been hard to let go of his resentment and frustration. But focusing on his own life and examining what really mattered to him and his family had helped him see past the fear and stop com-paring his situation to anyone else's. They're still in the condo, and I'm sure that financial regret rears its ugly head from time to time, but at least now he knows how to get perspective and appreciate what he does have and what he has done right.

Daniel wasn't the first client I've seen with financial regrets, and I know he won't be the last. Loads of people come in with crippling regret over real estate deals they didn't make and stocks they sold too soon or held on to too long. I've even had clients who lost more than $1 million in a Ponzi scheme. Imagine how hard you could beat yourself up over that one.

No matter how big the issue seems, the solution to financial regret of all kinds remains the same.

Step 1: Remember why you made that decision in the first place

The future is a mystery. All we know for certain is what is directly in front of us. If you could go back in time, armed only with what you knew then, you'd probably make exactly the same decision all over again, because it was the right one at the time. Try to recall why you made the decision, and you'll realize you're not bad with money or an idiot. Given the information you had, the choice made sense then.

I didn't buy the townhouse because I didn't want to be house-poor and miserable. Daniel bought the condo because it made sense at the time and was affordable for him. As for the couple taken in by the Ponzi scheme, they had researched the company, asked all the right questions and trusted that their investments were safe. What more could they have done? The answer is nothing, and they had to stop blaming themselves. All of us made the right decision based on the information we had at the time. Period. Full stop.

Step 2: Recognize that luck has a lot to do with it

Unless you're psychic, you can't see into the future. Neither could the people who managed to make the "right" financial decisions. Most of the time they just got lucky.

I cannot stand it when people try to disguise their financial luck as financial savvy. *We chose a variable-rate mortgage because we knew interest rates would stay low.* Did you? Did you actually *know*? Do you work for the federal bank? Did you have insider information? Probably not. You simply made a decision based on information at the time and got lucky when it played out in your favour.

It's the same with the investment and housing markets. Sure there are trends, and I'm not saying it's all dumb luck, but no one can know for sure what's going to happen. All we can do is research, make informed decisions, place our bets and hope that our strategy plays out over the long haul.

Comparing yourself to someone who has had more financial luck than you is like going to a casino with a friend who wins $1,000 while you lose $100. You can't help but wish you had played the same games they played. But there was no way you could have known how their games were going to turn out. And in truth, they were using just as much guesswork as you were.

Remember as well that life isn't fair. Bad things sometimes happen to good people, and vice versa. That doesn't make it easier to swallow, but it happens. And there's no point dwelling on things you couldn't have known in advance and cannot control.

Step 3: Recall the Beyoncé Factor

Unless you know the intimate numerical details of other peoples' lives, stop comparing yourself to them. The person who invested in medical marijuana early on may have made 20 percent on their stocks, but maybe they haven't told you about their 45 percent loss on a rogue junk bond. You likely don't know the whole picture.

Step 4: Shift your perspective: It's not all about the money

Think how different your life would be if you had made a different decision. What's great about your life now that wouldn't exist if you had gone the other way? You made the choice for a reason. It was one that probably reflects what's important to you, outside and apart from money.

For me, not buying the townhouse allowed me the financial flexibility to quit my job and strike out on my own. For the couple who lost money in the Ponzi scheme, it forced them to reassess what was important to them and realize that their marriage was strong and money didn't define them. For the people who missed out on the Apple stock, maybe they made that decision because they couldn't afford to buy in at the time. That wasn't a bad call at the time; it was smart.

•

We cannot go back in time. But we can keep moving forward. And that is where your financial future lies, full of hope.

CHAPTER 16

Call to Action:
Spread the Money Love

Everything you've read in this book so far has been about you, your finances and what you can do to get control, live a life that makes sense for you and stop worrying about money. But there's a bigger picture at play.

You now know that getting your finances under control means living within your Hard Limit and saying no to Unhappy Spending, both of which are easier when you are open and honest about your financial situation with your inner circle—but only if that circle is supportive. Being honest about money and saying no to overspending can be daunting because you risk being judged by those you love or care about, being labelled cheap or broke or, worse still, financially irresponsible. That's why cultivating a supportive and nonjudgmental attitude within your inner circle is essential to both getting and keeping your financial life in order. I call this attitude Money Love.

But here's the thing: you need to ensure that the Money Love doesn't flow only one way. You need to be equally supportive of the financial decisions of others, which isn't as simple as it sounds. At one time or another, I'm sure, we've all been guilty of spreading a little Money Hate, which involves any of the following:

- judging someone's purchases, big or small
- becoming resentful or jealous of someone's financial success

- using shaming language like *cheap, irresponsible, ridiculous* and so on when speaking about someone's financial choices
- not taking no for an answer when someone can't or won't spend money on something you think is important

A recent interaction between two of my friends perfectly illustrates what I'm talking about. Zach and Luke are brothers. Both are entrepreneurs, but in different industries. Luke is in construction and Zach is in the restaurant business. While they're absolutely best buds, an underlying sibling rivalry and innate competitiveness keep them from being honest with each other about their finances.

Because I am both a friend and financial planner for the brothers, I know that Zach (the older) is having a hard time financially, while Luke is killing it. I also know that Zach feels completely inadequate when he compares himself to his brother. His financial goals are often those that Luke has already achieved. Luke buys a house; Zach feels like he needs to. Luke gets a car; Zach immediately wants one too. Luke has become Zach's benchmark, representing his Life Checklist, his Joneses—the person against whom Zach measures his own success.

When the brothers joined our group at the Canadian National Exhibition this past summer, I was the only person who knew the whole picture and understood what was going on behind the scenes financially (it's fun to be me sometimes). The CNE ("the Ex" to locals) is Toronto's annual end-of-summer bash, famous for the deals to be had. It has a bazaar where you can get great stuff on sale. It's a real haggler's dream.

It wasn't long before Luke came bounding over, exclaiming that he had just struck a great deal for himself and Zach. A vendor of flat-screen TVs had agreed to knock an additional $100 off the price if they each bought one that day. As in right then and there.

"Zach, go in on this with me," Luke said. "It's so cheap!"

The problem was that Zach could not afford the TV, no matter how good the deal. It wasn't within his Hard Limit. This was something only Zach and I knew. Of course, I said nothing.

"No, I'm good," Zach said. "I've got a TV." (His first attempt to say no.)

"Come on, man," Luke pleaded. "This is such a good deal!"

Laughing it off, Zach tried again. "You're so funny. I'm okay, seriously." (Attempt number two to say no.)

"If you don't have the cash now, I'll lend it to you," Luke said.

Zach shook his head. "It's not that. I've got the money." (That was his Life Checklist yelling, *I'm not financially inadequate!*)

"Then let's do this," Luke said. "You were talking about getting a new TV a month ago, and this is the best best price out there. Don't be so cheap."

All I could do was stand back and watch as Zach caved. He pulled out his credit card and headed off with his brother to purchase a television he couldn't afford. I remember how ticked off I was at Luke for bullying his brother, but in reality both were at fault.

A little background is in order here. For anyone who's already hating on Luke, you should know that Zach's restaurant is featured all the time on those "Top 10 Places to Eat" lists and there are always lineups at the door. With visuals like that, it's only natural that his friends and family assume Zach is also killing it financially. He's not, but Zach's fear of being judged for being financially irresponsible keeps him from being honest.

When his family asks "How's biz?" Zach responds with "Great," and "Busy, but good busy" and "Awesome!"—perpetuating the problem instead of telling them what he tells me: "Things are tough. I love the restaurant business, but the margins are tight and it's a cash-flow struggle every month. I have faith that it will work out over time, but these first years are a cash-flow nightmare."

For his part, Luke wasn't spreading Money Hate on purpose. He wasn't trying to be a jerk, but he managed to nicely because he refused to take no for an answer and used shaming words like *cheap*. Perhaps Zach's refusal to buy the television felt like a judgment of his own financial choice, but because they don't talk about money in any real way, nothing productive came out of their exchange.

Imagine the relief Zach would have felt if the conversation had gone something like this instead:

Luke: "Zach, go in on this with me. It's so cheap!"

Zach: "I can't swing it right now. Things are tight and I need to pump as much cash as possible into the restaurant."

Luke: "No problem. I get it."

No judgment, no fear, no shame. And as a result, no swipe of the credit card to keep up appearances. Zach's fictional honesty and Luke's quick acceptance are perfect examples of spreading Money Love on both sides. Unfortunately they aren't the norm. When it comes to money, judgment can often be the go-to reaction for people, and it can come at us from all sides. From family, friends, co-workers, strangers.

If you earn too much, someone thinks you're an entitled jerk. If you don't make a lot, someone may think you have made bad choices. If you spend money on *this*, someone's bound to think it's foolish. If you don't spend money on *that*, someone else will say you're cheap. *Ay-yi-yi!* The list goes on and on, keeping us all on edge and making it nearly impossible to talk openly about money.

That is how the cycle of fear and guilt continues. As much as I hate to belabour a point, financial honesty is the only way to break the cycle and stop worrying about money.

Money Love vs. Money Hate

My clients Dwight and Janine are a perfect example of how spreading Money Hate perpetuates the cycle of fear and guilt and how Money Love is the way out. Dwight and Janine were in my office two years ago, very upset about a recent blow-up with their youngest daughter, Stacy, who had just finished her first year of postsecondary schooling. The family had a massive fight during spring midterms that left Dwight and Janine feeling guilty and Stacy feeling ashamed. All about money.

Working not only with Dwight and Janine but also with Stacy allowed me to see both sides of the financial story. They proved, once again, the importance of cultivating financial honesty with your family and friends.

Dwight and Janine's Side of the Story

Dwight and Janine weren't able to financially support Stacy through her postsecondary education. While they had saved enough over the years to sustain the family's lifestyle and keep their mortgage manageable and their retirement savings on track, they could not manage the extra squeeze for the education fund. Which, as you know (and as I told them repeatedly), is totally okay. However, they felt beyond guilty about it.

The fact that Stacy wouldn't have help paying for her education made them feel financially inadequate, as if somehow they had made bad financial decisions. Every time their friends who had kids in school said things like "School is so expensive these days" or "How are these kids going to pay off their debt when the job market is so tough?" Dwight and Janine felt broke, ashamed and guilty. Like they were bad parents.

"Every time Stacy came home, she would complain about being a broke student. We felt so bad," Dwight said. "We would give her money, maybe $50 or $100, to help her out that month. Then the next time she came home, it was the same thing. She'd complain about being broke and we'd give her some money."

"Then we'd see photos of her on Facebook or take a peek at her bank account," Janine added. "Here we were feeling like crap because she said she was broke, but there she was out for dinner or spending $50 on a Halloween costume. We just got so mad."

Every time Stacy came home, the money game they were playing grew more and more tense. It all came to a head during the spring midterms, when Stacy came home for the weekend and admitted that her student loan had run out. She needed money for rent to make it to the end of the semester.

"I just saw red," Janine said. "She needed rent and living expenses for the next two months. A thousand dollars! That's so much money—we don't have that lying around. We had to borrow on our line of credit, and we're still paying it off."

"Then what happened?" I asked

"We lost it with her," Dwight said.

"It was a massive fight." Janine looked down at her hands. "I yelled, told her she was blowing through money for stupid expenses. I told her we couldn't believe she was being so financially irresponsible and that we hadn't raised her that way."

"And?"

"And she yelled back that we have no idea how much life costs. Her student loan was barely covering her tuition and she'd had to get a part-time job to subsidize her life."

"We had no idea," Dwight said.

"She doesn't share anything with us now," Janine said through tears. "We have no idea how she's actually doing. She could be racking up thousands of dollars a month on a credit card. We have no idea. She just says 'I'm fine' when we ask."

Their blow-up was totally understandable. Who wouldn't be mad? For months they had been feeling guilty about not being able to help Stacy with her education. Yet every time she came home, they gave her more money. I felt for them.

Their anger was being fuelled by the fact that they already felt inadequate because they couldn't help as much as they wanted to, or as much as they assumed their friends were helping their kids (hello, Inadequacy Influence). Every time Stacy asked for money it was a direct reminder that they weren't able to do more for her financially.

Here's the thing, though: while their intentions were good, without realizing it, Dwight and Janine were not spreading any Money Love to Stacy. Every time they gave Stacy money, it came with a passive-aggressive comment or lecture about her spending. "Okay, Stacy, here's $100, but don't spend it on going out," or "Here's $50; don't spend it on clothes."

Now, in case you're thinking Stacy is an entitled spoiled brat, hang on a moment before you leap into Money Hate yourself, and hear her side of things. In an attempt to ensure that Stacy was faring okay financially, Janine and Dwight gave their daughter the ultimate gift—a financial planning session with me ☺.

Being able to sit down with Stacy on her own gave me insight into both sides of the story.

Stacy's Side of the Story

"They kept telling me that if I needed help I just had to ask. But whenever I did, they would judge the way I was living. My dad would make me log into my bank account so he could see my statement. Then he'd go through it line by line, ripping apart anything that wasn't school-related. It was so embarrassing! I never knew if it was actually okay or not to ask them for money. In one breath they would ask me if I needed money, and then as soon as I admitted yes, they would make me feel so guilty about it. I thought it was okay, but it obviously was not."

Stacy was clearly upset, both angry and confused, but willing to talk openly, which I appreciated. "How have you been getting by?" I asked.

"The student loans don't cover more than books and tuition, so I'm always on a budget," she said. "I've got a part-time job and, yes, I go out sometimes, but I don't spend more than $20. I'm so careful all the time, but it's hard. Everything is just so expensive."

"How do you see things shaping up going forward?" I asked.

She shrugged. "I've been approved for more loans for next year, thankfully. But I'll probably end up taking on some credit card debt this year. There's no way around it."

"And your mom and dad?"

This time it was Stacy who looked down at her hands. "I don't ask them for anything anymore, and I don't tell them what I'm doing. It's easier when they don't see my posts on Facebook or Instagram. It's weird, you know, to hide things from them, but I don't know what else to do. I don't want to fight with them anymore about money."

My take on the situation? From where I sat, I saw a family in turmoil and a destructive battle that could have been avoided with a single conversation and a little more Money Love on both sides.

Where Dwight and Janine Went Wrong

Dwight and Janine wanted to help out Stacy financially but couldn't do it with big payments for tuition or rent. While they were happy to reduce their spending by about $100 a month to help her out, their sense of financial inadequacy made them feel like that $100 wasn't good enough. As a result, they were never open with her about what they could and could not afford.

Sure, they said "Let us know if you need financial help," but that was too vague. Because they weren't financially honest about what they were willing to spend, they led Stacy to believe that help was there if and when she needed it. Problem was, she didn't know the boundaries. They were as frustrated with her over a $20 handout as they were for $200.

Every dollar they gave her came with strings attached: instructions on how to spend it and shaming about past expenditures, all of which made Stacy feel even more broke and financially irresponsible.

All kinds of Money Hate were present, perpetuating the feelings of broke-ness, guilt and inadequacy on all sides.

Where Stacy Went Wrong

Stacy was never honest with her parents about what she needed. She only complained about being broke, which was just as vague as their offer of help. Dwight and Janine had no way of knowing how she was doing financially but were poised to hear her complain about money every time she came home. Sometimes it happened, sometimes it didn't. It kept everyone on edge because the ask was inconsistent. Too often she said nothing until the financial stakes were extremely high and then blindsided them with a massive request.

Both sides were spreading Money Hate, not Money Love. As a result, Stacy blocked her parents on Facebook so they couldn't see photos of her going out. No one was talking about money. Dwight and Janine felt even worse than before and Stacy was about to take on credit card debt.

No one was winning. Everyone felt guilty. Everyone was ashamed.

•

Imagine, however, if the situation had played out like this:

Dwight and Janine crunched their own numbers and came to the conclusion that they could comfortably, and happily, afford to give Stacy $100 a month.

Then they sat down with her before school started and said, "Stacy, we can afford to give you $1,200 a year in monthly installments of $100. No strings attached. It's your money to spend as you please. However, you can't ask us for more than that. It's what we know we can afford. If you run out of money, you'll have to work out a solution on your own."

That discussion would have absolved them of their guilt that they weren't helping her at all and saved them the emotional frustration of trying to guess when she might need money and how much. They also wouldn't have felt the need to hold her accountable for her spending, to have a say on where her money went, because they had set the boundaries. If she needed more, she knew she had to find it for herself. No guilt. No shame. No fear.

Stacy could have accepted the gift without guilt and used the money as she pleased without fear of shame. Knowing the money would be there every month without her asking would have given her a bit of financial breathing room. Knowing the boundaries would have allowed her to prepare in advance in case she needed more. One single, honest family discussion could have avoided this whole mess.

•

I brought Dwight and Janine into the discussion and suggested this strategy to all of them for the upcoming year. Stacy's parents agreed to give it a try and Stacy agreed to unblock them from her social media feeds.

A year later, I am happy to report that the plan worked—not that it was easy.

Dwight and Janine sent Stacy $100 a month via email transfer and didn't comment on her spending. "It was so hard at first," Dwight said. "I just didn't understand how a beer tour could be a priority for spending money, but I bit my tongue." He laughed.

"Why do you think you are able to now, versus before?" I asked.

"Mostly I think it's because how she spends her money doesn't affect us anymore. Before if she ran out of money, I worried about how much we would have to give her or how much she would ask for. Now I feel like we've set the boundaries, so I'm less affected by her spending. It's good."

"What about you, Janine?" I asked. "How are you finding the new arrangement?"

"It's great. I mean, I still wish we could do more and I still feel guilty when she makes comments about being a broke student, but I just have to keep reminding myself that we've done what we can do, and that she's gaining her own financial literacy right now."

"You're absolutely right," I said. "Stacy is learning how to manage her own money, and it's such an important life lesson."

Then I asked, "Do you think you'll continue with this plan?"

"Oh, for sure," Dwight said. "It feels like a weight has been lifted from our shoulders."

"We don't have to be the bad guys anymore, trying to micromanage her spending. We are all getting along much better, and I feel like Stacy is slowly coming around to sharing more with us again."

Money Love wins again. Dwight and Janine weren't on edge anymore when Stacy came home because they weren't worried that she would ask for money. They knew that was off the table. It wasn't easy for them, but necessary so that they could spread Money Love and avoid Money Hate.

As for Stacy, being limited to $100 a month was a hard lesson at first, but one that she was grateful for. "It wasn't easy. Some months I worry I'll be short by more than $100, depending on tips. But at least this way I know there's another installment coming the next month. That's been helpful for budgeting, for sure," she said. "I've wanted to ask for more a few times, but I didn't because of this whole new deal. It was hard at first, but I guess I'm learning to be an adult. So that's a good thing."

"What about your frustration with your parents?" I asked.

"They've been so much better since we implemented this plan. They haven't checked my bank accounts once or made passive-aggressive comments about my spending. I'm sure they hate how I'm spending the money, but they are really trying not to say anything, and I appreciate that."

The $100 a month helped Stacy budget better and manage her expectations around what her parents were able and willing to help with. She knew she had some spending money she could count on, a consistent amount that allowed her to plan better. She also knew that she had only $100 a month—that some magical additional amount was not about to fall from the sky. She knew the boundaries, so she held on to her part-time job, ensuring that she wouldn't ever run out again.

Everyone won. No one felt guilty and everyone was less worried about money.

•

Financial honesty is a powerful and frightening tool. It opens a whole new door, inviting our inner circle of friends and family to share their money plans and money fears without judgment or recrimination. When we understand what Happy Spending looks like for others, we realize their decisions aren't judgments of our own. We all have the right to say no to things that don't give us a high Emotional Return on Investment. Resentments wither and die. Competitive comparisons are swept aside and no one has to be ashamed about their financial choices. No more Money Hate.

That's why it's important to initiate honest discussions about money, opening that door so others are free to do the same. Spread the Money Love and everybody wins.

You Got This

One of the best parts of my job is knowing that all the people who walk through the door want to make a change in their financial life. If they didn't, they wouldn't be there.

Knowing that you're reading this book because you want to make a change in your financial life gives me the same joy. Just by turning the pages you've already set the wheels in motion and you have the tools necessary to stop worrying about money and take control of your financial future. All you have to do is take the first steps. The choice is yours.

- Choose not to compare yourselves to others.
- Choose to figure out your Hard Limit and live within your means.
- Choose to say yes to Happy Spending so you can enjoy your life.
- Choose financial honesty with your friends and family.
- Choose to say no to overspending.
- Choose to redefine what success means to you in order to be truly happy.
- Choose to spread the Money Love.

There's no denying it, things are different these days. Our economic reality is a bit scary and we need to support each other more than ever; we need to work as a team. Let's make those changes, one by one. Let's help each other by talking about money. Let's step out of the judgment-driven, overspending financial pressure cooker that's been ruling our lives. Let's choose to stop budgeting and start living, knowing we will be okay.

It's time to take all your financial lemons—past, present and future—and make sweet, sweet lemonade. You got this.

XO
Shannon

Resource Library

NOTE: The following calculations are all based on estimates. Results cannot be guaranteed and are approximations.

Debt-Repayment Calculator

To find out how much you need to put towards your debt to pay it off in a specific amount of time, use the Debt-Repayment Calculator at http://www.worryfreemoneybook.com/calculators.

> **Example:** You have a $6,500 student loan at 5.2% interest annually with a $65 minimum payment, to be paid off over five years.

Calculate how much needs to go to debt each month in order to reach your goal.

Loan amount	$6,500
Annual interest rate	Enter the annual interest rate
Payment periods	60 (5 years × 12 months)
Minimum payment	$65

This gives you a total of $123.26 per month, which we'll round up to $125.

So, over and above the minimum monthly payment, $60 is the additional monthly amount needed to pay down this $6,500 loan in 60 months. That $60 is Meaningful Savings.

Debt-Payoff Calculator

If you want to figure out how long it will take you to pay off your liability at your current payment rate, use the Debt-Payoff Calculator at http://www.worryfreemoneybook.com/calculators.

Example: You have a line of credit for $4,500 at 3% with a $100 monthly payment.	
Loan amount	$4,500
Annual interest rate	3%
Monthly payment	$100

It would take you 48 months (four years) to pay down this loan at the current rate of $100 per month.

Online Mortgage-Repayment Calculator

An online mortgage calculator can be found at http://www .canadamortgage.com/calculators/amortization.cgi.

Example: You are able to put $6,000 extra per year towards a $418,685 mortgage at 2.7% interest with a 21-year amortization period and a five-year term.

Use the online mortgage repayment calculator to enter the following figures:

Loan amount	$418,685
Mortgage rate	2.7%
Payment frequency	monthly
Mortgage term	5 years
Amortization period	21 years
Annual payment	$6,000 per year

This gives you a minimum monthly payment of $2,175.

If you want to figure out how much extra you'll need to put in to be mortgage-free in 15 years, change the amortization period to 15 years and change "extra payments" to $0. The monthly payment will then need to be $2,828.

If your current monthly mortgage payment is $2,175, the additional amount you'll need to pay each month will be $653 ($2,828 – $2,175). But make sure you won't be violating any mortgage-prepayment restrictions!

Savings Goal Calculator

When you are trying to save a specific amount of money and want to calculate how much you need to save each year to achieve that goal, use the Savings Goal Calculator at http://www.worryfreemoneybook .com/calculators. Your Savings Goal Total is how much you'd like to save, and your Current Balance is how much you have already saved towards this goal. For the annual rate of return, use your estimated annual rate of return after fees, then enter the number of years.

Example: Your goal is to save $34,000 over the next 15 years, with a net average investment return of 4.2%. You are starting from zero.	
Savings goal	$34,000
Current balance	$0
Rate of return	4.2%
Number of years	15

The result? You will need to put aside $1,672.92 per year ($139.41 per month) for the next 180 months (15 years).

Long-Term Savings Calculator

Use this calculator to estimate how much your savings will be worth over time: http://www.worryfreemoneybook.com/calculators.

Example: You have a gross annual salary of $50,000 and want to save $5,000 per year (10% of $50,000). This means monthly contributions of $416 ($5,000/12 months, rounded down). You'd like to know how much you will have saved up over 30 years if your income increases by 2% per year with inflation and therefore your retirement contributions increase by 2% each year as well. Input the following into the online calculator:	
Initial amount	$0
Annual rate of return	5%
Annual savings amount	$5,000 ($416 × 12 months)
Increase deposits yearly with inflation?	yes
Inflation rate	2%

The result? In 30 years you will have a nest egg of $439,351.

Withdrawing from Your Retirement Savings

Example: You have $439,351 in retirement savings on which you receive 5% average net investment returns. You are now 65 and you want your money to last until you are 90 (25 years). You'd like to withdraw $2,000 per month (in current dollars). Using the same Long-Term Savings Calculator (above), enter the following:	
Initial amount	$439,351
Annual rate of return	5%
Regular savings amount	− $24,000 (the amount you'd like to withdraw, with a minus sign)
Increase deposits yearly with inflation?	yes
Inflation rate	2%

Extra Paycheques

If you are paid biweekly, you get two additional paycheques in a year. These can help to offset the amount you need to save to Short-Term Savings.

> **Example:** Your regular paycheque is $1,800 every other week and you have two additional paycheques in a year, one on March 30 and one on August 31. Your Hard Limit (Spending Money) is $650 per paycheque.

Step 1: Calculate how much you need to put away annually for emergencies and spikes in spending

Let's say your Short-Term Savings accounts need $7,800 per year. Here's how it might break down:

Predictable spikes in spending	
Holidays	$600
Vacation	$2,400
Emergencies	
Car repairs	$1,200
Job loss	$3,600
Annual savings	**$7,800**

So, without any additional paycheques, you would need to save $650 per month ($7,800/12 months).

Step 2: Calculate how much you can put towards Short-Term Savings each year from your extra paycheques

When you get paid, $1,800 goes into your Bills and Savings account. You then move $650 to your Spending account and you leave

$1,150 in Bills and Savings. However, for the paycheques on March 30 and August 31, you'll move $650 to Spending Money and put the remaining $1,150 in Short-Term Savings.

That way, twice a year, $1,150 goes towards Short-Term Savings, for a total of $2,300 per year. This means that the total of $7,800 that you need to put away each year is reduced to $5,500 per year ($7,800 – $2,300).

Step 3: Change the monthly amounts that go into your Short-Term Savings on a monthly basis

Because of those two additional paycheques, you need to put only $458.33 each month ($5,500/12) towards your emergency accounts instead of $650!

It is exactly the same process for weekly paycheques, only with four additional paycheques a year.

Side-Hustle Money

You can estimate after-tax income from freelancing by using this tool: https://simpletax.ca/calculator.

> **Example:** You live in British Columbia and earn $1,700 a year from self-employment (sole proprietor) income. Your employment income is $41,616 per year.

When you enter these figures into the calculator, you find that your marginal tax rate in 2017 is 22.7 percent. Therefore, of that $1,700, 22.7 percent will go to deductions, which comes to $385.90. So you get to keep $1,314.10 ($1,700 – $385.90) of your self-employment income.

Daycare Life

In general, in 2017 you can deduct up to $8,000 for each child age six or under and $5,000 for each child from seven to fifteen years old. The amount is increased for each child who qualifies for the disability tax credit. These amounts are subject to change over time and there may be other limitations depending on your specific circumstances. You can find more information on the Canada Revenue Agency (CRA) website at https://www.canada.ca/en/services/taxes/child-and-family-benefits.html.

Example: You and your spouse pay $1,000 per month for daycare. One spouse earns $60,000 a year and the other $55,000. The spouse with the lower net income can claim the childcare expenses, unless he or she is the only person supporting the eligible child—a deduction of a whopping $8,000 from their income. This would mean that the spouse who earns $55,000 per year would have their taxable income reduced to $47,000 ($55,000 – $8,000). This is a general scenario; every family is unique. Ensure that your child and the childcare you are paying for qualify for this deduction.

Further Reading and Resources

Aesop. "The Ant and the Grasshopper." Available online at http://www.eastoftheweb.com/short-stories/UBooks/AntGra.shtml.

Dahl, Melissa. "Yes, Shopping Can Be Addictive." *Elle*, January 6, 2017. http://www.elle.com/fashion/shopping/a41845/shopping-dopamine/.

Government of Canada. Canada Pension Plan: How Much Could You Receive. https://www.canada.ca/en/services/benefits/publicpensions/cpp.html.

Government of Canada. Old Age Security Payment Amounts. https://www.canada.ca/en/services/benefits/publicpensions/cpp/old-age-security.html#tbl1.

Harris, J. Rich. *No Two Alike*. New York: W.W. Norton, 2006.

Simple Tax Online Tax Calculator. https://simpletax.ca/calculator.

Wilcox, Keith, and Andrew T. Stephen. "Are Close Friends the Enemy? Online Social Networks, Self-Esteem, and Self-Control." *Journal of Consumer Research* 40, no. 1 (2013): 90–103. https://ssrn.com/abstract=2155864.

Acknowledgements

This book would not have been possible without the love, support and hard work of so many people:

Mom, again, for your endless support and brainstorming chats. I'm so lucky to have you as a sounding board and mentor. Dubs, you are simply the best.

My husband, for making the process of writing a book while very pregnant manageable, and for always encouraging me to go out and follow my dreams, no matter how financially terrifying ☺. You are amazing. I love you.

My family and friends, for being so understanding while I've been totally MIA under deadline. I'm back!

The team at New School of Finance, for your hard work and dedication to the cause. Thank you for picking up my slack and for loving the New School of Finance as if it were your own.

Martha Webb, my agent, for taking a chance on me. Thank you for all your help, from that day in the coffee shop to here! Woot!

Kate Cassaday, my brilliant editor, for your keen eye and your hard work to make this book the best that it could be.

To the team at HarperCollins in Canada for believing in this book as much as I do and for giving it a chance to shine.

I feel very lucky to have you all.

Index